CULTURE, CRIME AND PUNISHMENT

CULTURE, CRIME AND PUNISHMENT

RONALD KRAMER

First published 2021 by
RED GLOBE PRESS

Red Globe Press in the UK is an imprint of Macmillan Education Limited, registered in England, company number 01755588, of 4 Crinan Street, London, N1 9XW.

Red Globe Press® is a registered trademark in the United States, the United Kingdom, Europe and other countries.

ISBN 978-1-352-01086-2 hardback
ISBN 978-1-352-01082-4 paperback

This book is printed on paper suitable for recycling and made from fully managed and sustained forest sources. Logging, pulping and manufacturing processes are expected to conform to the environmental regulations of the country of origin.

A catalogue record for this book is available from the British Library.

A catalog record for this book is available from the Library of Congress.

CONTENTS

CONTENTS

LIST OF FIGURES AND TABLES

Figures

Tables

ACKNOWLEDGEMENTS

This book would not have been possible without the help of many people. I am especially indebted to Lloyd Langman, an incredibly supportive and patient editor, who has provided invaluable guidance and advice throughout the writing and publication process. Emily Lovelock, Amy Brownbridge and Peter Hooper have also helped to ensure timely completion of the book, for which I am appreciative. It was a pleasure to work with Pandurangan Krishna Kumar, who managed many aspects of the book's production and final stages.

I am also grateful to the anonymous reviewers who provided constructive criticism on earlier versions of the manuscript. As one can only hope from the review process, those who read earlier drafts did their very best to save me from embarrassing myself. Of course, I doubt very much that they (or anyone else) could succeed in such an endeavour, and so any errors, questionable interpretations, defective arguments – in short, whatever problems one might find with the text – are my own.

Finally, I would like to thank Neera Jain, a kindred spirit who knows that having homemade pizza for dinner every other night need not engender feelings of sorrow or guilt.

INTRODUCTION

An immediate dilemma confronts any book that promises to explore theory on how culture, crime and punishment are related: the meaning of each of these terms is far from settled and thus remains subject to intense debate. Several scholars have noted that, of all the words in the English language, 'culture' is one of the most difficult to define, perhaps in the 'top three' (see Smith 2001, p. 1; Williams 1976). 'Crime' and 'punishment' may not register so high amongst difficult terms, but that does not render the proffering of definitions an easy task.

If one were to begin by seeking out definitions for crime and punishment, criminology would appear to be the most obvious place to go. After all, criminology is conventionally understood as the:

> scientific study of criminal behaviour, that is of infractions of the law, especially criminal law ... Criminology also includes the more specific discipline of penology. (Abercrombie et al. 1988, p. 56)

It is, however, a peculiar discipline. At its core, one finds a concern with behaviours, practices and strategies that pertain to crime and punishment. As crime and punishment can be approached in numerous ways, a variety of 'larger disciplines' – such as psychology, biology, medicine, anthropology, sociology and, amongst others, philosophy – have all attempted to 'resolve' the problems that provide criminology with its *raison d'être*. As a result, one does not necessarily encounter a 'discipline of criminology' per se, but *biological* criminology, *psychological* criminology, *sociological* criminology and so on.

Arguably, herein lies the source of multiple meanings being appended to the same terms. In some strands of criminological thought, 'crime' is effectively understood as those behaviours that are rightly prohibited and thus punishable by law. This can perhaps be considered a 'right realist' definition: it assumes that crime can be taken as an objectively given phenomenon, as a property that inheres within a certain range of behaviours. At first glance, defining crime as a 'violation of law' may seem unproblematic. However, some may object that doing so means that how the state (i.e., sovereign power) carves up the field of human behaviour into its 'legal' and 'illegal' forms can safely be taken for granted. Accepting the state's view of which behaviours are not legally acceptable (and which behaviours are legal) generally supports criminological approaches that strive to theorise about those who do not follow such state-imposed prescriptions.

Corresponding to this view of 'crime', there is a tendency to regard punishment as a response to criminal behaviour. Embracing this 'punishment as response' position often entails assessing punitive reactions in terms of their capacity to deter individuals from offending, rehabilitate those who have broken the law, restore social balance via retribution, or possibly accomplish all three. Again, this may all seem very straightforward and consistent with common sense. Nevertheless, adopting this position often assumes that the state's 'right to punish' is beyond question and that the state pursues specific objectives in punishing, such as guaranteeing the greater social good by inhibiting crime. For the scholar inclined this way, assessing whether state-orchestrated punishments are effective is likely to become a central problem.

Crime and punishment, though, may be understood in very different ways by different kinds of criminologists. Sociological criminology, the importance of which will soon become obvious, generally embraces a constructionist approach to crime and punishment. This means that crime is not a self-evident category, but one that needs to be called into question and critically interrogated. To do this requires recognising that what passes for 'crime' is the outcome of social, cultural and/or institutional processes: how, for example, are policing resources differentially concentrated across public space; which individuals are more likely to be surveilled and prosecuted; whose perspectives tend to 'win' parliamentary debates about legislation; and which social groups possess the power to determine legal frameworks and codes?

Crime, then, may just as easily be understood as an outcome of political struggles, labelling processes and institutional practices. In this view, there is no such thing as 'objectively-given crime', only behaviours that people 'translate' into a 'criminal grammar'. And, what behaviours do become constructed as criminal are likely to reflect political interests and power arrangements. This is perhaps most evident when you consider that societies in different times and places are not unlikely to have different perceptions of which behaviours can be subsumed by the category of crime. Even within a discrete social order, the same behaviour may be framed as criminal under some conditions but not others.

Concerning punishment, sociological criminology has often rejected the idea that punitive strategies can be understood as responses that simply await the criminal act. Instead, punishment is likely to be understood as any given set of punitive practices that need to be understood independently of crime. Once understood as a problem in itself, a range of questions open up: why and how do specific punitive practices come to be understood as appropriate to a society? To what extent do broader structural forces and realities shape the use of punishment? Is punishment orchestrated in ways that are fair and impartial, or is punishment skewed by inequalities grounded in class, gender, race and so on?

By no means is this all that could be said about the difficulties of defining crime and punishment, but hopefully the substance of these debates is relatively transparent such that we can turn to 'culture'. As noted, this is also a very contested term, one that has been inflected with multiple – and often disparate – meanings over the course of its long history. In lieu of a lengthy exegesis, however, I will cut a long story short by appropriating Philip Smith's (2001, pp. 3–4) summary of how culture has come to be broadly conceptualised and understood within contemporary cultural theory. This current usage can be summarised according to three principles.

First, culture tends to be understood as distinct from material conditions and socio-structural arrangements. While it is certainly the case that culture, material realities and structural practices interact in complicated ways, culture can be 'weeded out' and treated as a discrete category for *analytical* purposes. As an analytic category, culture has typically come to designate that realm in which ideas, beliefs, values, norms, signs, symbols, discourses, mental frameworks – in short, *meanings* – circulate and play some role in determining the course of social, economic and political life.

Second, culture is often understood as 'relatively autonomous'. This is a tricky idea, but the basic claim is that culture cannot be regarded as a simple reflection of the economic conditions and power arrangements that purportedly constitute the 'base' of society. The import of this argument is that, while material conditions may explain cultural forms in some cases, we should also be sensitive to the possibility that culture may play a determinative role in social life. As will be evident at various points throughout this text, how to theorise the relationship between culture and material conditions has not been settled and this may lead to paradoxes and contradictions within or across culturally oriented accounts of crime and punishment.

Third, treating culture as an analytic category implies that many other ways of conceptualising it are sidelined, if not disqualified. The culturally inclined theorist, for example, is not interested in using culture to differentiate supposedly 'superior' intellectual products (e.g., artworks, literary texts) and 'ways of life' from those that are 'inferior'. That is, the cultural theorist refrains from utilising culture in its more common-sense meanings, especially if these entail normative assumptions geared towards the passing of judgement. This is an important point and it bears repeating: culture is an analytic category for critical theorists, one that facilitates building theory about social problems. By way of contrast, it is not a notion for rationalising normative assessments that hierarchically arrange social groups.

This view provides some clarity concerning the meaning of culture within cultural theory, but the attentive reader will have certainly noticed that many ambiguities remain. How exactly do cultural, social and economic forces relate to each other? Can general theory be developed on this problem? How 'autonomous' is culture? If culture can be 'weeded out' for analytical purposes, can it actually be observed as a distinct force in social life, or is it always confounded with material realities and power arrangements? Given that culture is understood as a realm that houses ideas, values, norms, discourses, mental frameworks, signs – not to mention further possibilities – how can such a category meaningful delimit analysis? Does not such a broad range of subcategories open space up for almost any kind of methodological approach and analysis?

Cultural approaches to crime and punishment

Despite the polysemic nature of culture, there has emerged an interest in utilising the concept to make theoretical sense of crime and punishment. To some extent, this has provided criminology with another subfield. Perhaps one should be a little more specific and say that interest in culture has led to a subfield within sociological criminology. Not surprisingly, this emergent area has often been designated as 'cultural criminology' and it is this approach that operates as a magnet for much of the content that follows in this book.

Delimiting cultural criminology, however, poses a number of difficulties. The borders of cultural criminology are quite porous, making it difficult to know where this subfield begins and ends. Indeed, it may not even be possible to imagine scholarship that organises 'culture–crime–punishment' into an analytic constellation as a siloed entity. For the most part, the amorphous nature of thinking crime and punishment through a cultural lens follows from the very fact that culture remains a 'hazy' concept, but it is also a product of culture somehow being linked to material conditions. In short, culture is hazy *and* inevitably linked to the problem of power.

There is a further problem: how does one translate an interest in culture, crime and punishment into methodological practice? If things like signs, discourse, or symbolic representations are taken as sites for the registering of culture, then it is highly likely that the scholar will gravitate towards the analysis and interpretation of 'texts'. If, however, things like mental frameworks, shared norms, or values are seen as cultural 'indicators', then in-depth interviews, observations or ethnography may become the most appropriate methods to employ. Of course, some studies may come to depend on both types of broad methodological approach.

And, one more problem: what normative assumptions concerning crime and punishment is the culturally inclined scholar most likely to embrace? Or, what political standpoint is the cultural criminologist most likely to bring to their work? Given that the concept of culture hints at human creativity, or the ability for humans to construct their social worlds, cultural criminologists generally veer towards the position that the category of crime needs to be regarded with scepticism. In other words, crime ought to be understood as socio-culturally constructed, rather than self-evident and objectively given. Similarly, it is important to recognise punishment and social control as practices that are heavily influenced by broader structural conditions and forces, rather than rational responses to behaviours that can unproblematically be categorised as criminal.

For those who appreciate visual summaries, Figure 0.1 provides one possible way to portray this emergent sensibility in which culture is central to theorising crime and punishment.

The purpose of this figure is to show that, like most strands of criminological enquiry, cultural criminology springs forth from a concern with criminalised behaviour and punishment. Its distinctiveness emerges in light of the broader categories and assumptions that build lenses for theorising such phenomena. Culture, or that realm of 'meaning production', is obviously important, but so too is an appreciation of the power asymmetries that structure social relations. This latter category is quite broad and, as Figure 0.2 shows, can include power asymmetries that stem from class, gender, race/ethnicity, gender, sexuality and so on.

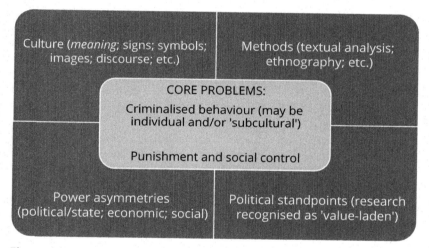

Figure 0.1 A 'visual summary' of cultural criminology

Dominant group	Wealthy, 'capital'	'Normative consumption'	White	Man	Adult	Able-bodied	Heteronormative
Basis of power differential	Class	Status, identity, or lifestyle	Race/ethnicity	Gender	Age	'Ability'	Sexuality
Subjugated group	Poor, 'labour'	'Pathological consumption'	Racialised 'others'	Woman; 'beyond the binary'	Youth	Persons with disability	Non-normative orientations

Figure 0.2 Power lines and the hierarchical organisation of social groups

While it places an accent on power asymmetries and while this opens up a wide range of theoretical possibilities, cultural criminology often focuses on the axes of 'age' and 'lifestyle'. This can easily lead to studying the subcultural behaviours of young, white men, typically from working-class backgrounds. The dimensions of gender, race, sexuality and so on, are often sidelined by such a focus. As such, these dimensions do not seem to play as significant a role in informing and structuring the analyses of cultural criminologists. To be sure, even the notion of class can easily end up riding in the back seat.

Cultural criminology has been heavily criticised for effectively concentrating on the behaviours of white, typically youthful, men. Feminist scholars, for example, point out that neglecting cultural constructions of gender, sexuality and the intersectional nature of power relations, leads to interpretations of subcultural crime that evince a masculinist bias (Naegler and Salman 2016). Critical Marxists have argued that the focus on age and lifestyle generates romanticised or celebratory readings of criminalised subcultures. This tendency is most evident, arguably, in construing subcultural practices as forms that resist the dominant order. Framing criminalised behaviour as resistant, however, can suppress discussion of the forms that effective political resistance against contemporary power asymmetries will need to take (Hall and Winlow 2007). We will return to these critiques – and a range of others that have been levelled against cultural criminology – at various points throughout the text.

Corresponding to the focus on culture and power are methodological and political concerns. Because cultural criminology construes meaning as central to inquiry, it requires methods that are attuned to 'capturing' this and related concepts. Hence, one often finds textual analyses and ethnographic approaches being utilised. Such methods are qualitative in nature, focused on generating rich descriptions and interpretations of crime and punishment. Finally, culture, power and methodological choices imply a political standpoint that the scholar is likely to adopt. Rather than construe scholarship as an objective, value-free process – as positivist criminology often attempts – the cultural criminologist is more likely to regard knowledge production as inherently political. One does not produce accounts that simply seek to map some external reality, but produces accounts that may actively shape social reality. As such, the scholar ought to pay attention to their own position in the world and the value judgments that they inevitably bring to research and scholarly analysis.

As Figure 0.1 intimates, it may be possible to represent cultural criminology as a field that underpins a range of approaches to theorising crime and punishment, but whether this field can determine if a particular piece of scholarship belongs to cultural criminology is open to debate. Imagine, for example, the scholar who prioritises some of the components associated with power asymmetries, while making only fleeting reference to any of the dimensions that demarcate culture, such as discourse or symbols. Would such fleeting references to culture be enough to consider one a cultural criminologist? What if the scholar is more inclined to self-identify as a Marxist criminologist?

Jeff Ferrell, often regarded as a major figure in the field of cultural criminology, offers a way to navigate this very problem. Ferrell (1999) suggests that at least three forms of scholarship can be regarded as important to any project that seeks to centre the cultural in criminological analysis. First, and most obviously, the scholarship that is produced by those who 'consciously identify their work as cultural criminology' (Ferrell 1999, p. 396). Second, the cultural criminologist ought to be concerned with work that explores the various ways in which culture, crime and/or criminalisation intersect. Third, it is important to acknowledge work that, despite being produced prior to the emergence of cultural criminology as a recognised label, can be retroactively considered as consistent with this broad orientation.

I will not depart too far from this logic and approach, thereby pulling into the text a variety of thought that, at least in my view, is important for the culturally inclined scholar to consider. By no means is the text exhaustive in these respects. Indeed, it is unlikely that a comprehensive text on culture, crime and punishment could take the form of a single volume.

This book, then, is quite modest in its aims. The goal is not to posit some essential criteria by which the cultural criminologist can be identified. Nor is the book designed to lay out a prescriptive set of rules that supposedly ensure one can think like or 'be' a cultural criminologist. And, I am certainly not on a quest to (re)label every scholar who has ever incorporated cultural dimensions into their work a cultural criminologist. Instead, the purpose is to explore culture as an ambiguous analytical device and the various ways in which conceptualisations of culture may enter into theories about crime and punishment. This is to suggest that sensitivity to the cultural dimensions of crime and punishment may generate critical analyses, insights and understandings of such phenomena. It is not, however, to advance the claim that we need to erect siloes or determine where the boundaries between, say for example, cultural criminology and Marxist criminology lie. Let's just get on with the business of critical analysis, incorporating cultural dimensions when and where they enhance such analyses.

The structure of the book

Chapters 1 and 2 essentially unpack the details embedded in Figure 0.1 (p. 5). Chapter 1 does this by focusing on the sociological roots to cultural criminology and how such an approach differs from what can be labelled 'positivist criminology' and 'radical constructivism'. Typically inspired by biology, psychology and cognate disciplines, positivist criminology generally posits that 'scientific' methods can be used to find the causes of crime and, from here, develop techniques that successfully intervene to control crime. In this perspective, 'individual defects' – such as self-interested rational calculations, biological properties, IQ, distinct brain patterns, genetic anomalies – are often posited as causative of crime.

Radical constructivism can almost be thought of as a polar opposite of positivist criminology. Heavily inspired by postmodern thought and the importance it accords to language/discourse, radical constructivism asserts that there is no reality outside of discourse. The things that we often assume to be 'real', or existing independently of us, only appear as such because of particular discourses. 'Crime' is no exception. As a result, crime needs to be understood as a language game that divides behaviours into 'legal' or 'illegal' forms and this at the expense of other possible designations. That crime is a language game is evidenced by its arbitrary nature; any given behaviour can always be framed otherwise. Smoking marijuana, for example, can be defined as 'criminal' or 'pleasurable', or 'medical', or 'necessary given the stress of contemporary life'. If smoking marijuana is successfully constructed as 'necessary', the counter-view that it amounts to a criminal offence is disrupted.

Sociological criminology and, by extension, cultural criminology sit somewhere between these two positions. On the one hand, sociological and cultural criminology do recognise that language, labels and meaning are necessary for certain behaviours to become widely understood as criminal. This is quite consistent with a radical constructivist position. Akin to positivist criminology, however, it is often acknowledged that crime exists independently of language/discourse. This is evident in the claim, echoed within sociological and cultural criminology, that crime amounts to 'symbolic resistance'. This argument presupposes that things like drug use, shoplifting, graffiti writing and so on, are criminal – and it is this very criminality that allows such behaviours to be interpreted as cultural challenges to mainstream society, moments of resistance that seek to question prevailing power relations. This amounts to a profound inconsistency within cultural criminology. Are we to understand crime as a cultural code that organises social life (which would parallel the radical constructivist position), or is crime to be understood as a real response, one loaded with cultural meanings, to material conditions and power asymmetries (which would parallel the objectivism of logical positivism)?

The other dimensions within Figure 0.1, or the methods and politics of research, provide the basis for Chapter 2. Here, a contrast is also drawn with positivist criminology but, rather than reinvoke radical constructivism, the sociology of science and technology will act as an important reference point. Although positivist criminology houses much diversity, it is often construed by the cultural criminologist as evincing a preference for the types of quantitative methods and epistemological standpoints that are typically associated with the natural sciences. As a correlative of this, positivist criminology often assumes that such methods are politically neutral, 'objective', or 'disinterested'. While sociologists of science reject the notion that scientific research can ever be conducted in ways that are free of political values, they often seek to recuperate it by emphasising the need for reflexivity and diversity in science (Harding 1986, 2015).

Those who are more culturally inclined tend to regard positivist criminology with horror and so their rejection of it is often expressed in no uncertain terms. On the basis of this rejection, they utilise different methodological orientations and claim to adopt political standpoints that are socially progressive. Methods that allow the scholar to trap or register meaning are preferred. Moreover, research is regarded as a fundamentally political activity: not only does the scholar bring value orientations to their work, but their work also amounts to the crafting of narratives that have political significance.

In the last part of the chapter, critiques offered by Pat Carlen (2011) and Dale Spencer (2011) will be explored. These critiques belong here because they follow from cultural criminology's tendency to situate itself against positivist criminology and, closely related, claim that its theoretical underpinnings, methodological orientations and politics amount to a substantively new and original variant of critical criminology. Carlen charges cultural criminology with 'evangelism', which is evident in its repeated efforts to distance itself from positivist criminology, invite others to join its 'intellectual crusade', and its insistence that science be understood as indistinguishable from politics. For Carlen, much of this is unnecessary and suggests that energy is diverted from actually conducting academic research that will lead to new discoveries. On a related note, Spencer (2011) also argues that cultural criminology fails to offer anything that is new, but posits that this is a product of remaining lost within contradictions that have long defined the sociological and critical criminology – especially labelling theory – from which cultural criminologists purportedly take their inspiration.

Chapter 3, the first of the more topical chapters that build the rest of the book, explores how the concept of culture has been differentially understood and brought into efforts to theorise crime and/or criminalised behaviour. Four distinct accounts are charted. Of these, the first is utilised to help contextualise how cultural criminologists have linked culture and crime. It begins with the view, pioneered by Walter Miller (1958) and subsequently echoed by Elijah Anderson (1990, 1999), that crime is a consequence of subscribing to a 'culture of poverty'. From here, we can slide into cultural criminology, where three distinct theories in which culture and crime are interrelated can be discerned. First, we look at the idea that crime is better understood as a logical extension of defects in mainstream culture (Nightingale 1993; Young 1999, 2003). In this view, crime is not the product of a simple exclusion, one that spawns a localised 'culture of poverty', but follows from the concurrence of inclusion and exclusion. In other words, while culture pulls people in to a world of particular desires or understandings of a meaningful life, they are simultaneously excluded from the fulfilment of such desires. Crime resolves this tension. Second, the argument that crime and/or risk-taking behaviour can be understood as a cultural response to socially constraining conditions is explored. This view can be found in the work of Stephen Lyng (1990) and Mike Presdee (2000), although the two offer slightly different takes on the significance of crime as a response. Third, the chapter examines arguments in which crime figures as a 'project of transcendence' (Katz 1988) or, relatedly, a manifestation of cultural resistance to hegemonic orders (Ferrell 1996).

This charting of positions on culture and crime will set the scene for Chapter 4, which is devoted to accounts that interrogate cultural criminology's interpretations of criminalised behaviour. A separate chapter is warranted because it is these theoretical claims concerning culture and crime that have attracted the most profound and engaged critiques of cultural criminology. Three broad critiques will receive our attention.

First, feminist scholars have argued that when cultural criminology focuses on power asymmetries, it becomes preoccupied with age and lifestyles and this to the neglect of gender, race, sexuality and the intersectional nature of power relations (Naegler and Salman 2016). This effectively leads to accounts that are partial, inaccurate and under-theorised. Many criminalised behaviours require sensitivity to gendered dynamics, but this seems to elude cultural criminology.

Second, a series of critiques have been sparked by cultural criminology's 'resistance thesis'. Hall and Winlow (2007; Hall et al. 2008) essentially argue that criminalised subcultures do not represent negations of capitalist relations and ideology, but logical extensions of such forces. Thus, when the cultural criminologist posits that subcultures are resistant, it amounts to an ideological claim that preserves capitalism and its inequalities. Cultural criminology has somehow come to construe the 'victims' of capitalism as agents of resistance. A related critique, advanced by Webber (2007), posits that the 'resistance thesis' is problematic because it fails to acknowledge the adverse consequences that can easily follow from engaging in criminalised behaviour.

Finally, the chapter explores Martin O'Brien's critique in some detail. According to O'Brien (2005), cultural criminology oscillates between 'idiographic' and 'nomothetic' notions of culture (O'Brien 2005). That may not sound like much of an issue, but the problem it poses becomes much more obvious when one notes that these two conceptions amount to mutually exclusive ways of defining culture. What O'Brien reveals is that cultural criminology tends to adopt an idiographic view for making sense of criminalised subcultures, but a nomothetic view for theorising opposition to such youthful behaviours. There is, however, no logical justification for jumping between conceptions of culture depending on which social group (youthful deviants or agents of control) one is attempting to theorise.

In the fifth chapter, concepts that can help us make sense of how crime and punishment are represented and the effects that such representations may entail, are explored in some detail. This chapter takes representation as a broad category, one that can encompass particular concepts and the theoretical frameworks to which they belong. Karl Marx's (1994a, 1994b) notion of 'ideology' provides our point of departure: ideologies are those ideas and worldviews that can be associated with the interests of the ruling, capitalist class. Due to the power of this class, it is their worldviews concerning crime and punishment that are likely to be met with widespread social approval. Ideology is contrasted with Michel Foucault's (1972) notion of 'discourse', which focuses on expert knowledges and how these shape institutional practices. Attention is then turned toward the notion of 'moral panics', which can be understood as over-reactions to behaviours or events that are relatively trivial. Nevertheless, moral panics can lead to new legislation, the intensification of policing and, amongst other things, alterations in cultural understanding of crime and deviance (Cohen 2011). Finally, the chapter discusses 'loops and spirals', or the tendency for mediated images of crime and punishment to reverberate throughout the media landscape and, oftentimes, exert profound effects upon actual practices (Ferrell et al. 2008).

Chapter 6 retains the interest in media, but focuses on what it means to consume crime and punishment. Crime and punishment increasingly saturate our mediated world, evidenced by their omnipresence in television, film, music, news reporting and throughout new social media formats. Not surprisingly, a variety of theories have emerged to make sense of our seemingly insatiable desire for mediated images of crime and social control. While some posit that overexposure to crime and violence spawns 'copycat' behaviour, thereby corroding social order, others have argued that it promotes an irrational fear of crime and punitive attitudes (Gerbner and Gross 1976; Oleson 2015). Some scholars have refined this latter perspective by suggesting that mediated images of crime and punishment displace rational anxieties – induced by the precarious social and economic conditions that define 'late-modernity' – onto the 'criminalised other' (Cheliotis 2010; Hollway and Jefferson 1997; Sparks 1992). In another view, attention is drawn to the maliciousness, victimisation and harm embedded in the very production processes that must transpire for crime and punishment to be transformed into commodities for public consumption and enjoyment (Ferrell et al. 2008; Presdee 2000). The chapter essentially explores these four lines of argument.

The problem of punishment is explored over the course of Chapters 7 and 8, albeit in different guises. In Chapter 7, punishment is approached as a field of interrelated punitive practices that, despite historical shifts and evolutionary moments, is typically overseen by the state. This is quite an abstract notion, one in which the socio-cultural functions of punishment are taken to be the fundamental problem. Critical and cultural scholars often begin from the premise that punishment does not follow from crime. In fact, punishment needs to be divorced from crime. Amongst those who accept this separation, punishment has opened itself up to a variety of theorisations. Those indebted to Marxist thought tend to posit that economic conditions and capitalist social structures determine punishment (Rusche and

Kirchheimer 2005), but others have emphasised the rise of particular expert discourses and how they instantiate new punitive practices (Garland 2001). Some suggest that a cultural obsession with 'order' underpins social life and that punishment is not immune from the demand to 'act in an orderly fashion' (Smith 2008). Somewhat related to this last view, feminist scholars have suggested that culture, because of its prescriptive nature, is inherently punitive (Young 1990). This is particularly evident when one considers how cultural constructions of femininity 'censure' those who are perceived as departing from gendered norms.

Chapter 8 explores an aspect of punishment that is, arguably, more concrete. Specifically, it looks at a range of policies that have emerged in much of the neoliberal, Anglophone world in recent years and which can be taken as evidence of a 'punitive turn' in penal policy. Such policies include things like 'three-strikes' legislation, mandatory sentencing schemes, preventive detention, 'zero-tolerance policing' and so on. These policies, and others like them, can be associated with the phenomenon of mass incarceration: a condition in which prison can be understood as an expected part of the life course, especially for those amongst society's most marginalised groups. The chapter explores three broader forces that help account for such punitive policy.

First, the media's tendency to fundamentally misrepresent crime, criminality and criminal justice. For Ray Surette (2015), such misrepresentations end up pressuring (perhaps indirectly) public officials to embrace 'tough on crime' rhetoric and practice. According to Michelle Brown (2009), the mediated nature of punishment excludes the very thing that is most fundamental to it: the infliction of pain upon some individuals by others. A mediated world that erases this pain effectively positions much of the public as a 'penal spectator': distanced from the realities of punishment, they come to passively endorse punitive practices. This is all the more problematic given that punishment is so profoundly structured by power asymmetries grounded in class and 'race'.

Second, and somewhat at odds with the idea of a passive public, some claim the rise of a public that is vocal and incredibly punitive. This punitive public often takes form in victims' rights movements and promotes harsh punishment strategies, even if such strategies are known to be ineffective, costly, or simply irrational (Pratt 2007).

Third, punitive policy has been seen as an outgrowth of those 'actuarial' discourses – in which the prediction and management of 'risk' is accorded priority – that now pervade criminal justice systems. Not incidentally, such discourses are coterminous with the rise of neoliberalism and the precarious social conditions it generates (Feeley and Simon 1992). As labour markets become more constricted, it makes little sense to rehabilitate offenders as there is minimal social space for their (re)absorption into conventional life. As a result, actuarial logic steps in to provide techniques for managing those who are ostracised from the economy and society.

In the concluding chapter, we return to the elements of Figure 0.1 (p. 5) and use these to explore the gap between the potential of cultural criminology and what it actually delivers. The emphasis on culture and power asymmetries makes cultural criminology rich with possibilities; it seeks to carve out a space that is nominally capable of hosting numerous critical positions. Judging by its substantive practice, however, it is difficult to realise this potential. As a subfield, cultural criminology comes to focus on quite specific problems, and it often ends up trying to accommodate concepts, methods and theoretical assumptions that are not reconcilable. A subfield plagued by contradictions is not peculiar to cultural criminology – every mode of scholarly inquiry will have its contradictions and limits. And so, the problem is not whether one can navigate cultural criminology's contradictions, but whether they are prepared to do so given the sacrifices that this will entail.

1 THEORETICAL FOUNDATIONS

Introduction

This chapter will begin sketching a picture of cultural criminology by situating it in relation to positivist criminology, sociological criminology and radical constructivism. Cultural criminology is very much an outgrowth of the sociological criminology that emerged in the 20th century in the Anglophone world, and it could be said that both sit somewhere between positivist criminology and radical constructivism. Given this, the two latter orientations seem well-suited as reference points that help outline the distinctiveness (but also non-distinctiveness) of cultural criminology.

To be sure, other criminological approaches could be utilised for such purposes, such as feminist criminology and Marxist/critical criminology. However, like cultural criminology, these approaches also tend to oscillate between ideal-typical conceptions of positivist logics and radical constructivism. As a result, feminist and Marxist criminologies are arguably not the best reference point for exploring the parameters of cultural criminology. Nevertheless, some major works produced from within these criminological approaches will appear in other sections of the text given the contributions that they make and, relatedly, the critiques that they level against cultural criminology.

The chapter begins by providing a sketch of positivist criminology and how it tends to approach the problems of crime and punishment. Positivist criminology attempts to reproduce the logics that are often held to define natural sciences in accounting for crime and punishment. This leads to a criminology in which crime is taken for granted and assumed to be a problem that requires scientific explanation. Positivist criminology generally seeks the causes of crime in the individual – either a defective biology or perverse use of rational calculation – and thus suggests punitive strategies in which the individual figures as the point of application.

Following positivist criminology, we take a brief foray into the world of radical constructivism. Radical constructivism is heavily indebted to postmodern thought, especially the latter's tendency to prioritise the notion of discourse and/or language. For the radical constructivist, a reality outside of language does not exist; our experiences and observations are never 'pure', but always culturally mediated in some way. In the context of criminology, this leads to the position that 'crime' cannot be understood as a category given to us by reality. Crime is one of many possible signifiers we could use to mark out any given behaviour. Absent any reality to crime, searching for its causes and remedies makes little sense. The scholar can only interrogate the representations and accounts of crime that others offer.

Over the next two sections, arguments that have been advanced by sociological criminologists and recognised as influential amongst cultural criminologists are discussed, and their reverberations within cultural criminology are briefly summarised. In the first of these sections, the focus is on sociological accounts of crime or criminalised behaviour; in the second, the focus is on punishment and social control. Given that cultural criminology acknowledges a debt to this sociological body of thought, it constitutes the bulk of the chapter.

In the chapter's final section, we return to some of the lingering, unresolved questions that haunt cultural criminology. These stem from what can be described as its unprincipled (or chaotic) embrace of sociological criminology and its ambiguous epistemological and ontological standpoint. The ambiguous, if not contradictory, nature of cultural criminology can be opened up by revisiting radical constructivism. From this vantage point, it becomes clear that cultural criminology has not come to solid positions concerning the epistemology and ontology by which it is informed. As we will see, a radical break with positivist criminology is often claimed, but the two enterprises make the same fundamental assumptions about reality, the viability of proffering knowledges in which causal relationships amongst variables are posited and the right to pursue strategic interventions in social life.

Positivist criminology: Theories of crime and punishment

Positivist criminology assumes that crime is a 'problem', the causes of which can be discovered via scientific methods. In this quest for a causal theory, it primarily concentrates on the individual, thereby leaving little room to question whether the origins of crime may be found within social structure or discourse. The focus on the individual has spawned theories that focus on biological properties of the body and our supposed capacity for rational decision making.

Writing during the late 19th century and often regarded as the founding figure of criminology, Cesare Lombroso (2006) is most known for positing that some individuals are 'born criminals'. Although the born criminal is Lombroso's most notorious category, he did develop a taxonomy of criminal types over the years, which included the 'criminaloid', 'habitual criminal' and the 'criminal of passion' (Lombroso 2006). Despite these shades of criminality, Lombroso maintained that all criminals, albeit to varying degrees, possessed distinct biological features. This led him to posit that criminal behaviour could be regarded as atavistic, a resurfacing of ancestral traits otherwise rendered redundant by the course of 'civilisation'. In describing the born criminal, Lombroso (2006, p. 91) suggests that such:

> ... criminals resemble savages and the colored races. These three groups have many characteristics in common, including thinness of body hair ... small cranial capacities, sloping foreheads, and swollen sinuses. Members of both groups frequently have ... thick skulls, overdeveloped jaws and cheekbones, oblique eyes, dark skin, thick and curly hair, and jug ears.

Lombroso's suggestion that there is a biological basis to crime has long been discredited. Aside from the obvious racism of the theory, there is little to support the view that biological features can explain variations in crime rates (Taylor et al. 1973, pp. 41–42). Despite such limits, biological theories were popular and they are still echoed today, albeit in somewhat modified forms. There is, for example, a 'new' biological criminology in which crime is generally understood to follow from how genes and environmental forces interact to shape individual dispositions and behaviour (Baker et al. 2010). Moreover, a range of technologies are still deployed in order to measure the body – brain scans, IQ tests, genome mapping, the penile plethysmograph (which purports to measure blood flow to the penis to determine if an individual is a sex offender) – in hopes of finding the biological source of criminality (see Carrier and Walby 2014; Horn 2003; Walby and Carrier 2010 for critiques of biocriminology). Arguably, arguments in which biological processes are accorded theoretical importance remain popular because they are consistent with broader power arrangements and the ideological forms that sustain them: 'criminality' can be regarded as an objective category (it can, after all, supposedly be detected in the natural body); criminal behaviour is the product of individual defects; the state's 'right to punish' need not be questioned.

For positivist criminologists who wish to avoid the pitfalls of biological criminology, but continue to construe the individual as defective and thus the fundamental cause of crime, 'rational choice' appears to have emerged as the preferred theoretical approach. One could easily argue that 'rational choice' is the most well-worn theoretical construct underpinning contemporary theories of crime in which the individual occupies a central place. To give a few examples, rational choice provides the foundation for routine activities (Cohen and Felson 1979), situational crime prevention (Cornish and Clarke 1986) and, amongst other theories, zero-tolerance or order-maintenance policing (Wilson and Kelling 1982; Kelling and Bratton 1998).

Models based on rational choice posit that individuals are essentially instrumental actors that weigh up the costs and benefits – or chances of punishment versus rewards – associated with any given course of action.

Criminal behaviour transpires when the commission of any particular crime is perceived as relatively low in risk and thus offering benefits that outweigh its possible negative costs. Construing the individual as a rational actor is generally conservative in its implications. Rational choice theories tend to legitimise strategies that make crime difficult to commit (e.g., target hardening) or intensify the force of punitive interventions (as in zero-tolerance policing). Instead of focusing on social changes that might mitigate the appeal of crime, such approaches are geared towards the suppression of criminalised behaviours that emerge within social orders premised upon inequality, exclusion and gross power asymmetries.

The causal theories of crime espoused by positivist criminology can be associated with distinct arguments concerning the purpose of punishment. To return to Lombroso, his notion that criminal behaviour could be traced back to biological deficiencies was met with an obvious criticism: if biology were the cause of crime and troubling behaviours, how could the state justifiably punish those found guilty of a criminal offence? Biology is, after all, beyond the control of the individual. How can one be held responsible for actions that would appear to be 'biologically determined'?

In response, Lombroso (2006, p. 165) was quick to truncate any such reading of his theory, lest the state's power to punish be inhibited. As he put it:

> [W]hile we may deny individual responsibility, for it we substitute social responsibility, which is much more exacting and severe. While we may reject the legal responsibility of criminals, we do so not to reduce their punishment, but rather to increase the length of their detention.

Rather than raise questions about individual responsibility and thereby problematise the power to punish, Lombroso turns his biological determinism into a rationale for punishment strategies that prioritise incapacitation. Because some individuals are predisposed to commit crime, the function of punishment becomes that of 'social protection', which is to be accomplished by intensifying detention.

In some respects, one could argue that this kind of logic, in which the state is encouraged to protect society by incapacitating offenders, is quite prevalent in numerous contemporary criminal justice systems. As some have argued, much of the Anglophone world seems to have given up on the idea of rehabilitating offenders, preferring to see imprisonment as a viable way to physically prevent some individuals from committing criminal acts (Feeley and Simon 1992; Wacquant 2010; see also Chapters 7 and 8).

Where crime is associated with rational choice, there is a tendency to construe deterrence and rehabilitation as the primary goals of punishment. This line of thought is often associated with utilitarian thinkers, such as

Jeremy Bentham and Cesare Beccaria. Perhaps its clearest illustration can be found in Beccaria's short tract, *On Crimes and Punishment* (1963). According to Beccaria, human nature guarantees that individuals will be governed by self-interest, and thus willing to sacrifice the collective good if it means securing private advantage. In this view, the exercise of rational judgment will not go too far beyond an assessment of what is in the best interests of the individual. Given this, Beccaria (1963, pp. 43, 47) held that punishment needs to be exploited for its capacity to communicate. A well-organised system of punishment could be utilised to provide a moral education of sorts, it will teach people that their self-interests will not be secured via crime. Several conditions need to be met in order for punishment to function in such a manner: it must follow every crime, no matter how small; the costs of punishment must exceed, albeit moderately, the rewards from crime; punishment should never be based on emotion, as this would lead to excessive penalties and thus a loss of the state's perceived legitimacy.

In much of the Anglophone world, the idea of using punishment to re-socialise the individual, to rehabilitate them such that crime would no longer be perceived as a rationally defensible choice, was a dominant penal logic for much of the 20th century and it is still discernible today. It has, however, increasingly been displaced by the logics of incapacitation and deterrence (Garland 2001). Where state-orchestrated punitive practices are governed by a logic of rehabilitation, they tend to take the form of 'correcting' the individual. This is especially evident in the recurrent use of cognitive-behavioural therapies, alongside a range of other approaches derived from the field of psychology, which assume that 'criminals' think in ways that involve 'distortions' or 'errors in reasoning' (Hannah-Moffat 2005; Kramer et al. 2013). By way of contrast, incapacitation is less concerned with re-engineering the thought processes of those who engage in crime. Instead, it prioritises strategies like confinement, chemical castration, intensive monitoring and surveillance of those released from prison and so on, such that offending behaviour cannot be practically enacted even if the motivation to offend remains.

Despite their obvious differences, these punishment philosophies (i.e., incapacitation, deterrence, rehabilitation) do have some important points of overlap. In all of these views, punishment is regarded as a legitimate state activity, a normatively appropriate response to criminal acts. This in itself takes for granted that the state's demarcation of criminal from non-criminal behaviour need not be questioned, presumably because it is imagined to correspond to some kind of broad social consensus regarding acceptable/unacceptable behaviours. It is against this imagined consensus that criminal offending occurs, thus rightfully animating the impulse to punish.

Perhaps of greater significance, these theories presuppose that there exists some 'technical' and/or individual-level solution to the crime problem, thereby rendering any need for broader social change redundant. In Lombroso, the central technology is the prison, reduced to a mechanism for isolating and thus incapacitating 'born criminals'. In this view, so-called crime problems can be solved by identifying offenders, especially those with 'biological signs' of criminality and ensuring they are quarantined from the rest of society.

Following his view that no human can escape the pursuit of self-interest, including those who occupy important positions within the criminal justice system, Beccaria (1963, p. 15) lays out a blueprint for determining punishments in a way that supposedly achieves the objective of deterrence, but also fairness and impartiality:

> For every crime that comes before him, a judge is required to complete a perfect syllogism in which the major premise must be the general law; the minor [premise], the action that conforms or does not conform to the law; and the conclusion, acquittal or punishment.

Punishment, it would seem, is a dish best served cold. What Beccaria seems to suggest is that criminal justice, particularly its capacity to punish, ought to operate like a technical piece of machinery. The judge in this scenario does not interpret the meaning of behaviour, analyse its context, its impact and so on. All that he or she does is ask whether any particular behaviour is classified as criminal and if the individual has engaged in such an act, then consult the law books to apply the corresponding punishment. Human judgment is excluded from the process of imposing punishment because human nature is seen as liable to error. But if this human tendency can be excised, the punishment and rehabilitation of individuals can transpire with some kind of technical precision.

Radical constructivism

Radical constructivism is heavily indebted to postmodern thought, especially the latter's tendency to centre the notion of discourse. Discourse is explored in more detail in Chapter 5, but a brief description is required here to clarify the radical constructivist position. Discourse refers to ways of speaking (and writing) about topics or objects. However, discourse does not simply reflect an external reality that can be imagined to exist independently of our capacity to observe. Instead, the notion of discourse suggests that the practices of speaking and writing actively construct the world they represent.

According to Michel Foucault (1972), an array of discourses are available at any given time to make sense of 'reality'. It is not the case, however, that some of these discourses do a better job than others of encapsulating the truth of reality. There is no 'truth' to be found outside of discourse according to Foucault. Instead, discourses compete to operate as *the truthful* account of reality. Those that come to be most commonly accepted can be understood as 'dominant' discourses, whereas those that do not acquire as much currency can be thought of as 'subjugated'.

The radical constructivist essentially pushes this notion of discourse to its logical limit. According to Nicolas Carrier (2006, 2008), there are at least three conceptual corollaries of discourse. First, once it is accepted that there is no reality beyond discourse – that all experience is textually mediated – it follows that any given knowledge claim cannot be privileged relative to others. There is no basis upon which discourses can be organised into a hierarchical order, with those that better approximate truth being pushed to the top. Knowledge claims are equal. Second, speaking in 'representational' terms, or believing that the account one produces simply maps reality, becomes delusional. Third, and closely related, the view that science involves the discovery of 'laws' or causal relations amongst discrete variables, which allow us to intervene and 'fix' problems, must be abandoned. As Carrier expresses it, we need to 'resist dreaming of a society (and of a penal apparatus) governed by God or Reason' (Carrier 2008, p. 176; see also Henry and Milovanovic 1996, pp. 122–150).

This perspective has important implications for thinking about crime and punishment and the theories that scholars develop about these problems. To put it as broadly as possible, radical constructivism rejects all of the fundamental tenets of positivist criminology (and, as we will see below, can be marshalled to critique sociological and cultural criminologies). For the radical constructivist, there is no such thing as 'crime'. Instead of crime figuring as some objective reality, it is a term that can be appended to particular behaviours, a signifier that can mark behaviour as somehow distinct. When any given behaviour is labelled as criminal, it is effectively contrasted against behaviours marked as 'non-criminal'. Using crime as a marker, however, is arbitrary – other ways of signifying behaviour are always possible (Carrier 2011; Hulsman 1986; Young 1996).

An example of this was provided in the Introduction. Smoking marijuana can be framed as 'criminal', but it can also be framed as 'medical', or 'necessary' and so on. Of course, this is not to say that how behaviours are framed is insignificant. Distinguishing behaviour as 'criminal' typically rationalises punitive interventions orchestrated by the state. The point is that the distinction cannot be justified by appealing to 'reality' or some notion of 'objective truth'. In other words, it is not reality that gives us the concept of 'crime', but 'crime' that makes smoking marijuana – or any other behaviour – appear as an objectively given violation of law.

Because crime is without an ontology – that is, because it does not exist in some pure reality – it makes no sense to search for its 'causes' according to the radical constructivist. If crime can be said to be caused by anything, it is the language game in which the distinction between legal and illegal, criminal and non-criminal appears. Because there is no reality outside of such language games, there is nothing in the body, or the mind, or the socio-cultural group to which one belongs, that precedes and somehow 'causes' criminal behaviour. This whole way of speaking does not make sense from a radical constructivist vantage point. It amounts to the fallacy of 'representational epistemology', or the belief that one can safely assume that their use of language is akin to a mirror that reflects objective conditions free of distortion.

And, of course, all of this also calls the right to punish into question. Radical constructivism posits that the tendency within positivist criminology – and many other forms of criminology – to suggest interventions or ways to control the 'crime problem' ought to be abandoned. Any such desire, whether it involves the moral re-education of criminals, incapacitation, improving social conditions, amounts to a 'will to power'. Such strategies and proposed interventions are often assumed to follow from objective, scientific analyses of crime, the human body and so on. And, they often involve promising that a better society would follow if implemented. Criminal justice would be governed by reason, the greatest good for the greatest number would triumph, the state would ensure the security of subjects. But all these promises are also discursive. Rather than map reality, they construct reality by securing their dominance. If biology is said to determine criminality, then pre-emptive and/or incapacitative punitive strategies will appear desirable; if crime amounts to a 'rational choice', then punishments with 'deterrent' or 'rehabilitative' potential will seem unproblematic.

Sociological criminology: Theories of crime

Many of the arguments advanced by positivist criminology are called into question by sociological criminology. However, sociological and positivist criminology tend to make similar assumptions when it comes to ontology (reality) and epistemology (knowledge). That is, they are often united in the view that reality exists independently of the observer, and that it is possible to produce knowledge that adequately reflects this reality. On the basis of knowledge that involves identifying variables and relations between them, logics of intervention can be developed. By no means is the sociological criminologist a radical constructivist in the sense outlined above.

Nevertheless, the 20th century did see something of an explosion in critical, or perhaps one should say sceptical, thought concerning crime. There was a movement away from theories of crime that concentrated upon supposed defects in the individual, which opened up space to consider the broader socio-cultural relations within which individuals and groups are invariably embedded. And, as evidenced by Howard Becker's work, the very category of crime was called into question. This section will briefly chart four sociological ideas of the period that cultural criminology has portrayed as influential to its development (Ferrell et al. 2008). These include crime as: (a) resolution to socially induced dilemmas (Merton 1938; Cohen 1955);

(b) embodiment of 'subterranean values' (Matza and Sykes 1961); (c) resistance or meaningful struggle against socio-structural conditions (Centre for Contemporary Cultural Studies/CCCS); and (d) socially constructed through labelling processes, rather than a category that captures some objective reality (Becker 1963). Having outlined these ideas, how they infuse cultural criminology can be discussed.

Robert Merton and Albert Cohen: Crime as resolution

Inspired by Emile Durkheim's notion of 'anomie' (a breakdown in regular social order), Robert Merton (1938) argued that much human behaviour could be understood when considered in light of how a society is organised. Any given society was liable to having deficiencies in its arrangement according to Merton and thus the cause of various strains in the lives of individuals. In 'Social Structure and Anomie', Merton (1938) suggested that society consists of cultural ideals and institutions. The cultural realm establishes 'goals' (or aspirations) for individuals; social institutions provide the 'means' for achieving culturally established ends. Writing in the United States, Merton posited that mainstream culture encourages individuals to desire wealth acquisition – the so-called American Dream – and to achieve this via formal education and stable employment in the legitimate labour market.

Merton does not pass judgment on whether this is a morally desirable arrangement, but focuses on how it can operate as a source of strain upon the individual. If people accept the goal of wealth accumulation and have access to education and jobs, then society may be relatively harmonious. What happens, however, when people are encouraged to pursue wealth while being denied access to education and work opportunities? Merton suggested that four behavioural responses might emerge when the individual cannot easily reconcile cultural goals with social means: innovation; ritualism; retreatism; and rebellion. Ritualism occurs when an individual plays by the rules but lacks investment in cultural goals. The retreatist is someone who has lost ties with both cultural goals and institutional means. The rebel is invested in society, but pursues the development of new institutional arrangements and cultural ideas (Merton 1938).

In relation to crime and deviance, it is the innovator that usually commands most interest. The innovator accepts culturally established goals, but is denied access to the institutional means that would ensure their fulfilment in a socially approved manner. Many types of property crime could be understood as innovative responses to this form of strain. For example, selling drugs and theft are often about the pursuit of wealth, but they are not typically regarded as legitimate routes to wealth accumulation. Such behaviours, however, might allow individuals to resolve the tension that follows from being psychically wedded to a cultural goal that eludes material, objective fulfilment.

Whereas Merton tended to assume that theory should account for individual-level behaviour, Albert Cohen focused on group responses to social contexts. In *Delinquent Boys: The Culture of the Gang* (1955), Cohen sought to explain the formation of deviant subcultures amongst working-class youth. He argued that young, working-class boys often find themselves in social settings that are implicitly governed by middle-class standards or norms. This is especially the case, for example, in schooling and/or educational settings where there is a heavy emphasis on being polite, docility, a certain kind of 'book smartness' and so on.

If tension resulted from a mismatch between aspirations and access to means for Merton, it is the clash between working- and middle-class norms, in which the latter are privileged, that produces frustration for Cohen (1955). The frustration is resolved by the formation of subcultural groups in which new cultural codes and standards of behaviour are deemed desirable. More specifically, working-class youth develop a subcultural response that is premised upon a repudiation of middle-class values and, as such, typically involves rejecting the school environment, minor forms of deviance and, amongst other things, pleasure-seeking activities.

Interestingly, Cohen (1955) does not see this argument as consistent with the concept of anomie. Cohen's reasoning is that the behaviours engaged in by the deviant subculture are not instrumental. That is, working-class youth do not appear to be much interested in accomplishing middle-class goals. However, it seems reasonable to assert that Merton and Cohen share similar ground insofar as they regard many behaviours – which positivist criminologists would be inclined to dismiss as inherently deviant – as resolutions to social arrangements that are beyond the control of individuals and/or marginalised groups.

David Matza and Gresham Sykes: Subterranean values

One of the critiques that could not only be made of Merton (1938), but also of Cohen (1955), is that the realm of culture is conceptualised in a fairly simplistic manner. Can 'culture' be reduced to an injunction to pursue wealth, or seen as premised upon a clash between relatively distinct working- and middle-class cultures? It was not long before Matza and Sykes (1961) came along and offered a more complicated picture of mainstream culture.

Also writing in the context of the US, Matza and Sykes (1961) recognise that the cultural realm encourages individuals to pursue all kinds of objectives, not just wealth. They posit that American culture is a bifurcated entity. Certainly, it puts a heavy accent on the values of 'hard work', 'delayed gratification' and 'wealth', but it also encourages things like 'risk', 'excess' and 'excitement'. To be sure, it is not that these value orientations are promoted equally, or receive equivalent forms of social approval. Instead, the first range of values are more likely to be publicly endorsed, or promoted without a sense of shame; the latter are promoted, albeit in more indirect or private ways. For instance, commodity advertisements typically encourage 'excess' in the form of reckless spending and making purchases according to *wants* instead of *needs*. Given their relatively subtle nature, Matza and Sykes (1961) suggest that the latter (i.e., risk, excess, excitement) can be understood as 'subterranean values' – they exist on the underside of what is publicly proclaimed and sanctioned.

According to Matza and Sykes, culture and society also establish appropriate channels for the pursuit of these subterranean values. One may go skydiving on the weekend, but does not let their interest in such a risky activity encroach upon work time; one eats and drinks to excess on specific holidays, but exercises restraint otherwise. If one sticks to these kinds of rules, it is unlikely that they will be regarded as deviant in any way. What Matza and Sykes (1961) are getting at, though, is that many forms of deviance can be understood as efforts to put subterranean values into practice, albeit during inappropriate times and within inappropriate places. Minor acts of vandalism, for example, may embody a quest for excitement and thrills, but society deems this an inappropriate way to pursue such desires.

The work of Matza and Sykes (1961) could easily be regarded as providing a further variation on a theme that was discernible within Merton (1938) and Cohen (1955): deviants and criminals are not necessarily 'pathological' or disconnected from their culture and society. Rather, criminalised and deviant behaviours are likely to follow when individuals are deeply connected to mainstream cultural currents and social realities. The individual who sells drugs to acquire wealth may be trying to live up to cultural expectations; the working-class deviant is struggling against the imposition of middle-class standards; those who seek excitement through criminal and deviant acts are enacting a mainstream cultural prescription, albeit in ways that are regarded as 'out of time' and/or 'out of place'.

The Centre for Contemporary Cultural Studies (CCCS): Subcultural resistance

The sociological perspectives covered thus far tend to construe individuals and groups as being pushed and pulled in various directions by broader socio-cultural currents. In this sense, there is a tendency to see those who engage in criminalised or deviant behaviour as lacking agency. Scholars associated with the Centre for Contemporary Cultural Studies (CCCS) – a research centre at the University of Birmingham, England, that was founded in 1964 and closed in 2002 – broke with this pattern. What the CCCS scholars saw in subcultural groups was an engagement with social contradictions; an engagement that amounted to symbolic resistance, or what one might perhaps term a 'cultural politics'. In other words, subcultural behaviour (which may involve deviance or violating the law in some instances) was to be regarded as meaningful to those who engage in it. Of course, the CCCS did not lose sight of structural contradictions and how these constitute the context within which subcultures arise. In fact, the CCCS reasserted the necessity of recognising how class structure plays a profound role in shaping many facets of social life. Given that class-based analyses seemed to have been falling by the wayside during the 1970s, reclaiming the significance of class as an analytic category was an important move.

Arguably, the most provocative statement concerning the relationship between class dynamics and subcultural formations can be found in 'Subcultures, Cultures and Class' (Clarke et al. 2006 [1975]) in which the authors open by revealing how 'youth culture' is an ideological construct. Youth culture was a term that the mass media embraced, along with some scholars, to make sense of the social changes that seemed to characterise the latter half of the 20th century. The term suggested that young people had emerged as a distinct group, marked by relative affluence and thus better positioned to engage in the consumption of commercial commodities made available in a post-war era marked by mass production (Clarke et al. 2006, p. 11). However, to talk of youth as a distinct group and to suggest that age is a major structuring principle of post-war society, is to render class irrelevant.

According to Clarke and colleagues, however, class is still relevant and much more so than age, in terms of ordering social relations. The salience of class is evidenced by the persistence of poverty, the stability of relative inequality between classes, the power of small groups to control large portions of private property and wealth and so on (Clarke et al. 2006, p. 17). Given that young people are also fractured along class lines, by no means can 'youth' be said to constitute a monolithic group. More importantly perhaps, we cannot hope to make sense of young people, the subcultural groups they form and their behaviours without a robust conception of class.

To understand post-war class dynamics in Britain, Clarke et al. (2006) draw heavily from Marxist theory, especially the work of Gramsci and his notion of hegemony. This is quite a complicated section of the text, but to put it briefly, capitalist societies are defined by discrepancies in the material positions of their core classes: 'capital' and 'labour'. The former refers to the propertied and thus more powerful group; the latter to those who lack private property and thus belong to the working class. The imbalance between the classes intimates that conflict exists at the base of society. Such conflict, however, is not always evident because the ruling, capitalist classes produce a range of ideas that 'manage' or conceal it. We have already seen 'youth culture' perform this kind of work: it became a widely promoted idea for making sense of society and young people because it denies the ongoing salience of class structure.

However, for Clarke and colleagues, class antagonisms are never completely contained. There always exists some degree of tension and negotiation between classes. Much of this struggle is expressed through cultural means, such as disputes over how reality ought to be understood, the policy positions that define different political parties, practical strategies and so on (Clarke et al. 2006, pp. 28–34).

With this theoretical underpinning, subcultures are said to arise because they provide 'a section of working class youth (mainly boys) *one* strategy for negotiating their collective existence' (Clarke et al. 2006, p. 35). Given that subcultures are typically set apart by the rituals and stylised forms they embrace, however, Clarke and colleagues are quick to point out that subcultural responses are unlikely to resolve the problems that class contradictions generate for working-class youth: the subcultural response is imaginary, or operates at a symbolic level. As such, subcultures cannot address substantive problems like 'unemployment, educational disadvantage, compulsory miseducation, dead-end jobs' (Clarke et al. 2006, p. 35).

A variety of post-war subcultures, such as Teddy Boys, Skinheads and Mods, are used to illustrate the limited resistance afforded by subcultural options. For example, Mod subcultures may revolve around consumption and hedonism, thereby suggesting that contemporary capitalist society should 'honour' its promise of greater freedoms, but such behaviour will not address the inevitably of returning to 'boring, dead-end work' on Monday morning (Clarke et al. 2006, p. 37).

Several scholars have criticised the CCCS for reducing subcultural phenomenon to class dynamics, often pointing out that a neat correspondence between class location and subcultural involvement cannot be so readily discovered (Bennett 1999). J. Patrick Williams (2007) emphasises that youth formations are incredibly diverse, such that some may be approached as class-based subcultures, but many others will not fit this theoretical model. Cultural criminology appears to have embraced such critiques of the CCCS approach: rather than reduce subcultures to class relations, cultural criminology appears to have adopted the CCCS' claim that crime or deviance is better understood as a form of resistance, an agentic response to the social contradictions and power imbalances that structure any given society.

Howard Becker: Crime as a label

Up to this point, the sociological theories discussed have sought to explain the individuals or groups who engage in behaviours typically regarded as criminal or deviant. Drawing from a symbolic interactionist framework, which posits that communication plays a decisive role in the formation of individual subjectivity and social practices, Howard Becker (1963) questioned whether particular behaviours, acts or events possess any inherent meaning. Becker suggests that a distinction between behaviour and meaning can, and should, be drawn. We engage in all kinds of behaviours, obviously enough, but the meaning of those behaviours is not necessarily stable, constant or 'pre-given'. In the context of crime or deviance, this position leads Becker to the view that behaviour needs to be successfully framed as deviant for it to be regarded as unacceptable.

Crime or deviance, in other words, is 'caused' by people labelling specific behaviours as 'criminal' or 'deviant' (Becker 1963).

This may sound odd or counter-intuitive and some may be inclined to respond by claiming that at least some behaviours are universally classified in a similar way. Surely, for example, most people would recognise killing another person to be wrong? We all know 'terrorism' when we see it, right? According to the logic proposed by Becker, however, this is not actually the case. What to make, for example, of murder cases in which 'self-defence' is raised and neutralises the possibility of punishment? There are quite a few people throughout the world who would argue that the United States is a 'terrorist' state. For the labelling theorist, whether a behaviour constitutes crime or deviance is a relative matter; it all depends on who is observing the behaviour, not the behaviour itself.

Having said that, power is not equally divided amongst all individuals or groups. And so, some are better positioned to make their interpretations and behavioural labels 'stick', or have greater socio-cultural impact. Courts, police, teachers and the mass media, to name a few, are better positioned to create and apply labels than, say for example, young people or those on the margins of society. In this sense, the most powerful social groups can be said to drive the labelling process, typically in ways that suit their interests.

The idea of labelling was soon taken up by scholars in Britain, such as Stan Cohen (2011 [1972]) and Stuart Hall et al. (1978), who developed it via the notion of 'moral panic'. As is explored in detail in Chapter 5, a moral panic can be understood as an over-reaction to a behaviour, event or practice that is relatively inconsequential. Often fanned via mass media, moral panics connect inconsequential behaviours to those that are typically regarded as major problems. Civil protests, for example, may be constructed as a precursor to urban violence (Hall et al. 1978). Even though such representations and links are specious, moral panics can forge cultural associations between notions like 'crime' or 'deviance' and particular behaviours.

Like all theories, Becker's notion of labelling is open to critique. There is a tendency, for example, to conceptualise social structure in terms of a society's institutions and its interest groups (e.g., mass media, courts, police, educators and so on). This does not leave much room to imagine social structure as an independent entity, or something that exerts a profound influence upon institutions, interest groups and everyday life. Many of our labels and ways of framing behaviour, for instance, may be consistent with remote, 'abstract' structural dynamics (such as those revolving around class, ethnicity, gender, sexuality and so on) even if those who promote such perceptions are unaware of this. Like much mid-range American theory, Becker seems reticent to engage in inductive analyses that would take him beyond what can be directly observed.

Nevertheless, labelling theory ought to be credited with offering an important insight or two. Perceptions of what behaviours should be considered criminal or deviant are somewhat arbitrary; in a different social order, or in different times and places, constructions of crime and deviance would most likely be quite dissimilar from our own. This should force us to consider the social processes, along with the rationalities and interests by which they are animated, that demarcate 'criminal' from 'non-criminal' behaviour, 'deviant' from 'non-deviant' acts. In other words, instead of fixating on the supposed deviant, or the marginalised subculture, the notion of labelling invites us to 'look upwards' and critically examine the work that powerful institutions, social groups and individuals do in order to construct certain behaviours as problematic.

Reverberations within cultural criminology: Criminalised behaviour

The influence of these sociological accounts of criminalised or deviant behaviour can be discerned within cultural criminology in at least three ways. First, both perspectives understand crime as a product of deficiencies in the underlying economic, political and cultural conditions that structure social life. Whereas sociological criminologists tend to focus on specific structural forces, cultural criminology is open to operating with a broad understanding of social context. Suggesting that structural forces drive crime is evident, for example, in Merton's (1938) argument that strain is produced when access to legitimate means to achieve cultural goals is blocked; in Matza and Sykes's (1961) notion that cultural prescriptions, even if unintentional, inspire deviance; Cohen's (1955) claim that class cultures emerge in light of underlying material, social relations; Becker's (1963) notion that crime is a label imposed by the powerful upon the powerless. Cultural criminology, as will be explored in greater detail in Chapter 3, often understands criminalised behaviours in light of the structural and cultural backdrops against which they emerge.

Second, and closely related, cultural criminology marshals much of sociological criminology to move away from the kinds of individual-level explanations of crime that are routinely found in positivist criminology. This has often led cultural criminologists to focus on criminalised behaviours that take collective, or 'subcultural', form. Subcultural groups may emerge for a wide variety of reasons within sociological criminology, such as problems shared in common (Cohen 1955), or as group quests to embody cultural demands (Matza and Sykes 1961). Cultural criminology tends to embrace the notion of subculture, using it to recognise that crime is unlikely to occur independently of peer groups. Such groups may be central to the commission of criminal acts in various ways: members of groups may practically help one another, awareness of the group may provide a sense that one is in dialogue with others, or they may provide a cultural set of codes and symbols that makes behaviour meaningful to the individual.

Third, and arguably most evident in the CCCS position, cultural criminology often adopts the view that criminalised subcultures offer members a way to express their resistance to the dominant social order and its injustices.

Rather than automatons, or instrumental actors akin to robots programmed by some external set of commands, human behaviour is just as likely to be governed by emotional investments. Human behaviours, especially those deemed criminal, embody the desire to articulate something of individual and collective experience. However, if the CCCS dismissed subcultural responses by portraying them as merely 'symbolic', cultural criminology is oftentimes more celebratory and sympathetic to the youthful subcultures it observes. For the cultural criminologist, subcultures may not offer an effective or perfect mode of resistance, but resistance rarely takes such forms. As such, it becomes elitist and overly judgmental to so readily dismiss subcultural resistance (Ferrell 1996; we return to this in Chapters 3 and 4).

Sociological criminology and the problem of punishment

As with theories concerning crime, sociological criminology may emerge from the same ontological and epistemological soil as positivist criminology, but from here it develops a range of distinct insights regarding punishment. Instead of simply accepting that punishment follows crime and instead of falling into the view that punitive interventions can control crime, sociological criminology critically interrogated and called such arguments into question. For the sceptical, sociological criminologist, punishment was not determined by the occurrence of crime, but a range of social forces (explored below and in further detail in Chapters 7 and 8). Moreover, punishment is not easily construed as an effective strategy for the elimination of crime. Indeed, one of the core claims of sociological criminology is that punishment is counter-intuitive, often exacerbating the very problems it claims to resolve. In what follows, these sociological accounts will be explored before summarising how they have operated as a reference point within cultural criminology.

Howard Becker redux: Rule enforcers and moral entrepreneurs

We saw earlier that Becker (1963) drew attention to the relative nature of deviant (and non-deviant) behaviour. The other side of his theory focuses on how rules, which need to be established for deviance to be identifiable and punished, emerge. According to Becker, there is nothing in human behaviour that tells us what is acceptable or unacceptable. Instead, socially acknowledged distinctions between wrong and right, criminal and non-criminal, can be traced back to rule enforcers and moral entrepreneurs.

In terms of the former – rule enforcers – Becker (1963, pp. 137–146) illustrates this notion by showing how marijuana became a social concern, quite suddenly, at a particular moment within US history. Prior to 1933, marijuana was not generally recognised as a cause for alarm amongst authorities or much of the public. In that year, however, a significant change took place: the federal prohibition on the production and sale of alcohol, initially introduced in 1920, was lifted. Presumably, this was great news for those in the alcohol business, and perhaps for much of the public, but it was not so well-received amongst those in the game of law enforcement, especially those branches that were tasked with enforcing prohibition laws. Without a set of laws to enforce, the careers afforded by some police divisions were in jeopardy.

And so, a new cause for social concern – a new 'evil' – was required. Marijuana fitted the bill quite well: it was enjoyed by a relatively small, but also relatively constant, portion of the population; it was known to alter one's mood; and it was generally produced outside of the United States. It was the kind of 'problem' that was common enough and thus capable of keeping police agencies occupied. Once this was recognised, marijuana was rapidly constructed as a threat to social order, something that necessitated a response from the state.

Agencies of social control are not the only source of rule creation according to Becker. A second set of actors, more likely to be driven by normative sensibilities than material concerns, can be identified: moral entrepreneurs. The entrepreneur is someone who comes to believe that the moral boundaries of a society, which typically constrain behaviour, are inadequate in some respect. The perception that something is amiss encourages the entrepreneur to embark upon a moral crusade, in which the objective is to 'fix the problem' by drawing attention to it, suggesting remedies and enticing others to join and support his or her campaigning efforts (Becker 1963, pp. 147–163). Attempts to censor popular music or entertainment can often be regarded as fairly clear illustrations of moral entrepreneurship (Wright 2000).

Moral entrepreneurs may or may not be successful in their quest to institute new rules, or perhaps have old ones revived. In some respects, however, success is tethered to the social location in which a moral crusade emerges. Those that emerge from within the middle and/or upper classes, or from amongst relatively privileged groups, are more likely to gather momentum and obtain some form of social recognition. Moral crusades do, after all, require resources such as time unencumbered by workplace demands and, oftentimes, freedom from financial constraints.

Hall and colleagues: Class structure, constructions of deviance and policing crisis

The claim that rules are the product of activities orchestrated by rule enforcers or moral entrepreneurs allows us to break with the view that distinctions between right and wrong are inherent to human understanding. Akin to his notion of labelling, however, Becker is hesitant to connect rule creation and social control to the broader, fundamental structural contradictions that characterise social relations. A more radical, critical Marxist theory that traces constructions of deviance and control efforts to broad social contradictions can be found in *Policing the Crisis: Mugging, the State, and Law and Order* (1978).

In *Policing the Crisis*, Stuart Hall and colleagues examine why 'mugging' and, by extension, 'violent crime' came to command the attention of the mass media and much of the public in Britain during the early 1970s. While muggings or street robberies certainly occur, the authors argue that the media attention devoted to the problem is disproportionate relative to its reality. In this sense, mugging cannot be reduced to a real, material event that is simply reported by the media. It becomes a socio-cultural phenomenon that requires explanation.

Hall et al. (1978) provide a very rich description of the specific structural context in which concern with mugging arose and which explains why it became such a focal point. It is well beyond the scope of this chapter to provide a detailed account of their text, but some broad outlines can be offered. As it existed in Britain, capitalism entered a period of crisis in the early 1970s. This was due to internal dynamics and global economic trends. The crisis in capitalism was marked by things like falling rates of profit, which meant the economy was in decline and wages stagnated; rising unemployment rates; sharp increases in the average costs of living; and so on (Hall et al. 1978, pp. 264–283). As is not uncommon when the cracks of capitalism begin to show, protest is likely to emerge and this was certainly the case in the 1970s. The period was marked, for example, by student protests and the re-emergence of working-class militancy (Hall et al. 1978, p. 261).

True to their Marxist roots, Hall and colleagues acknowledge that capitalism is premised on capital versus labour, but also point out that the labouring class is divided along racialised lines. Within the working class broadly conceived, one will find a black working class that not only experiences more intense forms of exploitation, but is compelled to absorb the worst failures of capitalism (Hall et al. 1978, pp. 338–395). This is due to discrimination in educational settings, housing markets and within labour relations. Given this internal differentiation of the working class, it is not surprising to find that the 1970s also witnessed the rise of black power movements (Hall et al. 1978, p. 280).

The conflicts between capital and labour, which underpin capitalism, are typically concealed or managed through hegemony, which involves the capitalist class convincing the working class to 'consent' to exploitative economic conditions. But, when class conflict becomes too hard to conceal in this way, dissent, opposition and organised forms of resistance are likely to emerge. As indicated above, the 1970s were just such a period according to Hall and colleagues.

Capitalism, however, has a further, secondary strategy in such contexts: it can move towards 'authoritarian consensus'. This essentially entails winning consent to the use of force, or draconian forms of social control, in order to preserve and protect capitalist relations (Hall et al. 1978, p. 217). The strategy, or at least one manifestation of it, hinges on the need to find a social 'evil' that can convince the working classes – the exploited majority – to lose sight of the social conflicts upon which capitalism thrives, if not re-commit to it as an economic system.

Given the upheaval of the period, the forging of authoritarian consensus became an important strategy and mugging supplied the 'necessary evil'. Mugging was attractive to the interests of capital for several reasons. Constructing it as a major problem encourages the public to see the distinction between the 'civil' and 'uncivil' – or 'law-abiding' and 'law-violating' – as a social contradiction that is more fundamental than the tension between unequal classes. If this view is accepted, the state can foster a self-image in which it appears to protect society from the threat posed by an 'uncivilised other' or 'criminal element' (Hall et al. 1978, p. 310). Moreover, mugging could also be inflected with racialised meanings, construed as a crime committed by black youth against a white majority. Such a strategy was quite successful according to Hall and colleagues, especially because of its power to re-inscribe the racial line that has historically – and contemporaneously – divided the working class into its white and black factions. A working class so divided amounts to a politically ineffective working class (Hall et al. 1978, p. 396).

None of this is to suggest some kind of conspiracy theory is required to explain mass media and public concern with mugging. It is not the case that some secret, capitalist group gets together and masterminds such a strategy. A better way to understand the work of Hall and colleagues, perhaps, is to recognise that it views a society's structural arrangements as requiring reproduction and as a powerful set of forces that run throughout everyday social life. Of course, individuals and groups engage in all kinds of activities – journalists write stories about mugging, politicians pass laws that increase punitive sanctions and so on. However, such activities occur within structural contexts and can either work to reproduce or challenge these. It is almost as though individuals and groups can be thought of as channels through which structural forces play out. Unlike Becker (1963), Hall et al. (1978) are suggesting the need to pay attention to these broader forces that precede individual or group action and set the parameters within which social struggle plays out.

Edwin Lemert and Stan Cohen: Secondary deviance and amplification

Sociological criminology did not limit itself to exploring the relationship between interests, structural needs and social control. It also revealed that punishment and control efforts were likely to be ineffective, if not counterproductive. Rather than deter, rehabilitate or ensure public safety as is often assumed within conventional criminology, punishment may intensify motivations to deviance according to sociological criminologists.

Edwin Lemert (1967) advanced one of the most influential statements along these lines, particularly via his distinction between 'primary' and 'secondary' deviance. Primary deviance is defined by what it does not do. It refers to deviant acts, which may have any number of causes, but do not lead the individual to alter his or her fundamental conception of self. Imagine, for example, an individual that engages in deviant acts but does not consider these to be the product of an internalised, deviant identity. For Lemert, this is to remain at a stage of primary deviance.

In contrast, secondary deviance occurs when the individual alters their fundamental self-conception such that they identify as deviant. Importantly, this recrafting of self-identity is caused by social reactions to deviant activity. To be more specific, secondary deviance arises because others react to an individual's behaviour by labelling it deviant and, oftentimes, enacting some form of social control. According to Lemert (1967), secondary deviance is to be regarded as more problematic than primary deviance: altering one's self-conception in a deviant direction amounts to internalising an identity that ensures a stronger commitment to deviant attitudes and thus behaviours. The deviant label becomes a self-fulfilling prophecy and the deviant lives up to the expectations that others have of him or her.

It was in this sense that Lemert (1967, p. v) could claim the usual formula in which 'deviance generates social control efforts' ought to be reversed:

> I have come to believe that the reverse idea, i.e., social control leads to deviance, is equally tenable and the potentially richer premise for studying deviance in modern society.

Whereas Lemert's distinction between primary and secondary deviance is pitched at an individual level, Stan Cohen suggests that social reactions can intensify deviance in other respects. Drawing from the work of Wilkins (1964) and Young (1971), Cohen posits that societal reactions may have the effect of 'amplifying deviance' (Cohen 2011). This notion is best illustrated, perhaps, when the mass media devotes attention to deviant behaviours. Cohen shows how the media attention devoted to the Mods and Rockers, two youthful groups that would travel to beach towns on British public holidays throughout the 1960s, intensified subcultural involvement and primed the audience for deviant events to transpire.

Prior to media interest, the Mods and the Rockers were not necessarily clearly demarcated and well-defined groups. However, in emphasising the supposed differences between them and their supposed differences from the adult community, the mass media superimposed a meaningful structure upon the holiday situation (Cohen 2011, p. 188). In drawing boundaries, the media suggested that the subcultures were defined by their rivalry, thereby creating an expectation that deviant, perhaps criminal behaviours can be expected. Moreover, Cohen (2011, pp. 198–199) suggests that the mass media play a vital role in crystallising identities, replete with role expectations that audiences may embrace and emulate. In short, creating images of 'social types' and publicising deviance may be enticing for many, thus amplifying deviant activity by drawing a broader section of the community into such behaviour.

Despite the theoretical tensions within the field, sociological criminology carries important implications for how to think about punishment and social control – implications that are quite distinct from those to be found within positivist criminology. First, there is a recognition that punishment and social control efforts operate in a manner that is fundamentally unfair, or inconsistent with important principles of justice. This is evident insofar as it is held that rules and the punishments pegged to their violation are, in many respects, devised by those with social power and wielded against the relatively powerless. Another way to put this might be to say that the creation of rules often reflects particular interests, even though such interests invariably masquerade as universal principles.

A second important implication is the recognition that most punishment and social control efforts will not successfully address crime and deviance – if by this we mean their eradication or minimisation. This is because most control strategies ignore the ways in which crime and deviance are products of social contradictions and thus fail to intervene at structural levels. Furthermore, many approaches to social control are likely to actively produce deviant individuals and groups due to their stigmatising and labelling effects or, as Lemert (1967, p. 17) might put it, their capacity to compel 'symbolic reorganisation at the level of self-regarding attitudes'.

Finally, but by no means exhaustively, sociological criminology implies that simply trying to control what is often assumed to constitute criminal and deviant behaviour is the wrong goal. Instead of this, a more appropriate objective would be to create economic, political and cultural conditions in which the subjective motivation to engage in crime or deviance does not so easily arise.

Reverberations within cultural criminology: Punishment and social control

Sociological critiques of punishment and social control have infused cultural criminology in various ways. Both perspectives embrace the view that punishment and control efforts are not simply triggered by crime. Instead, punishment often operates in ways that are consistent with political interests, often working to preserve the dominance of privileged social groups by criminalising and repressing those who are marginalised and relatively powerless. Punishment, in other words, is understood as a mechanism for protecting power asymmetries.

For both sociological and cultural criminology, that punishment preserves power relations indicates that there is something fundamentally unjust about its use. Rather than a justifiable response to wrongdoing, the draconian and authoritarian nature of punishment needs to be acknowledged. Its excessive nature is perhaps most evident in the tendency to over-criminalise behaviours that are relatively inconsequential, or associated with marginal social locations (Ferrell 1996; Hayward and Yar 2006; Snyder 2017).

There is, then, a general view that power relations and punishment are connected, but cultural criminology has come to focus on specific power asymmetries when punishment and social control enters its field of vision. The ways in which race profoundly structures punishment and social control, discussed in length by Hall et al. (1978), appears to have fallen out of view for cultural criminology. Instead, the focus is often on how adults police and seek to regulate young people. This is a disconcerting oversight given the extent to which power asymmetries grounded in 'race' profoundly structure many criminal justice systems.

Another extension of sociological into cultural criminology is discernible in that both approaches endorse an interventionist logic. In other words, practical implications and/or certain prescriptions follow from linking power, punishment and social control. Most notably, the use of punitive practices that label and/or stigmatise individuals should be minimised. Likewise, excessive criminalisation and intensifying punishment appears unwise. Such interventions run the risk of further ostracising individuals, thereby reaffirming their commitment to crime and deviance. There is also an important flipside to this: instead of trying to devise punitive practices that can be assessed in terms of how well they constrain individuals – the logic routinely endorsed by positivist criminology – sociological and cultural criminology suggests a need to shift the focus to social relations. It is only by shifting our gaze that we will see how society is just as responsible for what it considers to be 'crime problems'.

Some lingering doubts and unresolved problems

This chapter has chartered four theoretical approaches to crime and punishment: positivist criminology, radical constructivism, sociological criminology and cultural criminology. Cultural criminology often defines itself as an outgrowth of the sociological theories covered above. In acknowledging these sociological ideas as core to its own development, it strives to distance itself from positivist criminology. In other words, cultural criminology routinely portrays itself as offering a counter to positivist criminology via its sociological underpinnings (Carlen 2011). However, introducing radical constructivism allows us to question whether sociological and cultural criminology represent fundamental departures from positivist criminology.

Certainly, there are differences. Positivist criminology assumes that crime has a real, ontological existence, and that its causes can be found to reside within the individual. From here, it follows that crime can be eradicated by discovering its causes, and subsequently intervening. Sociological and cultural criminology are somewhat sceptical of the view that crime can be understood as objectively given, which is most evident in Becker's (1963) labelling theory. However, they often advance the view that social, economic, political or cultural conditions are generative of crime. In this, crime is assumed to be 'real', but a product of structural inequalities. This implies that different interventions are warranted: crime would be better addressed by improving social relations (i.e., creating conditions in which equality prevails), by adopting a more reflexive stance concerning criminalisation, labelling, stigmatisation and so on.

As intimated by the radical constructivist position, however, there are also similarities across these approaches. Both accept that a reality exists 'out there' and that it can be adequately represented in language. In this realm of reality, one will find problems (e.g., crime) and the causes of such problems. As Carrier (2006, p. 6) notes, in the case of crime, it is either the individual mind, body, or social body that is 'sick'. Different sites of pathology, to be sure, but something is always discovered to be 'sick' and in need of a 'cure'. And it is the scholar who can proffer the cure, be it punishments that incapacitate or rehabilitate, or a re-engineering of social relations.

These points of overlap amongst positivist and cultural criminology open up questions that are not easily resolved, but can be posed in order to provoke further thought. First, what is 'crime'; how are we to conceptualise it? Is it a label that adequately grasps a range of behaviours that have an objective, real existence? *Or*, is 'crime' purely discursive, a category that actively constructs the phenomenal realm it purports to simply map? Second, given this dilemma, does it make sense to search for the 'causes' of crime, whether this take form via an examination of the biological body, the mind/psyche or social contradictions? *Or*, must the search for a causal theory of crime be abandoned and replaced by analyses of the cultural/discursive processes that construct behaviour as criminal? Third, and also following from the questions posed above, is it the task of the scholar to 'intervene' by positing (perhaps intimating) strategies that are promised to 'resolve' crime problems? *Alternatively*, should scholars restrict themselves to 'deconstructive readings', that is, critical interpretations of accounts that claim to represent reality?

The problem these questions ultimately pose for cultural criminology may not be immediately obvious. But the content of this chapter should intimate why they have been posed. The questions that appear before the 'or' (and 'alternatively') in the above formulations belong to a particular epistemic framework, one that assumes reality is 'out there' and can be known. The questions that appear after the 'or' belong to a framework that assumes there is no reality outside discourse. Cultural criminology, however, has attempted to grapple with all of the questions posed above. To put it proverbially, cultural criminology wants to have its cake and eat it too.

2 METHODOLOGICAL APPROACHES AND THE POLITICS OF RESEARCH

Introduction

In the previous chapter we saw that positivist criminology offers theories of crime and punishment that differ from those advanced within sociological and cultural criminology. Drawing from radical constructivism, however, we also saw that these theories tended to differ in content more so than in form. That is, these divergent theories emerged from within similar understandings of ontology (reality), epistemology (knowledge) and the relationship between the two (the real world is knowable through its observation, it can be diagrammed in terms of causes and effects, interventions can be determined via such knowledge, etc.).

This chapter explores how cultural criminology seeks to distinguish itself from positivist criminology via its methodological choices and in light of its view concerning the relationship that exists between knowledge production and political standpoints. In the first part of the chapter, an overview of the 'positivism' in positivist criminology is provided. Positivism can be understood as a philosophy of knowledge production. It refers to a set of beliefs and prescriptions concerning how knowledge can/should be produced. Following this, some work from the sociology of science and technology is discussed. Drawing from Sandra Harding (1986, 2015), in particular, we will see how the sociology of science has disrupted the positivist claim that science can, and needs to be, free of political biases. For Harding and others, this is simply impossible as society and science are 'co-constituted': society finds its way into science and science harbours social relations. Despite this co-constituted nature, however, Harding does not reject science and its methods. Provided science can acknowledge its political and ethical dimensions, and provided it can diversify the perspectives from which it is produced, science can operate as a democratic institution.

The cultural criminologist is not so accommodating and is more inclined to dismiss positivism outright. Amongst many cultural criminologists, the methods preferred by positivism are understood as very limited because, far too focused on quantifying variables and finding correlations among them, they exclude meaning from analysis. To get at meaning – the emotive invest-ments, mental frameworks, significance that crime (and social control) has for its participants – cultural criminology turns to ethnography and textual analysis. An overview of these methods and some concrete illustrations will be provided.

Having outlined ethnography and textual analysis, the chapter turns to the political standpoints that cultural criminologists read into these method-ological orientations. These methods and their politics are commendable in many respects; they oftentimes end up generating critical accounts of power asymmetries and the unjust nature of prevailing social relations. They are not, however, without problems. Ethnography has often been criticised for its tendency to be inauthentic or deceitful, and to exploit the research par-ticipants on whose behalf it claims to speak (Stacey 1988). The researcher is never as committed to the groups under study as group members are and often advances a personal career on the backs of those researched. Textual analysis, conversely, can easily exclude the voices and perspectives of those it analyses (Clarke 1990; Williams 2007).

In a final section, we return to cultural criminology's presumption that positivist methods must be rejected to make way for a 'new', critical strand of criminology and the critiques that this position has inspired. According to Pat Carlen (2011), this amounts to 'evangelism' and, somewhat ironically, simply detracts from advancing new knowledge. Similarly, Dale Spencer (2011) is sceptical of the notion that cultural criminology offers a radically fresh perspective on crime and its control. Despite all its talk about departing from positivist criminology and breaking new ground by focusing on culture and meaning, Spencer (2011) suggests cultural criminology has not moved much beyond the sociological criminology from which it takes much of its inspiration. Old wine in sort-of-new bottles.

Positivist criminology: Methodological predilections and political values

Reading the work of positivist criminologists may lead one to conclude that research is governed by a series of inviolable rules and prescriptions that, if followed carefully, will guarantee the production of scientific knowl-edge. However, it is almost impossible for research to occur in the absence of a philosophy of knowledge production. And if there is one philosophy of science that dominates positivist criminology, it is, not surprisingly, 'positivism'.

When put into concrete practice, positivism generally appears in the form of 'deductive' models or 'deductive research design'. This involves start-ing with some general theoretical propositions and using these to develop 'hypotheses' or guesses as to what data will reveal if the theory is correct. The type of data that is fetishised in such models is that procured through some kind of sampling procedure – 'random sampling' being the 'gold standard' – and constituted by a large number of observations (Babbie 1995). Data, in other words, is often reduced to aggregated, quantitative data that is necessary for statistical analyses to be performed. This approach is defended by asserting that large data sets, random samples and so on, ensure that research findings will be reflective of an 'external truth' and 'generalisable'. The more numbers that get crunched by statistical manipulations, so the story goes, the greater our chances of 'discovering' general laws or causal relations.

The description just provided may sound abstract, but positivism is most likely a familiar idea. It is typically associated with the natural or physical sciences and, in this sense, arguably amounts to the common-sense view of how scientists operate. The notion that 'gravity causes objects to fall towards the earth' comes out of positivist logic. So too does the knowledge that NaCl (salt) dissolves in H_2O (water). Once such laws are known, other possible relationships may be inferred and empirically tested.

Many social sciences, such as sociology and criminology, have sought to appropriate the tenets of positivism in order to justify their existence, if not put them on an 'equal footing' with physical sciences. Like the natural scientist, apparently the criminologist can also observe and thus 'discover' causal laws that govern the social world (Crowther-Dowey and Fussey 2013, p. 41). Cesare Lombroso is often regarded as the figure who imported positivism into criminology and it led him to advance arguments that have become 'iconic' – perhaps one should say infamous – such as 'crime is caused by genetic atavism' (Lombroso 2006).

Positivism may appear at first glance as a set of methodological ideas and prescriptions that are politically neutral. For example, it would not make much sense to utilise positivist methods to fundamentally alter the natural world. It is hard to imagine that anyone would seriously suggest that we should try to change gravity to ensure that objects stop falling to the Earth's surface. Likewise, no one would argue that NaCl ought to be redesigned such that it is insoluble in water. It would be bizarre for any scientist to claim that the Earth's atmosphere ought to be re-engineered to control global warming. Certainly, knowledge of the physical world may be exploited in a wide variety of ways, but there is little sense that consciously recrafting fundamental features of the physical world constitutes a reason for seeking such knowledge.

Insofar as this is the case, the natural scientist may appear detached or, to be a little more specific, understood to analyse a physical realm that is distinct from the researcher and, in some very important respects, remains impervious to his or her activity. However, as detached as positivist science may seem, it cannot operate outside of the social contexts in which it arises. It is this fundamental relationship between society and science that ensures knowledge production and political interests will inevitably overlap.

Many sociology of science and technology scholars have demonstrated this point, but we will use the work of Sandra Harding (1986, 2015) to explore it in more detail. Much of Harding's work infuses the sociology of science and technology studies with critical, feminist perspectives. Sociologies of science and technology explore the ways in which society and science are co-constituted (Harding 2015, p. 47; see also Kuhn 1970). According to Harding, it is actually quite ironic that science often asserts that it should not be subject to the same kind of analysis that it constantly imposes upon physical and social worlds (Harding 1986, pp. 35–40, 56; 1993, p. 16).

Positing that science is socially constituted has many important implications. One can no longer accept that science is an institution devoted to the production of 'neutral' or 'objective' knowledge. Instead, the work that transpires under the banner of science always plays out in a broader set of socio-structural conditions. The types of problems, theories, methods, data, analysis strategies – in short, every element that constitutes science – will bear some relationship to the social conditions in which they emerge (Harding 1986, p. 100; 2015, p. 30). In her earlier writings, Harding marshalled the co-constitutive nature of society and science to demonstrate how science was a profoundly gendered institution. This was evident by considering who worked as a scientist and how labour was divided within scientific fields. However, the gendered nature of science – its masculinist biases and gaze – was also evident in its symbolic organisation and material effects. That is, science ultimately served the interests of men and this, somewhat obvious from a feminist standpoint, at the expense of women's interests (Harding 1986, pp. 238–239, 249–251).

Harding's argument, however, cannot be reduced to the importance it has for feminist theory. For it is generally the case that political agendas pass straight 'through the scientific process to emerge intact in the results of research as implicit and explicit policy recommendations' (Harding 1986, p. 77). And, in a slightly more provocative formulation, Harding (1986, p. 251) posits that 'science is no different from the proverbial description of computers: 'junk in; junk out".

To give this 'junk in; junk out' metaphor substance, Harding (1986, p. 76) offers the following illustration (among many others): cancer may be recognised as a problem, but precisely how it is formulated can vary. Some may suggest that we need to 'find a cure' for cancer; others may claim we need to 'eliminate the causes' of cancer. The first formulation assumes that cancer is best eradicated when it takes hold in an individual body. This suits the interests of those who are generally healthy and so worry about curing sickness if/when it occurs. The latter formulation suggests a need to focus on environmental pollution, the carcinogens associated with industrialisation and so on. In this framing of the problem, science would pursue the collective good and this at the expense of society's more powerful members.

Of course, Harding's image of 'junk in; junk out' could just as easily be applied to the forms of positivist criminology discussed in Chapter 1. In that chapter, we saw positivist criminology accord crime an ontological status (treating it as a category that is beyond question), construct it as a symptom of some defect in human nature and regard it as a 'technological' problem. This is the 'junk' that goes in to positivist criminology. The 'junk' that comes out is a fetish for the detection of crime or criminals, mechanical justice, containment or repression of (specific) bodies, moral conditioning of the population. But this is to construct the problem of crime in a very specific way. One could quite easily put a different kind of 'junk' into criminology, thereby ensuring that something else emerges on the other side. If, for example, 'crime' is understood as symptomatic of a defect in economic relations, cultural frameworks and so on, then social-systemic solutions are required. This second type of 'junk' is what sociological criminological typically puts into its criminology.

Despite pretensions to the contrary, then, positivism does not offer scientific accounts that are value-free. Neither does sociological criminology. Indeed, once it is posited that society and science are co-constituted, 'political-free research' becomes oxymoronic. And yet, Harding does not give up on science. Instead, she calls for 'successor sciences'. With this notion, Harding (1986) essentially suggests that because all knowledge claims are partial – they derive from occupying a particular location – science would be improved by opening itself up to a greater range of partial perspectives and recognising how all such perspectives are inseparable from a political agenda in one way or another (on this point, see also Haraway 1988).

Diversity in knowledge production would not, according to successor science, threaten objectivity. If anything, it is only through an incorporation of partial perspectives that a greater degree of objectivity can be accomplished. Harding (2015) frames the pursuit of objectivity through diversity as a viable way to build a science that is more democratic, one that would work to produce more equitable social relations. As an institutionalised activity, science ought not be divorced from political and ethical considerations. In fact, the opposite is more desirable: science will be more objective and democratic if it adopts a reflexive stance, one that considers how its knowledge production absorbs political and ethical commitments and is replete with normative implications (Harding 1986, pp. 249–251; 2015, pp. 126–129).

Cultural criminology: The quest for *meaning*

In Harding's view, the problem with positivist methods emerges when the political values that accompany their use are repressed/denied. Successor science, then, does not necessarily entail that the methods associated with positivism are rejected, only that they are used in conjunction with awareness of the political and ethical dimensions of research. Particular projects require particular methods and so no method can be rejected out of hand. But all research is political and so some research can be rejected for its political implications.

Cultural criminology is not as optimistic – perhaps one should say tolerant – concerning the methods typically associated with positivism. In fact, the cultural criminologist's critique of positivist criminology could fairly be described as brutal. Here, for example, is Jeff Ferrell et al. (2008, p. 165) summarising what happens to criminology when it succumbs to positivism:

> It becomes lifeless, stale, and inhuman... the thudding boredom of orthodox criminology stems from methodologies designed, again quite explicitly, to exclude ambiguity, surprise, and 'human error' from the process of criminological research. Coupled with a state control apparatus organized around similar ends, these methodologies bankrupt the promise of meaningful criminological scholarship, becoming instead the foundation for the sort of 'courthouse criminology' described by Ned Polsky – the criminology of the 'technologist or moral engineer' (citations omitted).

And, having offered a critique of several articles randomly selected from leading criminology journals in the United States, they are adamant that this orthodox criminology is not criminology, but 'madness, madness filling issue after issue of criminological journals that function primarily as warehouses of disciplinary delusion' (Ferrell et al. 2008, p. 166).

For the cultural criminologist, the problem with positivist criminology is that it omits meaning. As noted in Chapter 1, cultural criminology understands criminalised behaviour (and efforts to control it) as meaningful to the actors involved. Positivism, with its large-scale surveys and quantitative data, is ill-equipped to capture the mental frameworks that animate much human behaviour. A different philosophy of knowledge, one that authorises a range of alternative methodological approaches, is therefore necessary. Instead of positivism, the research of cultural criminologists is often grounded by 'interpretation'. Other possible terms to describe this orientation include 'hermeneutics' and 'verstehen' (Ferrell 1998).

The work of Max Weber – routinely regarded as one of sociology's 'founding fathers' – often serves as a key reference point for clarifying the idea of interpretation. In *Economy and Society*, Weber (1978) suggested that four types of rationality exist, each capable of influencing behaviour. For our purposes, 'instrumentally rational' and 'value-rational' action are the most important. The former is probably what most people have in mind when they think of individuals as rational actors. In this mode, an individual accepts and rejects possible courses of action by calculating the 'means' that will be most effective in achieving specific 'ends'. The latter, value-rationality, entails acting in accordance with what we consider to be important beliefs, values or ethical principles irrespective of their 'prospects of success' (Weber 1978, p. 25).

Value-rationality is especially useful because it encourages us to focus on how behaviour is driven by moral sentiments or what one might describe as internalised values to which emotional energy is attached. This type of rational action may conflict with instrumental rationality. Presumably, instrumental rationality derives from our capacity to reason, but value-rationality is much more likely to reflect the broader, socio-cultural relations in which our sense of self is inevitably fabricated.

To give a quick, perhaps controversial, illustration. Imagine a young, teenage woman who has become pregnant. Let's also imagine that this woman is concerned with her long-term economic security and independence. In such circumstances, instrumental rationality may well dictate that an abortion is the most logical course of action: having a child at a young age will likely interrupt one's education and the demands of childcare may entail adverse consequences in job markets. But let's now imagine that the young woman has been raised within a Catholic tradition of faith that places a 'prohibition' on abortion and socialised according to gendered ideals in which the essence of femininity is thought to reside in one's child-bearing capacities. This may ultimately lead her to have the child, thereby honouring deeply held sentiments, but perhaps sacrificing rational (i.e., instrumentally rational) courses of action.

An observer of this situation – perhaps one who has read a series of articles showing that having children at an early age is associated with relative poverty – may jump to the conclusion that the young woman is making a very bad decision. However, once it is understood that she is approaching the situation from a particular, morally inflected and gendered standpoint (perhaps 'unconsciously'), her behaviour becomes much more comprehensible.

Of course, this does raise a fairly obvious question: how do we 'get inside the heads' of actors in order to identify the cultural frameworks, moral sensibilities, mentalities, rationalities – or whatever other term one wishes to use – that are likely to provide a 'blueprint' for behaviour and thus explain it? Two broad methodological approaches help the cultural criminologist address this problem: ethnography and 'textual analysis'.

Ethnography

Ethnography is often associated with anthropology, especially to the extent that anthropologists try to understand 'other' cultures and their ways of life. The method entails spending extended periods of time in the field interacting with groups and individuals that we wish to understand. Assuming that action can tell us much about cultural sensibilities, the ethnographer observes people and typically takes detailed field notes that document behaviours. Alongside this, ethnographers often participate in the daily life of those they are studying and conduct in-depth interviews, where they can ask people about their activities, beliefs, life circumstances and so on (for a very well-known anthropological account in which ethnography is utilised, see 'the Balinese cockfight' by Geertz 1973).

Ethnographic methods need not be restricted to the study of 'other' cultures or those typically associated with regions of the world far removed from that of the scholar. The method and its basic principles can be adapted to study almost any identifiable social, cultural or subcultural group. In this sense, one of the great strengths of ethnography is its flexibility. However, it is becoming less feasible in many contemporary university settings, especially where there is growing pressure to publish articles in 'leading' journals, which typically evince a preference for quantitative data and statistical analyses (Ferrell et al. 2008).

Gregory Snyder's (2017) recent book on skateboarders in Los Angeles, entitled *Skateboarding LA: Inside Professional Street Skateboarding*, can serve as a good example of contemporary ethnography. Snyder (2017, p. 24) spent 8 years exploring the world of professional skateboarding, but was familiar with the subculture for over 20 years because his younger brother, Aaron, held a long-time interest in skating and worked as a professional skateboarder. Snyder's account relies on a variety of particular strategies to elicit information from skateboarders and those who have somehow made careers out of their interest in skateboarding (such as the professional videographers and photographers who document skateboarding tricks). He conducts in-depth interviews with skateboarders at popular skate locations, spends much time observing and participating in subcultural activities, takes an extensive amount of field notes and captures the subculture through photography and short video-recordings (Snyder 2017, pp. 27–30).

Snyder positions his interpretation of skateboarding against two other possible readings of the practice. First, he positions it against available subcultural theory. Second, he situates it against mainstream or common-sense readings of skateboarding. We will return to Snyder's engagement with the latter in the following section of this chapter, as this is where the politics behind his own research become most obvious.

Concerning scholarly work and theory, Snyder's main protagonist is the Birmingham School or Contemporary Centre for Cultural Studies (CCCS). As noted in Chapter 1, the Birmingham School famously argued that subcultures can be understood as motivated by the desire to resist, albeit 'symbolically', the dominant social order and its power asymmetries, especially those that stem from profoundly unjust class relations. For Snyder, however, what skateboarders actually say and do does not lend much support to such an interpretation.

If not 'symbolic resistance', what is going on 'inside' of skateboarders and those connected to the subculture? What draws people into the culture of skateboarding? Snyder suggests that several forces lead people to gravitate towards skateboarding. First, some individuals simply love skateboarding; it is a passion and something that Snyder's participants are deeply invested in. Skateboarders recognise that skating is the activity around which a much broader subculture has come to evolve and it is this to which they feel deeply connected. Skateboarders want to contribute to this subcultural world by performing tricks and feats that have never been done before. Their terminology for this is 'progression' (Snyder 2017, pp. 38–57, 70–75). This is such a powerful imperative that skateboarders may attempt a trick hundreds of times in order to perfect it and capture it on film, even though this may entail serious physical injury. In this sense, there is something imminent to the activity that attracts participants. Presumably, a profound sense of accomplishment must follow when one lands a trick on the 117th attempt.

Second, drawing heavily from the work of Angela McRobbie (1997, 2002), Snyder shows that skateboarders turn out to be very entrepreneurial and invested in the idea of a 'subcultural career'. That is to say, they recognise that they could make money from their skateboarding talents and they are generally open to such possibilities (Snyder 2017). Insofar as this is the case, their behaviour could be considered a manifestation of 'instrumental rationality': skating is a 'means' to the 'end' of financial rewards. However, being entrepreneurial or career-oriented turns out to be a little more complicated in this case. It is not simply that skaters are open to profiting through skateboarding, but that they are invested in carving a career out of something they are deeply passionate about. For many, skateboarding is about 'making your own way in life', securing independence in a way that resonates with one's sense of self. In Marxist terms, one might say it is driven by a desire to avoid the alienation that accompanies mainstream forms of work, without foregoing one's everyday needs.

Third, skateboarding fosters a sense of group belonging and community and this can often translate into concrete political action. Interestingly, skateboarders are not typically involved in abstract political action or general social critique. Instead, when they engage in political activity it tends to revolve around public space and the idea that, in a democratic society, space should be provided such that a diverse range of behaviours and collective interests can be meaningfully pursued (Snyder 2017, pp. 215–242). This is hardly surprising given the paradox that often engulfs skateboarding: while the activity is illegal in many US states, and often regarded as a public nuisance, it generally hinges on the appropriation of everyday, mundane spaces like benches, stairway handrails, ledges and other concrete infrastructure. As such, skateboarding is an activity that transpires at the heart of spatial politics, or those formal rules and informal norms that govern who is allowed to occupy public space.

Thus, those invested in skateboarding love what they do and most would be more than happy to turn their passion into a viable career that brings economic rewards. Given that skateboarding necessitates access to public space and infrastructure (i.e., benches, ledges, stairway handrails, etc.), many skateboarders may become involved in direct forms of political action, especially struggles that revolve around 'rights to the city'. Indeed, as Snyder shows, there are several instances of skateboarders organising to secure access to areas that are famous in skateboarding subculture and lobbying to have skate parks built (Snyder 2017, pp. 109–111). It is through deep, ethnographic immersion that Snyder can reveal the specific mentalities that motivate the behaviour of individual skateboarders and the broader skateboarding community. Rather than engaging in 'symbolic resistance', it would seem as though skateboarders are more concerned with creating niche economies that can sustain their activities, passions and the collective group to which they belong.

Textual analysis

In addition to ethnography, research that is carried out within the tent of cultural criminology often utilises 'textual analysis' of some sort. Textual analysis can be understood as an umbrella term that includes a variety of particular methods, such as 'semiotics', 'discourse analysis' and, amongst others, 'visual analysis'. To be sure, 'textual analysis' is a bit of a misnomer. Cultural criminologists do not understand 'text' in its conventional sense, where it is likely to be reduced to books or written form. Instead, text is understood very broadly, and thus refers to almost anything that can be 'read' and thus interpreted. Images, photographs, memes, advertisements, newspaper articles, television shows, films, documentaries, books, journal articles, videogames, government reports, official documents – by no means is this an exhaustive list – may be regarded as text by the cultural criminologist (Ferrell et al. 2008).

But how, one might ask, do such texts help us understand the meanings that accompany and inform action? Texts can be approached as artefacts that absorb cultural logics, collective sentiments, the common sense of this or that time period. As such, a close analysis of them can shed light on the value-rationalities that underpin social relations and everyday practices. To put it metaphorically, texts are akin to the fossil: through inductive reasoning and analysis, the cultural criminologist claims to understand something of the broader, social and cultural contexts in which texts emerge.

Depending on the particular method one selects, certain concepts facilitate analysis. It is well beyond the scope of this chapter to discuss every interpretive method. Nevertheless, semiotics can be used to indicate how interpretation may translate into methodological practice. (The notion of discourse, which is central to discourse analysis, will be treated at greater length in Chapter 5. Readers may want to consult this subsequent chapter to develop a stronger sense of interpretive methods.)

Semiotics is often associated with Ferdinand de Saussure (1972), a linguist who sought to understand how language makes meaningful communication possible. Saussure's ideas were 'popularised' in critical and cultural theory by Roland Barthes. Central to Saussure's thought was the notion of 'sign'. Languages make communication possible because they are essentially systems of signs. Each sign consists of a 'signifier' and 'signified' and implies a 'referent'. The 'signifier' can be understood as an acoustic sound or a word as it appears on a page (e.g., 'guitar'). The meanings that are associated with a signifier are the 'signified' (e.g., 'musical instrument with six strings', 'not a mandolin'). The referent is the physical manifestation, or the reality, that is referenced by a sign (i.e., signifier and signified).

In a series of works, but especially *The Fashion System* (1983) and *Elements of Semiology* (1973), Barthes adds to this by suggesting that the signified can be broken down into denotative and connotative dimensions. At the denotative level, one will find those layers of meaning that are relatively obvious; the denotative concerns those meanings that appear 'on the surface', so to speak. At the connotative level, the analyst is concerned with latent, or submerged, meanings. One might understand connotation as embedded in an everyday question that we ask ourselves or others in many situations, 'but, what do you think [his or her behaviour/text or email message/lack of response/the film's ending/etc.] *really* means'? As this question intimates, identifying the 'submerged meanings' of a text requires careful thought and analysis if one wishes to develop a plausible interpretation. (For a more straightforward account of Barthes and semiotics, see Smith 2001, pp. 107–114.)

Thus far, much of this may seem quite removed from criminology. However, consider that criminalised subcultures and those tasked with controlling crime emit, and oftentimes actively produce, many 'signs' or communicative texts.

An article by Randy Lippert and Blair Wilkinson, 'Capturing Crime, Criminals and the Public's Imagination' (2010), offers an illustration of semiotics in action. Using a combination of methods, some of which are interpretive, Lippert and Wilkinson (2010) analyse closed-circuit television (CCTV) images as they come to be used in *Crime Stoppers*. *Crime Stoppers* is an anti-crime initiative that operates in various countries. It publicises behaviours and social encounters that are presumed to involve criminal wrongdoing and encourages the public to supply anonymous information to police. Of course, such information is meant to help police locate and punish individuals for crimes they have allegedly committed. In semiotic terms, one might say that this understanding of *Crime Stoppers* – an initiative that simply publicises crimes to facilitate policing and crime control – operates at the 'denotative' level.

As Lippert and Wilkinson (2010) show, however, the fusing of images sourced from CCTV footage and *Crime Stoppers* is loaded with latent, connotative meaning, which becomes discernible when one looks at the formulaic nature of *Crime Stoppers* segments and their specific content. Imagine what would come to mind for most people if asked to think of a particular segment from *Crime Stoppers*? Or, alternatively, what comes to your mind? What kind of criminal act are you imagining? What does the perpetrator look like? What does the victim look like? Is a weapon involved? Where is the CCTV camera that is recording the action positioned?

Lippert and Wilkinson find that the segments publicised by *Crime Stoppers* typically involve crimes against businesses (e.g., convenience store robberies) and a narrative that explains what the viewer is seeing. Moreover, individuals who appear to belong to racially marginalised groups are over-represented, especially in terms of perpetrators and third parties who happen to be caught on camera as a crime supposedly occurs (Lippert and Wilkinson 2010, pp. 136, 146). For the interpretive, 'semiotically-inclined' scholar, the question becomes what kind of effect this is likely to have on audiences.

Five problems follow from how *Crime Stoppers* repeatedly uses CCTV images and narrative elements to depict crime. First, audiences are likely to develop a very narrow understanding of crime. This is mainly due to what is absent. Very rarely, if ever, does *Crime Stoppers* seek the public's help for cases that involve 'corporate malfeasance or manslaughter, state corruption, large-scale financial fraud, serious assault or theft by police, domestic violence, or racist or homophobic violence' (Lippert and Wilkinson 2010, p. 138). Instead, the focus is consistently on 'street crime' (robbery, assault).

Second, *Crime Stoppers* subtly conveys that CCTV is not an effective way to identify those who engage in criminalised behaviour. What CCTV images consistently reveal is that perpetrators take steps to conceal their identity by wearing masks or disguises. Third, and closely related, CCTV and public campaigns to control criminalised behaviour are generally unable to deter crime (Lippert and Wilkinson 2010, pp. 143–144). The very fact that crime stories can continually be produced, and embellished by images sourced from CCTV cameras, shows that retroactive control efforts are generally ineffective. Of course, those who tout the supposed benefits of CCTV and seeking out public help to 'solve' crimes would be very unlikely to admit either of these points, but a semiotic reading makes such an understanding possible. After all, that conventional modes of crime control are unlikely to deter offenders is being communicated 'beneath the radar', hence discernible by the interpretive analyst.

Fourth, and incredibly disconcerting, it is very likely that *Crime Stoppers* forges an association between 'crime' and 'race' amongst its audience. This happens in several ways. Most obviously, a disproportionate number of crime stories incorporate offenders that appear to belong to marginalised social groups. In addition to this, however, the third parties that often appear in CCTV footage are also disproportionally from marginalised groups. Such representations, repeatedly produced within *Crime Stoppers*, reinforce racist ideologies in which crime and race are inextricably linked and may encourage the state to concentrate its policing resources in marginalised communities or upon specific individuals (Lippert and Wilkinson 2010, p. 146).

Finally, through narrative elements in which it is asserted that a crime has been committed and that the police wish to speak to a 'particular individual', not to mention the use of 'birds-eye' camera angles that make CCTV images appear impartial, *Crime Stoppers* undermines the legal principle that one is presumed innocent until found guilty. As Lippert and

Wilkinson (2010, p. 140) put it, *Crime Stoppers* operates as a form of 'counter-law'; it effectively amounts to 'trial by media' and allows for individuals to be criminalised in informal ways. Formally, and in principle, the democratic state is supposed to guard against this type of extra-judicial criminalisation. And yet the state and its crime control apparatus (legislative bodies, courts, police) appear to see *Crime Stoppers* as unproblematic; if anything, such programmes are often endorsed by the state.

All this by closely examining patterns in the representation of crime and the specific content of the images and narrative elements upon which such representations depend. If one were to restrict their analysis to the 'denotative' layer of *Crime Stoppers*, they would most likely accept that it does what it purports to do: solve crimes by seeking out information from the public. However, once the analyst operates with the notion of 'connotation' – the idea that much more is happening 'beneath the surface' – a whole realm of new, subtle, perhaps unintended meanings, becomes discernible. In this particular illustration, *Crime Stoppers* is no longer a 'public service' or 'social good'. Instead, it is a social problem, an endeavour that undermines important principles of justice and fairness.

The politics of cultural criminology

The pieces of scholarship that illustrate interpretive methods also tell us much about the political standpoints that are likely to inform cultural criminology. In talking about 'political standpoints that inform cultural criminology', I am not referring to the fact that scholars often read political meaning into the individual or collective behaviours that they analyse. Rather, I mean to suggest that producing academic texts inevitably entails that scholars adopt a political standpoint. As Howard Becker (1967) put it, the question that knowledge producers ought to ask themselves is not whether they are impartial – that is impossible – but 'whose side are we on?' The same problem was evident in Sandra Harding's (1986, 2015) critique of science discussed above: research simply cannot be divorced from the socio-political contexts in which it is conducted.

And, to be sure, because of the inequalities and power imbalances that structure society, there are 'sides' here. Cultural criminologists often view the work that they produce as 'speaking back' to power; rather than 'looking downwards', they emphasise a need to 'look upwards' and question the inequalities and everyday injustices that structure social life. The political task of the cultural criminologist is posited as one of intervening to challenge problematic practices, especially those orchestrated by the state and society's more powerful social groups.

This can take various forms, but two broad tendencies are discernible. On the one hand, cultural criminologists may produce accounts that are 'sympathetic' to the marginalised social groups that they study, often trying to see the world through their eyes (recall, however, Figure 0.2 from the Introduction, which indicated that the cultural criminologist is likely to focus on particular dimensions of social marginalisation at the expense of others). That an account may strive to be sympathetic is not to suggest that it is therefore doomed to inexcusable biases – one can be accurate *and* sympathetic. On the other hand, they emphasise how dominant cultural frameworks and practices are profoundly unfair, and oftentimes the source from which injustices follow.

In terms of siding with socially marginalised groups, we can return to Snyder's ethnographic exploration of skateboarding. As noted above, Snyder interrogates the notion that subcultures can be understood as symbolic modes of resistance, but he also questions the common-sense view that skateboarding can be dismissed as nothing more than an 'illegal, destructive, and stupid' activity (Snyder 2017, p. 198). Were one to accept this common-sense view, it would follow that individuals ought to be policed and punished for skateboarding in public spaces. Likewise, this view also provides a foundation for informal modes of social control to be enacted against skateboarders.

Rather than condemn skateboarding, Snyder suggests that it merits social recognition and approval. Skateboarding is incredibly difficult and it requires an enormous amount of devotion. A glance at the history of skateboarding shows that it contains many 'miraculous' moments: complicated tricks that were long thought to be physically impossible to execute are suddenly performed and documented. Furthermore, the subculture makes important contributions to local economies and vitalises urban environments (Snyder 2017). With this, we are quite far from those interpretations in which skateboarding is imagined as 'stupid'. The practice is better understood as a physically demanding sport, a form of professional athleticism. When interpreted this way, the warrant that common-sense perceptions provide to police and control skateboarding suddenly loses its legitimacy.

Insofar as it generates a discursive account, ethnographic research may be said to speak back to power and authority, as Snyder's work does appear to do. It is important to point out, however, that ethnography has been heavily criticised for the power relation between the researcher and the researched upon which the method can be said to hinge. Judith Stacey (1988) identifies at least two ethical problems that stem from the relationship between the researcher and the researched. First, ethnography entails various forms of deceit to generate a scholarly account. The researcher, for example, simulates belonging to the group being researched, but can typically leave the research setting whenever this is deemed convenient. Moreover, while the ethnographic account may seem to be the product of a genuine collaboration between those being researched and the scholar, it is typically narrated by the latter. It is, in other words, an individual interpretation that masquerades as a composition of voices from below.

Second, ethnography often demands that the scholar exploit those being researched. As Stacey (1988, p. 23) notes:

> The lives, loves, and tragedies that fieldwork informants share with a researcher are ultimately data, grist for the ethnographic mill, a mill that has a truly grinding power.

The relationship is exploitative because it is the researcher that gets more out of the final ethnographic account than those researched. The researched tell their stories, reveal the inner recesses of the self, so that the researcher can transform this into a product that helps build and secure an academic career. The subjects of ethnographic research, to put it metaphorically, are raw material that is spun into a commodifiable account from which the researcher benefits.

The interpretive methods favoured by cultural criminology are, arguably, less susceptible to the pitfalls of ethnography. This has a lot to do with the fact that interpretive methods do not necessarily require research participants and because they can more readily focus on culturally meaningful outputs of the powerful. The article by Lippert and Wilkinson, 'Capturing Crime, Criminals and the Public's Imagination' (2010), is illustrative of this tendency to call the cultural frameworks and practices of society's more powerful members into question. Their analysis of *Crime Stoppers* reveals how such programmes reinforce racist ideologies that link 'crime' and 'race', construct the category of crime in a very limited manner (i.e., crime is equated with 'street crime' or crimes against businesses) and undermine the presumption of innocence. This analysis, however, goes beyond a deciphering of the latent meanings that *Crime Stoppers* conveys to its audience and has important political implications.

There is a need, for example, to recognise that crime is committed by many individuals, not just those who belong to socially marginalised groups. Indeed, criminologists have often noted that the harms associated with state, corporate and white-collar crime dwarf the damage (in physical and economic terms) done by all aggregated street crime (Coleman 2005). By ignoring offences of the powerful, the resources of the state can remain focused upon marginalised individuals and communities. The political significance of this, perhaps obvious by now, is that *Crime Stoppers* makes an irrational use of resources appear entirely rational; such programmes 'turn reason upside down'. Shouldn't crime control strategies be focused on those forms of offending that entail the most serious harms and costs?

Another important political undertow within Lippert and Wilkinson's analysis revolves around calling the legitimacy of the state into question. This is evident in their suggestion that *Crime Stoppers* operates as a form of 'counter-law' (2010, p. 140). The notion of counter-law refers to that range of norms, rules and practices that undermine formally recognised rights and legal protections. It is a difficult idea, but an example can make it more transparent. Democratic societies formally recognise that the state is required to prove an individual is guilty of any given criminal offence for which they have been charged. As a result, accused individuals have a right to trial, and they should not be punished for exercising this right. However, it is common practice to impose harsher sentences upon individuals who are found guilty at trial (National Association of Criminal Defense Lawyers 2018).

This tension has fostered legal systems in which most criminal cases involve some kind of plea bargaining, often affording more power to prosecutors who can threaten defendants with harsher penalties if they exercise their right to trial but subsequently lose the case. The fallout of this is that individuals cannot really exercise their right to trial without absorbing some degree of risk. That is, the formal right to trial is fairly meaningless because the actual operation of criminal justice is grounded in a range of counter-laws that turn any exercise of rights into a dangerous prospect. Of course, if the fundamental protections associated with democracy are a sham, it follows that democracy does not really exist.

Lippert and Wilkinson, then, are ultimately saying that programmes like *Crime Stoppers*, which are often tolerated, if not actively endorsed by public officials, cannot be easily reconciled with the types of formal rights that effectively define democracy. Publicising CCTV images that proport to document criminal offending, a practice orchestrated by powerful social groups, therefore becomes a problem. Street crime may well be undesirable, but so too are the strategies utilised by dominant social groups to curtail such behaviour. In this case, the presumption of innocence is undermined and society's most marginalised members are unfairly portrayed as inclined towards criminality.

When applied to the cultural outputs of the powerful, textual analysis may well avoid the deceitful and exploitative dynamics that accompany ethnography. However, textual analysis may become problematic if the scholar chooses to examine the cultural artefacts of subjugated or marginalised social groups. As various scholars have said of the CCCS approach to subcultures (discussed in Chapter 1), the dependence upon semiotics and hermeneutical readings often meant that what subcultural participants actually thought or had to say was simply excluded from the analysis (Clarke 1990; Williams 2007, p. 577). If ethnography is problematic for its tendency to include research participants in a manner that is exploitative, the problem for textual analysis may well be that it excludes those it talks about entirely.

'Nothing new to see here': Pat Carlen and Dale Spencer

In addition to its theoretical, methodological and political limits, scholars have also posed something of a broader question: does cultural criminology actually offer anything that is new to the field of criminology? Do we actually need yet another strand of criminological thought? What can it do for the development of knowledge that other approaches have not already done? Along these lines, Carlen (2011) considers three distinct types of criminology: those that operate under the label of 'critical', 'cultural' and 'public'. Carlen's core claim is that each of these strands, unfortunately, is haunted by four 'evangelical' tendencies, which minimise the likelihood that they will succeed in advancing new knowledge.

The first of these evangelical mantras is that cultural criminology is necessary as an antidote to positivist, 'mainstream criminology'. Cultural criminology, apparently, spends far too much time and energy construing the mainstream of criminology as positivistic and thus limited. This is problematic for various reasons. First, it is simply not accurate according to Carlen because cultural criminology is now a 'mainstream' approach within university settings. Second, and arguably of more importance, defining oneself as a negation of positivist criminology can stifle theoretical creativity and the production of new knowledge (Carlen 2011, p. 98). A constant iteration of what one negates runs the risk of remaining locked within an oppositional stance, thereby subtracting energy from the development of new insights.

Closely related, this obsession with defining oneself in opposition to a purported mainstream has methodological consequences as well. According to Carlen, the methods favoured by cultural criminology – such as ethnography, semiotics, interpretation and so on – are not inherently critical or politically progressive. Likewise, quantitative methods are not inherently conservative (Carlen 2011, p. 102; see also the preceding discussion of Harding). Methods are simply possible ways of doing research, and method selection should hinge on the type of problem that one is interested in. Thus, as much as cultural criminologists may assert otherwise, methods and politics cannot be equated, and the use of specific methods does not guarantee the production of knowledge that carries particular political meanings or implications.

A second evangelical tendency is evident in claims to be doing something new simply by focusing on 'meaning, representation and power'. It is all well and good to posit that paying attention to such themes is necessary, but their importance can be regarded as a 'taken-for-granted assumption in academic criminology since at least the 1960s' (Carlen 2011, p. 99). Construing what are long-standing concerns in criminology as 'new themes' is problematic because it can generate an ahistorical criminology, one that does not go beyond reproducing earlier ideas.

The third sign of evangelism is discernible in calls to 'join forces with the new cultural criminology'. Cultural criminology has described itself as a 'loose federation of outlaw intellectual critiques' (see Carlen 2011, p. 99) and invites those who are critically inclined to identify with the cultural criminology label. Attempting to bring critique together under one roof, however, may be problematic if it entails diminishing the force of particular critiques. In other words, to say that 'cultural criminology' can encompass the diversity of critical positions may exert a homogenising effect, and thus a dilution of 'outlawed' critiques.

Finally, the tendency in cultural criminology to see science and politics as inseparable and to insist that one ought to embrace the intertwined nature of knowledge production and political orientations, detracts from advancing new insights because it encourages prescriptive statements concerning what types of intellectual work can make meaningful contributions (and thus what types of work cannot contribute) to academic criminology. As this conflation of politics and science comes to command focal attention, cultural criminology is likely to become increasingly preoccupied with drawing boundaries that demarcate 'authentic' from 'inauthentic' knowledge.

As a counter-image to the one effectively drawn by these evangelical tendencies, Carlen (2011, p. 107) is adamant that criminology is better approached as a 'scientific art':

> The primary motivation is usually an intellectual curiosity... And the interest will be in the artful production of new knowledge – on puzzling over something – maybe data but maybe just a hunch or observation of a social phenomenon – and then getting something produced.

Rather than tell criminologists how they should operate as moral agents, Carlen (2011) suggests that it might be more important to focus on what actually needs to be done in criminology!

Dale Spencer (2011) offers a critique that, like Carlen, ultimately posits that cultural criminology does not offer much that is 'new'. From here, however, Spencer takes things in a slightly different direction and offers two additional critiques. First, he suggests that cultural criminology has not advanced our understanding of crime and criminalisation because it has not resolved the theoretical, and thus methodological, tensions discernible in those critical criminologies that emerged throughout the 1960s and 1970s. In this sense, cultural criminology exists within the past and, worse yet, continues to get lost in long-standing contradictions. Second, because it is premised upon a variety of unresolved contradictions, cultural criminology has failed to develop a grammar capable of significantly challenging administrative or positivist criminology.

These two critiques are demonstrated by juxtaposing cultural criminology with the critical, labelling theories that came to exert a profound influence in social thought during the 1960s. Spencer's comparison is structured by an examination of how the two strands of criminological thought engage with the themes of *power*, *identity* and *knowledge/epistemology*.

In social sciences and critical thinking, the concept of power has generated intense debate. In what is probably the more common view, power is understood as something that inheres in social structure. This view of power manifests in numerous schools of thought, but it is perhaps most discernible in Marxist scholarship. For many Marxists, it is the broader organisation of economy and society that fundamentally patterns everyday practices; political economy thus exercises power over the individual. In criminology, this has led to construing crime (and social control) as real behaviour that can be understood and empirically explored as a product of economic contradictions (Spencer 2011, p. 200).

In opposition to this view, power has also been understood as a force that traverses social life through knowledge and/or discourse. Once power and knowledge are seen as bound together, it follows that no practice can be understood outside of language. This view is often attributed to Michel Foucault (see Chapters 1 and 5), but something very much like it is central to labelling theory. Howard Becker (1963), for example, argued that privileged social groups (e.g., white men, adults, upper classes and so on) possess the power to create labels and apply such labels to others. In the context of criminology, this position has led to the notion that behaviours do not have any inherent meaning and so there is no behaviour that is inherently criminal. Rather, beliefs about what constitutes criminal behaviour embody the prejudices and moral sentiments held by relatively powerful social groups.

According to Spencer (2011), cultural criminology has contributed little to the advancement of critical thinking because it has not worked out its position on this very important point: do criminal acts have an objective basis in reality, or is the supposed reality of crime nothing more than a label that powerful groups use against the powerless? Somewhat obviously, how one answers this question will shape their sense of what counts as a problem worthy of scholarly exploration. After all, different conceptual understandings entail distinct research questions and methodologies. Amongst those who identify as cultural criminologists, some seem to accept that crime has a reality and can be understood as a product of structural inequalities (e.g., Young 1999, 2003. See Chapter 3); others regard crime as the outcome of discourses and labelling processes that reflect the normative standpoints of privileged social groups (e.g., Hayward and Yar 2006; see also Spencer 2011, pp. 200–202). Moreover, irrespective of which view is promoted, it would be fair to say that neither is without precedent.

Concerning identity, much academic thought has construed the individual as possessing a stable or 'essential' identity. Against such essentialist accounts, it has been suggested that the subject is better understood as 'fluid' or always in-flux. In this construction, our sense of self forever remains in a constant process of becoming and, as a result, our identities are never fixed. In Spencer's reading, cultural criminology claims to be influenced by the latter view and so it is this position that should be reflected in how cultural criminologists speak about the social groups that come to occupy centre stage in their analyses.

Cultural criminology, however, does not really seem to follow its own promise to recognise the subject as in a constant state of becoming. Spencer's point of comparison, once again, is labelling theory. In that school of thought, it was understood that individuals develop a sense of self in light of the social interactions in which they are embedded and move through. As such, individuals may drift into deviance and, depending on social reactions to their behaviour, may come to embrace a deviant identity. This identity may be sustained by subcultural membership, but it may also be destabilised and produced anew as social circumstances change (Spencer 2011, p. 206). For Spencer, this kind of delicacy is hard to discern in cultural criminology. Instead, the weight of social structure is seen as profoundly constraining individuals and subcultural groups in their ability to move across identities and possible subject positions.

Knowledge/epistemology constitutes Spencer's third theme for critically evaluating cultural criminology's claim to offer something new. As noted, cultural criminology tends to embrace a particular side in debates concerning how meaningful knowledge is produced. On the one hand, we have positivists, who tend to prioritise quantitative data and statistical analysis and who have often been portrayed as apathetic towards those who are criminalised. On the other, one finds the anti-positivist position, in which qualitative and interpretive approaches are favoured and where sympathy for those who are criminalised supposedly exists.

In the context of this broader debate over epistemology, the question posed by Spencer (2011, p. 207) is whether cultural criminology is any more critical than labelling theory in its adherence to the latter view. By now, the reader can probably pre-empt the response: there is little in cultural criminology that represents an advance over the labelling theorists that came before. More specifically, labelling theory rejected all the fundamental tenets of positivism, such as the tendency to accept that crime and deviance could be adequately understood via official statistics and quantitative techniques, the view that knowledge was objective or beyond politics and so on. Consistent with this rejection, labelling theorists prioritised ethnographic methods, thereby recognising the importance of deep immersion in the worlds of those deemed deviant if we truly wish to develop rich theoretical accounts.

Spencer (2011) acknowledges that cultural criminology has produced important ethnographies and, in this sense, the field has extended upon labelling theory. However, cultural criminology has also come to advocate for new methodological practices, such as 'instant' and 'liquid' ethnography. This move is seen as one that cultural criminology is more or less responsible for, but its desirability is questionable. The idea of 'speeding up' the ethnographic process – quickly getting into and out of the field, analysing a series of images or a particular media event – amounts to a 'McDonaldization' of research (Spencer 2011, p. 209). In other words, rationalising ethnography in such ways appears to be very much at odds with cultural criminology's refrain that better knowledge will follow from methodological immersion in the meaningful worlds that individuals and social groups inhabit.

Conclusion

As with Chapter 1, the methodological and political standpoints endorsed by cultural criminologists may be commendable in some respects, but they raise a series of problems that remain unresolved.

There is, for example, the claim that cultural criminology's preferred methods generate politically progressive accounts, or knowledge that disrupts a positivist criminology intent on serving the interests of the state and society's more powerful members. While positivist criminology certainly operates as an adjunct of power in many respects, this does not automatically guarantee that cultural criminology – because it purports to reject positivism – will serve a critical agenda. Ethnography can generate written accounts that communicate politically progressive messages, but the actual research processes entailed by the method may well be exploitative of those it researches. Indeed, Stacey (1988) argues that ethnography, because of the demands it places on participants and the extent to which it intrudes upon the lives of groups, might be more exploitative than positivist-type surveys, which demand relatively little of respondents. Is, then, ethnography able to claim progressive credentials given the power imbalances between researcher and researched upon which it hinges?

A comparable point could be made concerning textual analysis. There is nothing about this method that ensures a critique of power asymmetries will emerge from its use. Of course, this is possible, but by no means is the 'default setting' of the method one that reads 'speak back to power'. Much appears to hinge on whose textual output is subject to analysis. If one selects the communicative output of the powerful and privileged, the chances of disrupting power relations would appear to increase, but this is not guaranteed. A 'weak' interpretation is always possible. Applying the method to the relatively powerless – youthful groups, subcultures, etc. – seems to increase the likelihood that a politically disruptive text will fall by the wayside. This is precisely what the CCCS were criticised for (see Clarke 1990; Williams 2007). In examining the textual outputs of subcultures (i.e., their symbols, argot, styles and so on), the actual perspectives of participants were excluded from the analysis. Is this a critique of power, or academic elitism that mirrors the tendency of dominant social groups to dismiss the practices of young people?

And, although not exhaustive, a final dilemma raised by this chapter: does the rejection of positivism, and the turn to meaning by which it is accompanied, generate an approach that is new as is often presumed by cultural criminology? Cultural criminology has come under heavy attack for styling itself as an emergent, critical alternative and inviting others to join its ranks. For Carlen (2011), producing this type of propaganda is a distraction and simply withdraws energy from critical analysis. According to Spencer (2011), there is nothing in this turn to meaning, ethnography, immersion in subcultural worlds and so on, that takes us beyond labelling theory. To formulate the problem somewhat provocatively: does cultural criminology amount to an approach that is genuinely new, or is it little more than 'old wine in new bottles'?

3 THE CONCEPT OF CULTURE AND CRIMINALISED BEHAVIOUR

Introduction

The fundamental elements of cultural criminology – its theoretical origins, conceptual repertoire, methodological preferences and political orientations – were treated over the course of Chapters 1 and 2. In this chapter, we turn to how cultural criminology has sought to theorise criminalised behaviour, a topic that would seem unavoidable given that criminology and crime are so thoroughly interrelated.

Within cultural criminology, crime is not a straightforward concept. As noted in Chapter 1, there is a strand of thought in which crime is understood not as behaviour that transpires in the real world, but as a category that constructs some behaviours as criminal. In the theoretical pantheon of cultural criminology, this view is often attributed to Howard Becker (1963) and his notion of labelling, but it is also discernible in the radical constructivist position. Despite seeing crime as a cultural construct, the concept of culture has simultaneously been utilised to develop theoretical accounts concerning the motivations to criminalised behaviour. To be sure, and as noted in the concluding remarks of Chapter 1, there is a major dilemma here: crime cannot be understood as something that inheres in actual behaviour and, at the same time, a cultural or discursive resource that constructs reality. These views are logically incompatible. As such, crime is either real and can be explained, or crime is discursive and its use as a category warrants interrogation.

This chapter is organised around accounts that accept – at least to some degree – the first of these propositions (crime exists and can be theorised). Four broad ways in which a concept of culture has figured in attempts to explain crime are discussed. The chapter begins with 'culture of poverty' arguments, in which poverty is seen as generating specific cultural sensibilities that are conducive to crime. This argument is not one that has been advanced by those who identify as cultural criminologists. Nevertheless, it appears here as a reference point, one that can provide some sense of how culture takes on quite specific meanings within cultural criminology.

Bringing us into the realm of cultural criminology, the chapter then discusses theories in which dominant culture is seen as an important driver of crime. Arguments along these lines owe a debt to Merton's use of anomie or strain (see Chapter 1), but some subtle variations in theory can be detected here. This section begins with the work of Carl Nightingale (1993), which has been cited approvingly and appropriated by cultural criminologists. Nightingale shows how mainstream American culture suffuses poor inner-city communities. This is conducive to crime because the cultural realm encourages all kinds of desires and aspirations but, because of economic exclusion, these are rendered impossible to realise. The problem for those in poor inner-city communities, essentially, is that they are simultaneously included (via cultural values) and excluded (via unemployment, precarious employment) by society. Jock Young (1999, 2003) extends upon this notion of inclusion/exclusion by showing how it can explain crime, but also punitiveness. Furthermore, Young argues that inclusion/exclusion (i.e., the simultaneity of cultural inclusion and economic exclusion) implies that crime needs to be understood as transgressive, an emotionally charged rejection of dominant social order.

Following this, the chapter looks at the notions of 'edgework' and 'carnival', which intimate that crime may also entail escape from repressive social structures and playing with boundaries. Finally, the chapter considers arguments in which criminalised behaviour is interpreted as a 'project'. For Jack Katz (1988), crime amounts to a project in the sense that individuals are seduced by its promise to restore order to one's moral universe when this is disrupted. For Jeff Ferrell (1996), crime is a project insofar as it provides subcultural groups a mechanism of resistance or 'cultural politics'. Table 3.1 provides a schematic overview of these four arguments:

Table 3.1 Concepts of culture and criminalised behaviour

Theoretical approach	Culture–crime nexus	Strengths	Limits
Culture of poverty	Cultural worldviews as adaptation to poverty and, once formed, conducive to crime	Recognises culture as important to explaining crime	Tendency to 'pathologise' those in poverty
		Recognition of culture as complicated, multifaceted	Has been characterised as victim-blaming discourse

Theoretical approach	Culture–crime nexus	Strengths	Limits
Poverty of dominant culture	Mainstream culture (e.g., sanctioning of violence) as conducive to criminalised behaviour	Avoids reducing crime to problem at individual or social group level	Hard to explain why crime is not more common (given that mainstream culture, which suffuses social life, is problematic)
		Construes culture as an independent or antecedent force	Somewhat simplistic view of (mainstream) culture
Escapism	Culture as oppressive, crime to escape feelings of constraint	Rich contextual account of risk-taking and/or crime	Struggles to explain criminalised behaviours that are mundane
		Draws strong links between socio-cultural dynamics and the psyche	Romanticisation of crime and deviance
Transcendent projects and cultural politics	Crime to 'honour' cultural sentiments	Can explain a wide range of non-rational crime (and behaviour)	Like 'escapism' above, tendency to romanticise crime
	Crime as embodying political standpoints	Recognises creative capacity of subcultural groups	Difficult to construe many crimes (e.g., murder) as political

The last three accounts of culture and crime – inclusion/exclusion, escape, project – are often regarded as the core of cultural criminology, its most fundamental contributions to making sense of criminalised behaviour. It is not surprising, then, that it is this area of cultural criminology that has been subject to intense critique. In fact, the efforts of cultural criminology to link culture and crime have generated such intense debate that the critiques warrant a separate chapter. Given this, the present chapter keeps critical commentary to a minimum as this is explored subsequently in Chapter 4.

Culture of poverty arguments

Culture of poverty arguments are typically premised on the notion that the class structure of a society generates specific cultural worldviews. That is to say, one will find a cultural framework that is particular to the working class, another cultural framework that corresponds to the middle class and so on. In the late 1950s, Walter Miller (1958) adopted this logic in order to explain 'juvenile delinquency'.

The distinct nature of Miller's argument becomes clear when contrasted with Albert Cohen (1955), who suggested that youthful offending was a manifestation of working-class youth rebelling against middle-class norms and values (see Chapter 1). Miller rejected this, arguing that delinquency was better understood as an attempt to embody the 'focal concerns' of lower-class culture. In other words, the offending behaviours of young, working-class youth are motivated by a desire to conform to peer-group norms.

The core concept in Miller's argument is 'focal concerns', which summarises the structure of working-class culture and pinpoints how it can motivate the behaviour of individuals from the working class. According to Miller, there are six main focal concerns: trouble, toughness, smartness, excitement, fate and autonomy (1958, p. 7). Each of these concerns is essentially a spectrum consisting of two opposing points. For example, 'trouble' ranges from a concern with law-abiding behaviour to law-violating behaviour; 'toughness' ranges from exercising caution to displaying physical strength. Due to their spectral quality, different orientations to these focal concerns are possible, depending on one's social role. Miller (1958) illustrates this by noting, for instance, that a working-class woman with children will certainly be preoccupied with 'trouble', but will gravitate towards the law-abiding end of the spectrum: if her children were to bring home potential partners, she would most likely wish that they were not engaging in law-violating acts. Some teenage youths, however, may accord more prestige to the 'non-law-abiding' end of the 'trouble' spectrum.

With this framework in place, Miller proposes that crimes and deviant acts, especially those committed by teenage men, are a product of valuing the 'negative side' of the focal concerns that structure lower-class culture. In this sense, criminalised and deviant behaviour may accord status to young men within their immediate peer group. Given the shared working-class cultural milieu, it is hard to posit that such acts amount to rebellion as Cohen (1955) claimed. Rather, they can be better understood as moments of conformity, attempts to fit in and belong with one's immediate peer group.

Such an argument is important insofar as it utilises culture as an explanatory variable, and suggests that the notion is necessary to understand crime and deviance. It also has the merit of positing that cultural frameworks are likely to be complex. Much to his credit, Miller refrains from painting working-class culture with broad brushstrokes. However, as scholars have said of similar arguments, there is a subtle way in which Miller's use of culture amounts to 'blaming the victims' for their criminalised behaviour (Ryan 1976; Goode 2002; Steinberg 2011). In some respects, Miller offers what could be called a 'pathologising discourse'. In claiming that individuals can gravitate towards focal concerns in variable ways, they are construed as choosing to engage in deviance. Given the force of structural conditions, however, criminalised behaviour is arguably a much more complicated matter.

More disconcertingly, perhaps, Miller suggests that working-class culture is inherently problematic or deficient. This is evident insofar as it is working-class focal concerns, or aspects of those concerns, that are construed as the source of deviant behaviour. This effectively portrays crime and deviance as endogenous to the working class. Material conditions (e.g., exclusionary labour markets) and cultural orientations (e.g., consumerism) that originate well beyond the working classes and which may be conducive to criminalised behaviour are rendered invisible.

Although Miller's account may seem dated, and although the logic underpinning it has been criticised for blaming the victims, it is by no means a relic of the past. This is perhaps most evident in Elijah Anderson's notion of a 'code of the street'. In *Code of the Streets* (1999) and *Streetwise* (1990), Anderson draws from ethnographic fieldwork to explain violent interpersonal behaviour in predominantly black, urban communities within the United States. He suggests that the deindustrialisation process, combined with racial prejudice, has adversely affected the economic status of black communities. A major development in the US economy during the 1960s and 1970s, deindustrialisation involved companies relocating their production centres to other parts of the world in order to exploit cheaper labour power. Prior to this, many black Americans found some semblance of job security by working in factories, especially as unskilled or semi-skilled labourers. As these jobs were relocated outside the US, however, poverty quickly became a defining feature of working-class communities.

As communities became more impoverished, middle-class black people fled to the suburbs. This middle-class flight ensured the exodus of middle-class values, or as Anderson might put it, the 'code of decency'. It was as this moral vacuum opened up, in conjunction with growing joblessness, that the values associated with a 'code of the street' emerged and became entrenched (Anderson 1990, pp. 57–69; 1999, pp. 145–150; see also Wilson 1987). The core value within the 'code of the street' is respect or deference which, for several reasons, is intimately tied to violence. Using violence becomes a way to accumulate respect from others, thereby affording oneself some protection in dangerous environments. Furthermore, according to the code of the street, one must demonstrate a willingness to use violence, which may be manifested in a number of ways – through their attitude towards others, their clothing and/or style and so on. Demonstrations of the willingness to use violence, however, can often lead to actual violence.

While Anderson acknowledges the importance of broader economic relations, and how these are shaped by racial inequalities, the claim that poverty fosters a particular set of cultural orientations that, in turn, cause violence (and a host of other social problems) is not without controversy. As with Miller's argument, this effectively suggests that poor people are responsible for fabricating a cultural framework that causes problems within their urban environment. Moreover, it is this culture of poverty that may reproduce impoverished material conditions of existence. In some sense, the theory implies that the problems stemming from material deprivation could be addressed via some sort of process focused on 'fixing' the morals of poor people.

Poverty of dominant cultures: The problem of concurrent inclusion and exclusion

Against the view that a culture of poverty exists and can be used to explain crime, others have drawn attention to the problematic nature of dominant cultures. This view can be regarded as an offshoot of Merton's (1938) focus on the tensions between culturally established goals and social means, and even Matza and Sykes's (1961) notion of 'subterranean values' (see Chapter 1). It amounts to a strong rejection of culture of poverty-type approaches. In the culture of poverty view, those who engage in crime are reduced to their social exclusion, as if they could exist in some kind of socio-cultural bubble that is cut off from the rest of society. This allows mainstream society to elude analysis: the problem of crime emerges 'over there', in the culture of the 'other'. The politically conservative implications of such a view are somewhat obvious. It is this shortage of reflexivity, the failure to locate crime in the broader socio-cultural order, that the notion of inclusion/exclusion seeks to correct.

In terms of the relationship between mainstream American culture and crime, the work of Carl Nightingale (1993) has often been appropriated by cultural criminology. Like Elijah Anderson, Nightingale draws from ethnographic fieldwork conducted in an impoverished, predominantly black, inner-city community and begins by drawing attention to racism and the economic conditions that emerged in the wake of deindustrialisation. The relocation of industrial jobs to far-flung suburbs and other countries left many inner-city residents out of work and thus excluded from the economy. However, instead of claiming that an idiosyncratic culture has been spawned by poverty and racial marginalisation, Nightingale finds that many poor people are deeply invested in mainstream culture. It is this inclusion in mainstream American culture, combined with social and economic exclusion, that is conducive to crime.

There are four core currents in mainstream culture that profoundly shape the worldviews and behaviours of those in Nightingale's study. First, the belief that physical punishment is the most viable way to promote moral sensibilities and control behaviour. This leads many parents to use corporal forms of punishment in raising children (Nightingale 1993). Second, the persistence of negative racial stereotypes, most notably those that link the black body with sexual promiscuousness and violence (Nightingale 1993, p. 127). Particularly evident in the dominance of advertising, the third cultural current concerns conspicuous consumption, which dictates that one's social standing and worth is evidenced by their consumption choices. Fourth, the glorification of violence that can be discerned in militarism and even more so in a countless number of television shows and movies produced by culture industries (Nightingale 1993, pp. 167–177). Such glorifications of violence typically convey the message that aggression constitutes a legitimate way to solve problems and achieve justice.

The reasons for poor, inner-city residents developing strong investments in these cultural currents are complex. Nightingale suggests that racial marginalisation and economic exclusion generate a profound sense of internalised humiliation, especially among younger people. This leads many to seek out compensatory strategies, or ways to secure a sense of personal adequacy (Nightingale 1993, p. 42). Mainstream culture is spread through very powerful mechanisms that often saturate inner-city life. Television, cinemas, radio and advertising, not to mention places of commerce, dominate our mental and physical environments. Mainstream culture is everywhere and turning to it can go some way towards alleviating feelings of humiliation: acquiring the latest mass-produced status item, even if it is stolen, can mitigate one's awareness of being excluded from society; living up to racial stereotypes can take the sting out of the damage they do to one's psyche; given the way cultural industries routinely portray violence as the ultimate panacea, it is not hard to see why some would turn to it when others insult them or obstruct the pursuit of their interests.

According to Nightingale, much of the crime and deviance recorded in poor inner-city communities can be attributed to this potent combination of extreme economic exclusion and cultural inclusion. The solutions that mainstream culture promises its adherents, however, often turn out to be illusory or invite further problems. For example, the sense of competence that may come from acquiring new clothes or shoes is short-lived; utilising violence to address insults may lead to entanglement with the criminal justice system.

Nightingale's work appears as an important influence in Jock Young's (1999, 2003) account of how the cultural realm engenders crime. Young, however, stretches the notion of inclusion/exclusion – which he often refers to as social 'bulimia' – in some novel directions, leading to a nuanced theory of criminalised behaviour and, in addition, an explanation of the punitive and vindictive ethos discernible in late-modernity (a theme to which we return in Chapter 8).

Consistent with Merton (1938) and Nightingale (1993), Young acknowledges that culture operates as a force of inclusion – by infusing the subject with desires and expectations – and that the economy operates to exclude. According to Young, however, it is not that culture simply includes while the economic excludes. Instead, the dynamic of inclusion/exclusion operates in all of society's fundamental institutions. To give a few illustrations, education brings many into its orbit, but simultaneously excludes in its tendencies to normalise and reproduce social inequalities; the labour market does expand to provide jobs, but these jobs are often precarious and poorly paid such that one cannot participate as a full member in society; the political sphere constantly invites us to pay attention to the happenings of government and to participate by voting, but the majority of people are probably correct in assuming that they do not have any real political power, that their voices are irrelevant to political decision-making; consumerism produces subjects that conflate their sense of self with commodities, but does not make these commodities readily accessible (Young 2003, pp. 397–398).

The concurrence of inclusion and exclusion has important implications for theorising crime. Echoing Merton, but also Nightingale, Young acknowledges that crime can be understood as an instrumental response to inclusion/exclusion. That is, crime allows one to alleviate strain, to close the gap between culturally induced promises of fulfilment and empty realities. However, crime must be understood as more than instrumental in the sense just described. It is also expressive, emotionally charged and driven, and meaningful to those who engage in it. It is precisely because crime occurs in the context of an inclusive/exclusive, 'bulimic' society that Young sees it as 'transgressive': it involves 'delight in excess, a glee in breaking the rules, a reassertion of dignity and identity' (Young 2003, p. 408). In crime, one 'speaks back' to the precarity, humiliation and frustration spawned by a set of structural relations in which much is promised, but very little honoured in reality. We will see these themes of transgression, resistance, crime as agentic response, reappear in some of the accounts summarised below.

What is perhaps most interesting about Young's account is its attempt to explain the rise of a punitive and vindictive public – particularly obvious amongst the middle classes according to Young – via the trope of inclusion/exclusion. For it is not only the socially marginalised who are subject to late-modernity's bulimia, but the entire social body. Everybody is just as included/excluded as everybody else. Granted, this has particular manifestations and implications depending on one's social location. Amongst the middle classes, a category that Young treats in some depth, the primary problem appears to be the precarious and thus illusory nature of their inclusion. The middle classes may have access to forms of employment that keep them out of poverty, but the security of these jobs is tenuous. At any moment, it seems that jobs can be lost and, if this transpires, one will be cast adrift in an ocean of insecurity.

Occupying such a middle location is not eased by the fact that one can peer upwards and/or downwards. Looking up, one sees a class of people that is incredibly wealthy, but inexplicably so. What does such a group of people do that justifies the rewards they receive? Those occupying the middle rungs of society sense that they have made just as many sacrifices, worked just as hard, but somehow remain insecure (Young 2003, p. 399). Looking downwards does not provide comfort either. Gazing down, those in the middle class are likely to see a group of people who reject work but receive public welfare, engage in hedonistic lifestyles, and live carefree. Of course, this is a stereotypical view, but the middle class is easily led to it via discourses available in the mass media, the political realm and so on (Young 2003, p. 405).

In Young's view, occupying such a location, and the comparisons to others that it invites, ultimately generates a strong sense of relative deprivation and resentment. The middle class sees itself as sacrificing, renouncing its own hedonistic desires in order to play by the rules, and yet unable to secure the basics of a secure life. Their sacrifice, in short, is not socially recognised or appreciated. Hence the resentment and 'secret envy' of those below: they refuse to sacrifice, but appear content nonetheless. It is this smouldering jealousy that quickly turns into a wish to punish the 'other' (Young 1999, 2003). An interesting idea, to be sure, but one may wonder why the classes at the top of the social order do not seem to emerge as targets for this middle-class resentment?

The escapism of edgework and the carnival

Rather than emphasising how crime embodies conformity to dominant socio-cultural forces (that it can be thought to reveal how subjects are so fundamentally interpellated by the hegemonic order), some theory has accentuated 'escape'. One of the most influential ideas within cultural criminology in these respects is Stephen Lyng's concept of edgework. According to Lyng (1990, p. 852), edgework is most clearly discerned in a range of risk-taking activities that are voluntarily chosen, such as skydiving, scuba diving and rock-climbing. What unites these kinds of activities is that they are likely to expose individuals to serious injury and perhaps even death. It is not hard to see that many other types of behaviour could easily fit into this kind of analysis. Individuals who engage in 'joyriding', for example, may routinely threaten their personal wellbeing in the course of such behaviour. Insofar as such activities draw individuals towards the border that separates life and death, safety and danger, order and disorder, Lyng (1990, p. 857) frames them as forms of edgework.

Lyng emphasises the subjective dimensions of deviance or edgework alongside the structural contexts in which they are embedded. At the subjective level, individuals who engage in forms of edgework are benefitted by it in several ways. Most notably, they gain a sense of self-realisation or omnipotence through risk-taking (Lyng 1990, p. 860). One might be inclined to say that they get a feeling of accomplishment through such activities; the sense that they have successfully done something. Feelings of omnipotence and self-realisation transpire because edgework demonstrates to participants that they are capable of exercising control over dangerous situations. This 'inflated' sense of one's power can be used to negotiate threatening situations that may arise in the future.

But, why would individuals seek out such experiences? What drives the need for such feelings of control? Lyng draws from Karl Marx and George Herbert Mead, who had much to say about the kinds of forces that exist beyond individuals and shape subjectivity and behaviour, to explain risk-taking activity. From Marx, Lyng takes the idea that individual freedom and fulfilment resides in the ability to objectify one's creative capacity through labour. There is, according to Marx (1994a), a certain kind of satisfaction that comes from working in a way that embodies an individual's creative capacities while addressing human needs.

Under capitalism, however, individuals are not free to work in ways that are consistent with their creative desires. Rather, having been robbed of a direct connection to land and nature, they are forced to sell their labour power to a capitalist class in order to survive (Marx 1906). Driven by a relentless quest for profit, the capitalist class is not concerned with the idea of fulfilment through work. The demand for profit necessitates that the production process be scientifically managed and constantly sped up. In this system of production, workers are compelled to become extensions of machinery, reduced to isolated and repetitive tasks (Marx 1994b). For Lyng, this is the first source of constraint that leads individuals to seek out forms of edgework.

Mead was more interested in the problem of the 'self' and how it is produced. To elucidate the development of a 'self', Mead posited a distinction between the 'I' and the 'me'. The 'self' is an outcome of an ongoing dialogue between the 'I' and the 'me' (Mead 1934). According to Mead, the 'me' is that part of my consciousness that absorbs social attitudes and cultural values. It is, in other words, the internalisation of society's norms and expectations concerning my own attitudes and behaviours. As I go about engaging in action, or think about future actions, this 'me' is likely to be there, acting as a check on my thoughts and desires. In this sense, the 'me' compels reflexivity; it demands that I constantly evaluate any proposed course of action in light of social and cultural expectations.

The 'I' is that internal force that is always in dialogue with the 'me'. Although it seeks to represent and embody individual desires, it is likely to be called forth by the 'me'. Defined in this way, the 'me' can be construed as a second source of constraint on individual choice and freedom. I might have a strong compulsion to urinate in public, walk to the supermarket in my underwear, randomly throw rocks through store windows and so on. However, the socialisation process – internalised in the 'me' – works to ensure that I do not depart from social norms and expectations. The 'me' suppresses my 'I'.

It is these sources of constraint – the exploitation of my labour power under capitalism and a socialisation process that enforces a constant self-monitoring of my desires – that are eluded through edgework. In exposing oneself to situations that involve a considerable degree of danger, the individual must rely on their wits and their 'instincts' to survive. In doing so, they can gain access to 'pure' experiences of creative control and escape the repressive nature of the 'me' (Lyng 1990). In dangerous situations, one must 'do'; action must be immediate and non-reflexive. In short, the repressive 'me' is repressed and the 'I' occupies centre stage.

The work of Mike Presdee (2000), also quite an influential figure in the field of cultural criminology, has some parallels with Lyng's account but is distinct in several important respects. Much like Lyng, Presdee also focuses on constraining social conditions and escape, but the underlying logic or meaning of escape is not quite the same across their accounts. The major theoretical influence in Presdee's work is Mikhail Bakhtin and his notion of 'carnival'. Carnival can be understood as those moments of 'time out of time' during which indulgence, excess, irrational behaviour and the mockery of those in power is permitted. Carnival allows its participants to play with the border between order and disorder, to invert the social roles that predominate in everyday life (Presdee 2000, p. 39).

This is an abstract definition, but it is not hard to identify concrete examples. I recall, for example, that my elementary school hosted a celebration at the end of each school year. One of the most enticing attractions was the 'dunking booth', which involved a teacher sitting on a plank hoisted above a small pool of water. The plank was connected to a target board, and if you hit it with a thrown ball, the plank would drop and the teacher would fall into the water. All of this embodies elements of the carnivalesque: rather than the student, it is the teacher that is subject to possible humiliation; the power relation that typically prevails between student and teacher is inverted, with students given the chance to subjugate the teacher. Of course, this is 'time out of time' that only lasts for a specified period. At the end of the day, the dunking booth is packed up and taken away and business as usual quickly resumes.

For Presdee, the carnival is a necessity and social order hinges on its existence. Its historical forms, however, have been eviscerated within modernity. The main threat to the carnival has come from the state and capitalism: the former insofar as it promotes bureaucracy and rational order, the latter because it seeks to commodify the carnival. What, for example, has become of Christmas and New Year's Eve? Things may well vary depending on where you live, but the time allocated for these holidays dwindles and both events become increasingly commercialised. In New York City, the Times Square approach to New Year's Eve reduces the event to watching some ball drop and then going home. The consumption of alcohol is forbidden by state laws and, because approximately one million people are aggressively competing for viewing spots, you might want to wear a diaper in case you need to urinate lest you miss the event (Myers 2018). If this were an 'authentic' carnival, by contrast, you would most likely get incredibly drunk and urinate in public or perhaps your pants.

Presdee (2000, p. 45) suggests that despite the best efforts of modernity to eviscerate carnival, if not because of them, it has shattered and dispersed throughout society. In fact, as the unbearable rationality of modern life intensifies, carnival becomes all the more necessary (Presdee 2000, p. 160). It can now be found in the crevices of everyday life, in pockets of subcultural practice, such as joyriding, body modification, S&M, raves and recreational drug-taking to name a few. As carnival splinters off, however, it is increasingly criminalised by the state (Presdee 2000). Body modification practices, for example, are regulated by the state; raves have effectively been rendered criminal in some places. This essentially leads to the claim that many criminalised practices constitute the current ways in which carnival survives. Crime is carnival.

While carnival is an escape, it is not the same kind of escape described by Lyng's edgework. To frame criminalised behaviour as a carnival implies that it is not so much about finding the pure self or regaining control over one's existence, but the pursuit of pleasure. For Presdee, the carnival of crime is about letting go and being out of control; it is hedonistic (2000, p. 121). Related to these characteristics, and especially given the now-fragmented nature of carnival, it no longer has 'closure' or a period that marks its end and return to routine existence. Instead, it is interspersed throughout life, often unplanned and able to erupt at any given moment. Finally, Presdee's aligning of crime and carnival suggests that criminalised practices often involve a direct engagement with hegemony, an undermining of those in power and a critique of broader social power relations. Lyng's edgeworkers may seek escape from oppressive social structures, and this may imply a critique of contemporary socio-cultural arrangements, but many forms of edgework do not threaten those in power. Thus, carnival implies that crime is always a social relation; edgework does not necessarily have this quality.

Crime as project: Restoring one's moral universe and meaningful political engagements

Our last set of accounts in which culture plays an important role in explaining criminalised behaviour is embodied in the work of Jack Katz (1988) and Jeff Ferrell (1996). Their work is not at odds with Lyng and Presdee, but it is nuanced in some respects. The contribution they make stems from the notion that crime might be best interpreted as a project. To be sure, they offer slightly different takes on exactly how crime is a project. For Katz, many crimes are non-rational quests for moral transcendence; for Ferrell, crime often amounts to a cultural politics.

In *Seductions of Crime*, Katz (1988) begins by suggesting that it is important to recognise the subjective dimensions that accompany our behaviours, especially those at the borderline of legality. He refers to such subjective dimensions as the 'foreground' of crime and differentiates this from the 'background' of crime. Prior to Katz, much criminological work conducted in a critical vein focused on background factors. With this distinction in mind, he seeks to draw attention to the situational factors that drive an individual to commit a deviant act. Many people live in poverty (a 'background' factor), but not all of them engage in property crime in order to overcome 'strain', as Merton (1938) may have suggested. So, according to Katz, there must be something in the very moments that precede a crime, and that define its duration, that ensure its occurrence. What, then, is occurring in these specific foreground moments of a crime?

Katz resolves this dilemma by showing how criminals are trying to accomplish something through their actions (hence the notion of 'project'). His most provocative example to demonstrate the foreground of crime is what he refers to as 'righteous slaughter'. In conventional terminology, righteous slaughter might be understood as murder that is not premeditated. Katz (1988, pp. 3–43) identifies three moments to righteous slaughter and, by extension, other forms of criminal behaviour. In the first moment, the offender perceives events as somehow threatening or perhaps as a challenge. Before a hot-blooded murder, for instance, one may have their sense of self-importance undermined by an insult. This insult triggers an emotional reaction that typically begins with humiliation and escalates to a feeling of rage. Once this state is reached, an individual is likely to act in a way that 'transcends' or 'honours' their emotional condition. In this sense, 'righteous slaughter' accomplishes something for the individual who engages in it: the act of murder addresses a perceived wrong, thereby restoring balance to one's 'moral universe'.

Individuals who commit violent and other forms of crime often have a hard time explaining why they acted in such ways after the fact. For Katz, this makes sense given that one is seeking to transcend powerful emotions during crime. Such emotional states are likely to suppress rational thought and judgement, thereby making a logical account difficult. However, while many forms of offending may well be non-rational, this is not to say that those who commit crime have some kind of psychological problem that sets them apart from the rest of us. Indeed, the subjective processes that precede crime are not unusual according to Katz. From this perspective, what is most alarming about righteous slaughter is not that it seems so extreme, alien and inexplicable, but that we recognise the ways in which we are likely to be familiar with the subjective processes that underpin murder and other types of criminal conduct (Katz 1988, p. 324).

In suggesting that crime is a moral project, Katz's explicit focus is very much on subjective processes, or what is happening within the individual. But it is difficult not to recognise that much of the inner processes described by Katz have cultural origins. The variability of cultural sentiments that appear to interpolate subjectivity is perhaps evidenced by some of Katz's empirical examples. Katz references the case of Francine Hughes, who killed a violent male partner who was preventing her from acquiring independence through education. He also references a case in which a man kills his wife after she calls out another man's name during sex (Katz 1988, pp. 14–15). In the former case, the aggressor is said to be defending an interpretation of the American Dream in which independence and self-improvement is prioritised; in the latter case, it is the idea of marital fidelity that is being defended. Although Katz does not necessarily focus on broad cultural forces and how these shape subjectivity, it seems somewhat obvious that respect for individual autonomy and fidelity are leitmotifs of deeply ingrained cultural frameworks. As much as crime may be a personal project to restore one's sense of how the world ought to be, conceptions of what is morally correct appear to be culturally conditioned.

Taking his lead from Katz, Jeff Ferrell (1996) also focuses on the foreground of criminalised behaviour. Rather than seeing crime as an attempt to honour one's moral code, however, Ferrell suggests that various forms of criminalised behaviour have important political dimensions. That is to say, some forms of deviance offer a critique of contemporary social relations and hint at what a more reasonable or ethical society might look like. Ferrell builds this line of interpretation from an ethnographic exploration – conducted in Denver, Colorado around the late 1980s and early 1990s – of graffiti writing culture and official opposition to the subcultural practice.

Ferrell intimates that the practices of writing graffiti and official opposition to it can be thought of as projects. Furthermore, the tension between the two pursuits offers an ideal way to observe the politics of crime. Through participant observations, Ferrell begins by charting the everyday realities that surround the illegal painting of graffiti. He finds that the production of graffiti can involve the need for planning and collaboration amongst numerous individuals. Insofar as this is the case, it is typically a dialogic and democratic process. However, oftentimes the best-laid plans of graffiti writers are thwarted by spray paint cans that run out earlier than anticipated, the sudden presence of others at proposed locations, and urges to paint something different from what was initially intended (Ferrell 1996).

Alongside a range of other qualities, these ensure that graffiti has something of a chaotic nature: graffiti writers must adapt to the immediacy of the situation, they must be flexible and fluid in their creative desires. In addition to this, graffiti itself is something of a chaotic, unexpected rupture within the urban landscape. Painted overnight, it is suddenly 'there' the next morning. Its content is often cryptic to those unfamiliar with the dynamics of graffiti writing subcultures, but it may also be playful and witty. In either case, the passer-by is likely to be stopped by the presence of graffiti and some kind of attempt to decipher its meaning may take place. And, of course, when graffiti is painted without permission it inevitably takes up some relation to the legal context in which it has been produced (Ferrell 1996, p. 26).

But how does any of this amount to graffiti being read as a political project? According to Ferrell, such an interpretation becomes plausible when the core features of graffiti are juxtaposed with those of anarchism (Ferrell 1996, pp. 160–166). As a political standpoint, anarchism promotes decentralised modes of power in which collective decision-making is dominant, accepts that multiple realities and truths are possible, and often utilises playful ways to disrespect authority. Ferrell points out that much of this political philosophy resurfaces in graffiti writing: its creative content is often premised upon collective discussion and taunts those in authority; it questions the aesthetic appearance of the urban environment and which social interests effectively determine this; and, amongst other things, it breaks with the routinisation of everyday life insofar as it is haphazard and produced in the 'off-peak' hours of the week.

When these aspects of graffiti are counterposed with the rhetoric and practices of those who oppose it, its political meaning becomes even clearer. The most organised opposition to graffiti often comes from local political elites and business interests. They often insist that graffiti is nothing more than mindless vandalism that undermines the city's visual appearance (Ferrell 1996, p. 178). And, not surprisingly, they frequently charge that graffiti is a 'problem' because it violates the rights of private property owners. Heavily funded campaigns geared towards the removal of graffiti or painting over it with various shades of grey usually follow such arguments. Anti-graffiti efforts that obey this logic demonstrate an alliance between the state and privileged social classes, one replete with a preferred urban aesthetic premised upon uniformity of appearance (Ferrell 1996, pp. 180–184). Their efforts are likely to be directed against those who are relatively marginalised or, perhaps a little more precisely, those who lack power within economic and political domains.

It is these underlying social relations that are playing out in struggles over the aesthetic appearance of the city and the heated debates that surround graffiti. On the one side, we have those in power who insist on hierarchical forms of social organisation and, on the other, those who are relatively powerless but still resistant. Insofar as all this plays out under the cover of aesthetic practices, it becomes possible to frame graffiti as cultural politics. Ferrell is quick to point out that graffiti writers may not necessarily be aware of how their practices constitute a political project, and that graffiti may not amount to a very effective mode of political action. But, then again, what forms of resistance are perfect? Are protests that involve seeking a permit from the state and which take place in pre-approved times and spaces any better? (Ferrell 1996, pp. 177–178; see also Chapter 4). More important in the present context, however, is the theoretical interpretation made of graffiti and, by extension, comparable forms of crime. To what extent can we read criminalised practices as projects that embody politics by cultural means?

Conclusion

Organised according to four strands of thought, this chapter has explored some of the ways in which scholars have theorised the relationship between culture and criminalised behaviour. Although there are similarities across accounts, differences in theory often stem from how the notion of culture is understood. Amongst culture of poverty theorists, culture is construed as a product of occupying specific class and social locations. Against this, some have suggested that culture may come from specific social locations (such as business interests and/or mass media), but emphasise how cultural values and orientations are promulgated throughout society. This often leads to seeing culture as a problem because it is 'imposed from above' rather than 'produced from below'. In theories that revolve around the quest for escape, culture is seen as a force that constrains the individual and thus partially responsible for behaviour that deviates from the norm. Others see culture as a heteroglossia of sentiments, some of which may be recognised as worth honouring or defending through action.

Despite multiple accounts of how culture may influence crime, the body of thought discussed in this chapter is not without limitations. We have already had opportunity to note the kind of critique that radical constructivists would make of the theoretical ideas described above (see Chapter 1), but it is worth briefly reiterating the substance of this position and the challenge it poses.

According to radical constructivism, all of the accounts summarised here can be charged with ontologising crime (Hulsman 1986). That is, they presume that crime is a real behaviour, the causes of which can be identified in some reality held to exist independently of our capacity to observe. Operating within such an epistemological space, crime is always construed as a 'symptom' of some underlying sickness or pathology. For the culture of poverty theorist, it is the cultural worldviews that, stemming from poverty, are causative of crime. For those who emphasise inclusion/exclusion, the sociocultural order is 'sick' and crime is a symptom of this sickness. Likewise, the notions of edgework, carnival and resistance presuppose that the social order can be understood according to its pathological properties (see Carrier 2006). Such perspectives, according to the radical constructivist, are problematic because they fail to call the very category of crime into question. As such, they can no longer explore how 'crime' is a discourse (or a label) that hierarchically organises the social body into distinct groups (Young 1996).

Even if, however, one accepts that crime is a reality that can be theorised – that it makes sense to search for its causes – problems remain. For example, questions concerning the general applicability of these theories linger. This is perhaps most obvious in light of some of the causal forces that appear in Nightingale's account. One can easily imagine that mediated images in which violence is glorified are common enough, but how the 'fetish' for militarism plays out in the context of the United States is, arguably, quite peculiar to that country.

More broadly, those interested in the culture–crime nexus often draw data from specific sites and social groups and tend to focus on particular forms of offending. In this chapter, we have seen several accounts that focus quite heavily on the activities of young men and behaviours that, although deemed criminal, are relatively innocuous (e.g., Ferrell 1996; Miller 1958; Presdee 2000). To what extent do the theories described here account for the crimes of individuals from different social locations? Are they effective as general explanations of crime? Or, are they not meant to be taken as all-encompassing theoretical models?

Despite these kinds of limits, some of the theories discussed above have important implications for thinking about how the state typically addresses crime. Suppose we accept that many forms of criminalised behaviour are driven by subjective processes that supersede rational judgement (Katz 1988), or that cultural forces beyond the control of individuals are heavily implicated in criminal acts (Nightingale 1993; Young 2003): what then is the role of criminal justice? In many respects, criminal justice systems pre-suppose rational actors and individual responsibility in order to justify punishment. It is these same presuppositions that lead many of those tasked with administering justice to the view that punishment has a deterrent value. Much culturally oriented theory, however, shows that a sizeable portion of offending is not at all rational and that it stems from culturally induced desires that are not easily suppressed or controlled.

Given all that, a series of questions arise. How should the state punish? Or, under what conditions can it punish? What are the chances that punishment systems premised upon rational action and choice will be effective in curtailing crime? (See Chapters 7 and 8 for more on punishment.) Cultural theories intimate that we need to focus on solutions at cultural, social and economic levels if we are serious about preventing the harms that accompany some interpersonal behaviours. It is hard, however, to actually imagine how such changes can be brought about. How, for example, are we to take con-crete steps to change deeply engrained cultural frameworks that, conducive to crime and violence, are often promulgated by powerful media industries? In some respects, theory is often silent on these kinds of problems, or they are side-lined by a greater concern with analysis and interpretation. Then again, perhaps the role of the cultural criminologist is to identify the com-plex nature of the contexts in which behaviour transpires, rather than pro-pose practical courses and intervening strategies.

The limits identified immediately above, admittedly, merely scratch the surface of cultural criminology. A much more formidable range of critiques awaits cultural criminology and its attempts to organise the categories of culture and crime into an explanatory framework. It is to these critiques that the next chapter is devoted.

4 CRITIQUES OF CULTURAL CRIMINOLOGY ON CRIME

Introduction

This chapter explores some of the critiques that have emerged in light of cultural criminology's attempts to account for criminalised behaviour and how cultural criminology might respond. By no means exhaustive, three critiques will command our attention.

First, feminist theorists have argued that cultural criminology pays insufficient attention to important dimensions of power, especially those that revolve around gender, race and sexuality. On a related note, cultural criminology has been construed as lacking an appreciation for intersectionality, or the ways in which axes of power may overlap to compound the injustices associated with social marginalisation (Naegler and Salman 2016). This occurs because cultural criminology is far too concerned with young men and their subcultural styles. This leads to accounts that are written from a masculinist standpoint and thus poorly theorised. Insights that should appear obvious are missed. Given that cultural criminology asserts that an awareness of power asymmetries is central to critical scholarship, it is odd that it appears to operate with a fairly narrow conceptualisation of power relations (see Figure 0.2 in Introduction).

A second line of critique hones in on cultural criminology's tendency to 'romanticise' or celebrate criminalised subcultures. The romanticisation of crime can be said to occur in those moments where it is interpreted as a mode of resistance to the hegemonic order. For the critical Marxist, this narrative of resistance amounts to ideology and thus demands demystification (Hall et al. 2008; Hall and Winlow 2007). Chapter 5 discusses ideology in more detail, but it can provisionally be understood as ways of portraying capitalist social relations such that they appear natural and thus beyond questioning. In being portrayed as natural, capitalist relations are taken as self-evident and thus reproduced. Arguing that subcultural crimes are best understood as resistant is problematic because it provides a distorted image of what resistance looks like. For the Marxist, resistance occurs when society's labouring classes – as the majority group who are exploited by a relatively small capitalist class – collectively organise into a political force such that the fundamental social relations of capitalism can be overthrown. When resistance is understood this way, it becomes hard to see how petty crimes – no matter how collectively organised – could mount an effective challenge to the power relations that structure capitalist societies.

Craig Webber (2007) also posits that the resistance thesis is problematic, albeit for reasons that are distinct from those advanced by the critical Marxist. For Webber (2007), the problem is that arguments about resistance entail that the scholar restrict their gaze to the 'background' and 'foreground' of crime. However, a critical criminology should also recognise the problem of 'foresight'. In other words, what of the future consequences of engaging in criminalised behaviour? For Webber, the story should not end with the criminalised subculture and its allegedly resistant ethos, but should consider the longer-term consequences. The state, for example, often responds to crime in ways that not only entail punishment, but create permanent criminal records that can stigmatise individuals for a very long time. In this, cultural criminology's resistance thesis may actually be irresponsible: it celebrates some forms of crime, but does not provide full disclosure concerning the risks that accompany crime.

In the third critique to be explored, the emphasis moves away from the political or ideological implications of cultural criminology and towards its conceptual foundations. An examination of these foundations suggests that cultural criminology does not operate with a coherent concept of culture (O'Brien 2005). On the one hand, culture is understood as primary, a creative force that humanity can use to organise – and endlessly reorganise – social life. On the other hand, culture is often understood to be secondary, a response to the constraints imposed by material realities. According to O'Brien (2005), these conceptions are mutually exclusive: culture is either the source of human creativity and 'free will' (for lack of better terms), or it is determined by the constraints within which we live. Cultural criminology, however, jumps between these two notions of culture, leading to a perspective that is effectively incoherent and muddled. If its foundations are so confused, it is not clear how its attempts to theorise crime or punishment – or any other problem for that matter – will elude the same fate.

Before exploring each of these critiques, it is important to note that they tacitly assume the same realist principles that underpin cultural criminological accounts of criminalised behaviour. That is, the perspectives in this chapter also operate within the boundaries of a specific epistemological and ontological standpoint, one that is at odds with the radical constructivist position that has been utilised elsewhere in this text. By no means should the relative absence of the radical constructivist position in this chapter be read as a tacit endorsement of 'realist' criminology and its tendency to ontologise crime. Rather, given that the radical constructivist critique has already been noted, it seems unnecessary to repeat it here. However, perhaps it should be said that the radical constructivist position has important implications for the critiques of cultural criminology that are explored below. For the radical constructivist, these critiques would be regarded as sharing much in common with cultural criminology insofar as all posit that crime is a reality in need of an adequate causal theory. This amounts to ontologising crime, thereby failing to interrogate and deconstruct the power of 'crime' as a discourse. In short, radical constructivism should be borne in mind throughout, as it reminds us that critique of those who criticise cultural criminology is warranted. All may work from within the same circle of 'realism' and 'representational epistemology' that radical constructivism rejects.

Feminist theory, criminology and cultural criminology

As explored in Chapter 1, cultural criminology was (and remains) influenced by a variety of texts that were published throughout the 1960s and 1970s. But some texts, such as Carol Smart's *Women, Crime and Criminology* (1976) and Angela McRobbie and Jenny Garber's 'Girls and Subcultures' (2006 [1975]), have commanded much less attention. McRobbie and Garber (2006 [1975]) argued that a feminist sensibility is necessary for fully understanding subcultural formations because broader, gendered hierarchies skew how girls and boys come to form and participate in such social groups. That is to say, the subcultures of young women are likely to be shaped by the particular cultural, economic and social contexts that delimit their experiences and life chances.

Likewise, Carol Smart (1976) also posited the necessity of recognising gendered dynamics and the specificity of women's experience if we wish to develop theories on crime and its control. In *Women, Crime and Criminology*, Smart offers a detailed critique of mainstream criminology, especially its habit of failing to consider how crime, criminal justice *and women* are interrelated. When criminologists do consider women's criminality, they tend to do so from within common-sense perceptions and dominant ideological frameworks. Within such frameworks, women's offending is understood as a function of biological and/or psychological 'defects'.

Smart (1976, p. 185) therefore called for a criminology that was attuned to the 'wider moral, political, economic and sexual spheres which influence women's status and position in society', suggesting that an attentiveness to such broad forces was necessary for making sense of female criminality and processes of criminalisation. If criminology continues to neglect women, the discipline will amount to little more than the study of men's behaviour and criminalisation, which inevitably ensures that our understanding of 'crime, law and the criminal process' (Smart 1976, p. 185) will remain partial at best.

Forty years after Smart's monograph was published, Naegler and Salman (2016) could still argue – quite convincingly – that cultural criminology has not done much to incorporate important theoretical insights from the fields of feminist criminology and theory. This is somewhat surprising given that cultural criminology, at least in its rhetoric, is not antagonistic or opposed to feminist thought.

Naegler and Salman (2016) suggest that at least three core concerns of feminist theory could be incorporated into cultural criminology and that, were the field to do this, its interpretive accounts would only be strengthened. First, cultural criminologists ought to consider the culturally constructed nature of gender, especially the dominant definitions of masculinity and femininity that circulate throughout society and work to normalise specific behaviours for men and women (see also Chapter 7). Second, cultural criminology would be enriched were it to bring feminist concerns around sexuality into its analytical repertoire. Here, Naegler and Salman refer to sex and sexual desire as an important motivational force. Finally, cultural criminology has neglected the notion of intersectionality to its detriment. Intersectionality encourages a focus on how gender, race, class, sexuality and so on, can overlap to shape one's experiences and biography (Naegler and Salman 2016, pp. 357–359).

Concerning gender (i.e., masculinity and femininity), Naegler and Salman point out that many of the subcultural activities that cultural criminologists construe as 'resistant', and thus celebrate, are effectively 'masculine' activities. Graffiti writing, for instance, is a subculture dominated by young men, lending credence to the view that it can be theorised as a quest to develop a masculine sense of self (Macdonald 2001); it also happens to be men that populate Lyng's (1990) ethnographic account of those 'edgeworking' skydivers who seek to master risky situations.

Overlooking the relationship between masculinity and these kinds of subcultural pursuits opens up several problems. For one thing, such an oversight suggests that cultural criminology's central concepts are tainted by a masculinist bias. From here, it follows that cultural criminologists effectively normalise particular cultural constructions of masculinity when they valorise deviant subcultural practices associated with men. Moreover, they fail to recognise how their own concepts might be refracted by gendered dynamics, and thus fail to see how they could be important for understanding women's experiences. To give but one quick illustration, in terms of 'edgework' or 'risk-taking activities', Naegler and Salman suggest that women may not need to go skydiving because their everyday lives entail significant risks. As they note:

> But far from being averse to them, women take risks – and develop the skill orientation necessary to do so – on a daily basis by virtue of simply being women in patriarchal and misogynistic societies. Women are forced to take risks in the most mundane situations such as walking home alone at night or engaging in intimate relationships that can turn violent. (Naegler and Salman 2016, p. 361)

Were cultural criminologists to pay more attention to constructions of masculinity and femininity, and how these permeate society and culture, not only would they recognise the masculine biases in their interpretations, they might also see how the very concepts that they prioritise could be extended even further and used to illuminate women's experiences.

In terms of sexuality, Naegler and Salman argue that cultural criminology tends to ignore the role that sexual desire plays in assuring the seductive appeal of subcultural practices. Here, they discuss some of the efforts that cultural criminologists have made to theorise terrorism and political violence. Although men who participate in violent subcultures have noted that they found the promise of access to women appealing, the scholars who step in to theorise such groups tend to gloss over this fact (see Naegler and Salman 2016, p. 364). Of course, subcultural practitioners need not articulate their sexual desires for the broad point about sexuality to be recognised. In all likelihood, the law-breaking activities and/or risk-taking behaviours that define various subcultures afford individuals the opportunity to enact a form of masculinity that may well be socially recognised as sexually appealing. Opportunities to actually act out one's sexual desires and fantasies may not transpire, but the belief that risk-taking will open up such possibilities may nevertheless operate as a powerful motivational force.

Naegler and Salman's (2016) final point concerns cultural criminology's omission of intersectionality. To explore how this notion would enhance cultural criminological analysis, they draw from Mark Hamm's (2004) work on white supremacist terrorist groups in the United States. Hamm finds that supremacist groups generally attract young, working-class, white men. In this sense, there is some dependence upon the notion of intersectionality: to understand such groups, we probably need to pay attention to how race and class intersect and forge subject positions. Hamm's study, however, discusses in detail Peter Langan, who founded the Aryan Republican Army (see Naegler and Salman 2016, p. 368). In this part of the analysis, it is noted that Langan was 'pampered by his mother' and that he was interested in 'cross-dressing'.

Importantly, Hamm does appear to acknowledge a relationship between broader gendered relations and white supremacist groups when he claims that Langan effectively endured a 'crisis in masculinity' (Hamm, quoted in Naegler and Salman 2016, p. 369). As Naegler and Salman emphasise, however, one could be a little more precise by noting that Langan's 'crisis' is actually quite specific: it is a crisis in *heteronormative masculinity*. In other words, Langan's struggle stems from an inability to embody dominant codes of gender (according to which being a 'mama's boy' is stigmatised) and normative sexuality (evidenced by cross-dressing). The white supremacist group may offer a way to address this more particular crisis because such groups typically 'flatten' and 'repress' non-normative identities and practices (Naegler and Salman 2016, p. 369).

Throughout their critique, Naegler and Salman (2016) seem sympathetic to cultural criminology, often acknowledging that it makes many important contributions to critical scholarship. And, they tend to position their critique as one that, if incorporated, would only strengthen cultural criminology. However, it seems that the critiques they raise are not easily accommodated; they effectively identify a series of problems that reside at the heart of cultural criminology.

Revising the conceptual armature of cultural criminology is not a simple matter of splicing some additional concepts into its analyses. Instead, it will be necessary to consider how the incorporation of additional concepts will refract the meaning of other concepts, and have important implications for how behaviour and social practices are interpreted. To provide but one illustration of the difficulty, we can return to the notion that constructions of masculinity and femininity refract 'edgework', or 'risk-taking behaviours', in gendered ways. If we accept that sex/gender is fundamental in structuring social relations, it becomes difficult to maintain that *men's* risk-taking behaviours inevitably constitute 'resistance'. They are better understood, perhaps, as efforts to embody 'hegemonic masculinity', and thus congruent with broader power asymmetries grounded in sex/gender. No longer resistant, the risk-taking subculture is now complicit with power asymmetries grounded in sex/gender.

My point is not to adjudicate between these differing interpretations, but to emphasise that they obviously differ in substance, and thus their implications. A meaningful incorporation of additional concepts into cultural criminology, or shifting its gaze such that it comes to emphasise the other axes of power that it is theoretically open to (see Introduction), will require rethinking a range of assumptions and understandings that currently underpin the field. Whether this makes for better or worse analyses – or analyses that are more theoretically coherent and compelling – will depend upon the substantive content of future works that strive to integrate the types of analytic concepts that, as feminist critics note, have historically been marginalised within cultural criminology.

The ideological import of 'resistant subcultures': Critical Marxism and the neglect of 'foresight'

Writing within a critical Marxist tradition (see Chapter 1, especially where *Policing the Crisis* is discussed), Steve Hall and Simon Winlow (2007) develop a critique of cultural criminology in light of its tendency to romanticise deviance. Hall and Winlow (2007) are driven to this critique by their own account of how cultural and economic forces provide the motivational force to criminalised behaviour (Hall et al. 2008).

Interestingly, Hall et al. (2008) endorse a theory of criminalised behaviour that is very much inspired by Merton (1938). In this sense, their work has parallels with that of Nightingale (1993) and Jock Young (2003), which was discussed in Chapter 3. For Hall and colleagues, however, drawing from Merton leads to a critique of the 'resistance' or 'transgressive' thesis advanced by many a cultural criminologist. Given this, it is worth briefly recapping how Hall et al. (2008) locate crime in broader social, economic and cultural relations before discussing their critique of cultural criminology.

Hall, Winlow and Ancrum (2008) recognise that contradictions between a society's culture and economy are a source of tension, but they identify particular tendencies that can be said to define these domains. To be more specific, their focus is on the strain produced by the forces of neoliberalism and consumerism, and how this fosters deviance among young men and women living in urban areas. Neoliberalism and consumerism can be understood as two contemporary logics that have become dominant in much of the Anglophone world, especially the United States, United Kingdom, Australia and New Zealand.

Neoliberalism has been used in many ways by scholars. In this context though, it encapsulates the social insecurity that arises in 'post-industrial' societies. After corporations in the industrialised world outsourced labour power to third-world countries, what scholars refer to as a service economy subsequently emerged (Braverman 1974). If one can find employment in the service economy, it is likely to pay relatively little, lack opportunities for career development, and it will typically be insecure. In countries that have embraced this kind of labour market, inequality has worsened and most people have effectively become worse off since it took shape. Further, as working environments and conditions degrade, individuals are not very likely to develop a sense of identity through work as they may have done in the past. Alongside these shifts in the economy, neoliberalism is marked by a retraction of the welfare state, which may involve the withdrawal of funding for public education, unemployment benefits and healthcare. This effectively means that governments do less to ensure the social security of citizens.

In conjunction with neoliberalism, a logic of consumerism has increasingly defined many societies in the post-World War Two era. Consumerism may be understood as an extension of conspicuous consumption, but there is a distinction between the two notions. Within the logic of conspicuous consumption, social groups consume in order to signify their distance from others. This implies that it is underpinned by some form of instrumental rationality: once distance is achieved, further consumption becomes unnecessary. In the accounts of Veblen (1899) and Bourdieu (1984), for example, privileged classes sought to naturalise social inequality through distinct patterns in consumer choices. Even in Nightingale's (1993) analysis, poor inner-city residents prioritised consumption to distance themselves from the symbolic markers of poverty. With the rise of consumerism, however, consumption becomes unhinged from any such restrictions and is driven by the relentless pursuit of desire (Bauman 2001).

Motivated by profit, major corporations foster the logic of consumerism, which dictates that all social groups be encouraged to engage in reckless spending (Belk 1984; Dunn 1998; Hayward 2004; Schor 1998, 2004). Consumerism does not discriminate on the basis of class, race, or gender: it targets all of us and we are all affected by it. In this world of shiny commodities, we become increasingly interested in objects for their power to shore up status rather than their actual quality or usefulness. Furthermore, our sense of self constantly needs validation. Why, for example, do people camp out at an Apple store to purchase the latest iPhone when their current mobile device works perfectly fine?

The ability to consume, however, obviously hinges on the wealth we have at our disposal to buy things, and such disposable income is strongly tied to one's place in the labour market. What, then, are individuals supposed to do when they are excluded from labour markets, or poorly paid even if working a 40-hour week, but bombarded with inducements to consume or risk social exclusion? According to Hall et al. (2008), it is precisely this predicament that generates a powerful impetus for crime, especially those forms in which commodities clearly play a central role.

This theory implies that criminal acts are manifestations of conformity: individuals who engage in crime to participate in consumerism are simply trying to live up to the socio-cultural expectations of neoliberal, consumerist social orders. The most obvious example, perhaps, is that of young men involved in illicit drug subcultures who spend the proceeds from drug sales on things like expensive sneakers. Given the broader context in which this occurs, such behaviour can be said to embody society's expectation that the meaning of life is to 'earn money and consume'.

Whereas cultural criminologists would be inclined to interpret these kinds of criminalised subcultures as bastions of resistance to the hegemonic order – consider, for example, the arguments advanced by Jeff Ferrell (1996) or Jock Young (1999, 2003) from Chapter 3 – those with a more Marxist orientation tend to reject any such interpretation. As noted, Hall and Winlow (2007; see also Hall et al. 2008) posit that criminalised subcultures are better understood as modes of expression and practice that logically cohere with dominant cultural imperatives, especially the demand to consume the commodities that, profitable to capitalism, operate as symbolic markers of 'success' or 'individuality'. Supposedly 'resistant subcultures', then, are obeying dominant cultural prescriptions despite emerging against a backdrop of profound exclusion from legitimate labour markets and/or economic relations.

From this perspective, the cultural criminologist's tendency to romanticise deviant subcultures runs the risk of reproducing, if not actually promoting, an ideological understanding of 'resistance'. Because the cultural logic and commodities of capitalism – which obviously includes physical objects, but also refers to mediated images or styles of transgression – are deeply interwoven with subcultural practices, it becomes difficult to see how the latter can 'resist' or 'critique' the former. Accordingly, claims of 'subcultural resistance' echo what one might call an 'optimistic postmodern' position, which posits that the neoliberal iteration of capitalism provides individuals with an unlimited freedom to construct a sense of self or personal identity as they see fit. Apparently, inequalities grounded in gender, ethnicity and class belong only to the 'old', modernist world; they have been surpassed in an era that tolerates and celebrates 'lifestyle choices' that the market makes available.

As Hall and Winlow (2007, p. 83) express the point, this is quite a 'comfortable place' for the cultural criminologist, it demands

> ... nothing more onerous than acting as a sort of freelance wildlife warden, imagining with undying sanguinity the arid desert of consumerism to be bursting with new life amongst the cacti and the rattlesnakes, diligently scanning the dull normality of the post-political landscape and slapping the label 'POSSIBLE AUTHENTIC RESISTANCE: DO NOT CRITICIZE!' on anything that snores, murmurs or growls in a slightly unusual tone.

This line of critique makes much more sense when juxtaposed with Hall and Winlow's historically grounded understanding of resistance. In their view, the only effective resistance that has been levelled against the injustices of capitalism, and the social order it instantiates, has taken the form of large-scale, well-organised movements that unite those from precarious classes into a political force. It is worth quoting them at some length:

> It was the tireless activity of morally driven and resolutely organised collectivist labour movements on both sides of the Atlantic that created what has thus far been western history's *sole effective resistance* to the brutal excesses of free-market capitalism. This general movement... laid the relatively secure and hopeful ground upon which could be born dreams of more radical change in the future. These periods, between 1904 and 1965 in the USA and between 1850 and 1979 in Britain, saw the historically lowest rates of predatory violent crime amongst the working classes coincide with the greatest hope, solidarity and genuine political gains yet seen. (Hall and Winlow 2007, p. 88; emphasis in original)

Of course, despite the broad-based, general nature of the movements referred to, even they did not curb the excesses of capitalism. Given this, it becomes all the more difficult to understand how a series of discrete, loosely organised youthful subcultures could ever mount an effective mode of resistance, one that would fundamentally alter contemporary power arrangements and transcend social injustices.

Like Hall and Winlow, Craig Webber (2007) also proceeds from cultural criminology's tendency to romanticise subcultural deviance. For Webber, however, this is problematic because it amounts to neglecting the actual outcomes that follow for many of those who engage in criminalised subcultural practices. Some subcultural activity leads to criminal records, and the associated stigma of such records, thereby limiting the life chances of many subculturalists; some individuals may be socially ostracised and, worse yet, some may meet an untimely death due to subcultural membership.

Subcultural activity that leads to the imposition of a criminal record is significant given the neoliberal backdrop against which this now occurs. Neoliberalism entails the development of tighter and tighter labour markets, where very few professional jobs are available and where an increasing range of jobs do not allow individuals to meet basic needs of subsistence. This economic tendency is accompanied by excessively punitive strategies that aim to manage and control those who are most excluded from the economy (see Chapter 8). Obviously, a criminal record is not very likely to enhance an individual's capacity to successfully negotiate this kind of social order.

Given this, one must question what it means to portray criminalised behaviours as meaningful manifestations of 'resistance' that strike back against the hegemonic order. As much as scholars may wish to offer such interpretations, criminal practices cannot necessarily be reduced to resistant acts. They may just as easily be pathways into a criminal label; a series of roads that dead-end at permanent social exclusion or, perhaps one should say, relatively permanent inclusion within those institutions devoted to 'warehousing' deviant groups.

To be sure, for Webber (2007) this does not amount to saying that cultural criminology should be cast aside and forgotten about. The more important point is that while cultural criminology routinely focuses on the 'background' and 'foreground' of crime, it should extend its gaze such that the 'foresight' of crime also comes into view. To put this quite simply, whereas the 'background' concerns those broader socio-structural forces that prefigure any individual act, and whereas the 'foreground' revolves around dynamics that transpire in the immediacy of crime, 'foresight' entails an appreciation for the future consequences that criminal activity has for individuals. As Webber (2007, p. 154) suggests:

> [C]ultural criminology tells fascinating stories of edgework and transgression, but leaves the conclusion unfinished. The outcome is that those policy makers, agents of social control and less sympathetic academics are able to write their own conclusions. Moreover, those whose stories are told in such detail are left on the pages once the book is closed, their fractured futures left untold.

In the absence of exploring these 'fractured futures', the narratives produced by cultural criminology may elucidate how some 'speak back' to power, but will struggle to recognise that power also speaks back to resistance, usually with vengeance.

Can the 'resistance thesis' be rescued?

Of these two critiques, Webber's (2007) does not necessarily entail entirely jettisoning the 'resistance thesis'. Rather, it seems oriented towards adding further dimensions to the analysis, such that the possible costs of resistance are also explored. And, to be sure, Webber is generally sympathetic to cultural criminology. The critique offered by Hall and Winlow (2007), however, does appear to strike at something much more fundamental. As such, it is this critique that will be explored in more detail below.

At first glance, the claim that it is erroneous to construe criminalised subcultures as modes of resistance may seem a relatively minor, interpretive squabble. But this is only the 'tip of the iceberg', so to speak; much more is transpiring beneath the surface. Claims about the 'meaning' of subcultures hinge upon a broad theoretical surface for comprehending the nature of social relations. And it is this 'theoretical surface' that is ultimately at stake. For Hall and Winlow, positing that subcultures are resistant entails suggesting that social groups can (re)appropriate the objects of consumer capitalism, and do so in ways that serve critical purposes. Rather than amounting to a theory of subcultural motivation, the 'resistance thesis' is better understood as embedding a particular discursive construction of resistance, one that turns out to be ideological and thus complicit with the interests of capitalism.

Subcultures, according to Hall and Winlow (2007), are better understood as logical extensions of broader economic and cultural relations, rather than a negation of them. And, effective resistance will require organising the working classes such that they become a force in political life, one capable of implementing better working conditions, wages that allow for more than the bare reproduction of labour power, a state that recognises its duty to serve the collective good and so on. Going skydiving on the weekend or adorning the latest unconventional look will hardly create better social conditions. How can one argue otherwise and simultaneously claim to be producing politically relevant scholarship?

This critique is persuasive. However, I am not sure that cultural criminologists would entirely disagree with Hall and Winlow. In *Crimes of Style*, for example, Ferrell is adamant that while criminalised subcultures may be interpreted as resistant, this is not to make any claims concerning their actual effectiveness. As Ferrell (1996, pp. 177–178) expresses the problem:

> Can we therefore conclude that graffiti writing constitutes an ideal act of anarchist resistance? Probably not... [But to] dismiss

graffiti writing – and similarly, hip hop music and culture – as 'flawed' is not only to buy into elitist, intellectualized assumptions about culture and cultural change, but to throw away the lived experience of resistance. And if indeed graffiti writing is a flawed act of resistance, it is surely no more flawed than peace marches which file along permitted routes while singing the songs of million dollar rock idols, or political campaigns which will, at best, elect 'progressives' into a representational system of compromise and corruption.

When it comes to the question of effective resistance, then, it is not an 'either/or' problem for the cultural criminologist. Some social practices may 'go against the grain', and thus present a challenge to the dominant social order, but this is not to assert that they are the most practical or effective ways to alter social relations. Moreover, for the scholar to believe that they are capable of sorting acts that are resistant from those that are not, and positioned such that they can hierarchically organise modes of resistance along a scale that goes from 'effective' to 'ineffective', is elitist. In other words, it is to make an evaluative judgment that is dismissive of everyday practices, akin to the way in which 'popular culture' is often dismissed for lacking qualities supposedly found in 'high art'. For the cultural criminologist, it is this type of elitism that may well be ideological.

Is cultural criminology without a concept of culture?

If feminist critique focuses on the androcentric nature of cultural criminology, and if critical Marxists focus on the ideological significance of its interpretations, it is cultural criminology's foundational concept – 'culture' – that causes fundamental problems according to Martin O'Brien (2005). More specifically, O'Brien (2005) posits that one will find a glaring contradiction at the base of cultural criminology, which emerges because the intellectual endeavour does not operate with a clear, logically coherent concept of culture. Obviously, one would expect that something labelling itself as *cultural criminology* would have a robust and consciously articulated notion of culture. This lack of a cogent and consistent definition stems from the fact that cultural criminology has failed to engage with debates occurring amongst social anthropologists, especially those that concern culture as an analytic category.

Having ignored social anthropology, cultural criminology has effectively come to embrace 'idiographic' and 'nomothetic' conceptualisations of culture (O'Brien 2005). This is a problem because the two understandings are irreconcilable. According to the idiographic view, which is routinely associated with the work of Clifford Geertz, culture can be understood as a fountain of possible meanings. In this view, humans are regarded as fundamentally cultural beings, and thus capable of producing an endless array of 'symbolic forms through which to organize collective life' (O'Brien 2005, p. 60). According to O'Brien, Geertz's position on culture suggests that because culture is a creative space, the possibilities for collectively organised life are endlessly variable, or 'infinite'. Associated with Marvin Harris, the nomothetic approach understands things differently. In this model, culture is construed as an effect of material constraints. Humans are understood as constrained by environmental pressures, which engenders patterned, cultural responses to technical-economic limits. To put this otherwise, variations in cultural forms will be limited or 'finite' due to environmental constraints (O'Brien 2005).

O'Brien posits that the major texts in cultural criminology oscillate between these competing, if not mutually exclusive, conceptions of culture. Given its standing in the field, it is not surprising to find O'Brien utilise Jeff Ferrell's *Crimes of Style* to illustrate the tension. In making sense of graffiti writers, Ferrell (1996) adopts ethnographic methods that lead him into the minutiae of graffiti writing, such as which brands of spray paint are preferred by graffiti writers, how they work together under cover of darkness, the feeling they get from such experiences and so on. For O'Brien (2005), such detailed ethnographic description amounts to evidence that the idiographic approach animates the analysis.

When it comes to those who oppose graffiti, however, different methods are employed. Ferrell, for instance, claims that anti-graffiti crusaders, especially the mass media and political elites, can be understood as a product of their politico-economic circumstances and interests. Such an argument is said to entail the adoption of a nomothetic view of culture.

According to O'Brien (2005), this oscillation between two opposing conceptual understandings does not make logical or methodological sense, and it does not amount to a theory in which culture accounts for crime and efforts to control it. Apparently, it can only be understood as a political or normative move that is made by the cultural criminologist. The idiographic approach leads to a sympathetic, celebratory portrayal of graffiti writers; concerning the anti-graffiti crusaders, the nomothetic approach ensures that they figure as one-dimensional dupes who, lacking creativity, reproduce a worldview that is circumscribed by the broader political, economic and urban contexts in which they operate.

To be sure, Ferrell's account of graffiti writing is not the only key text in cultural criminology to evince conceptual ambiguities concerning culture. O'Brien also critiques Lyng's (1990, 1998) account of skydiving and Jock Young's (2003) claims of late-modernity as 'bulimic' (discussed in Chapter 3). In these respects, O'Brien appears more concerned with how cultural criminology seems ill-positioned to link culture and crime. Lyng's (1990) account, for example, provides a rich, ethnographic description of skydiving subcultures, which is then marshalled into a nomothetic model for understanding such risk-taking behaviours. However, forcing such ethnographic detail 'to travel a very long theoretical way' does not specify how culture fits into the theory: does skydiving illustrate the endless novelty of human culture, or is it to be taken as evidence of our limited capacity to respond to environmental circumstances (O'Brien 2005, p. 607)?

Likewise, Young's theory of late-modernity as 'bulimic' incorporates a cultural dimension, but remains vague as to precisely how this fits its associated theory of crime. In using the notion of bulimia, Young (2003) offers a revised Mertonian take on the relationship between economy, culture and crime. Late-modernity is said to be bulimic because it brings individuals into its cultural orbit of rampant consumerism, but spits many out from its economic possibilities. Those who are economically excluded, yet culturally included, are seen as occupying a social location that is conducive to criminal behaviour: such individuals are encouraged to acquire commodities that populate the consumerist landscape, but cannot do so through legitimate economic channels. What weight, however, is to be accorded to the gravitational pull of culture (i.e., consumerism) in relation to the exclusionary thrust of the neoliberal economy? Moreover, why is it that only young men appear to be trapped in this bulimic moment and why do they appear incapable of generating critical responses to the cultural logic of consumerism (O'Brien 2005, p. 609)?

Can the duality of culture be resolved?

O'Brien's (2005) critique hinges on a particular premise: cultural criminology has not been able to move beyond the contradiction between idiographic and nomothetic views of culture. It is unlikely that a coherent paradigm will be advanced without addressing this duality. There are at least two possible responses to this. The first is rather straightforward, but probably too simplistic and thus unlikely to address O'Brien's point. I will call this the 'just make a choice' resolution. The other is arguably more complicated, and may resolve the problem, but by no means is this guaranteed. I will call this the 'develop a dialectical sensibility' solution.

To start with what seems a relatively straightforward resolution, that of 'making a choice'. O'Brien effectively identifies two manifestations of this problem: (a) the duality of culture manifesting within the same account and (b) the duality of culture surfacing across accounts that are said to belong to a cultural criminology approach. The first reality is certainly a problem. Any given account will make contradictory claims if it utilises irreconcilable understandings of the same concept. This is not, however, insurmountable. All the cultural criminologist needs to do in this case is operate with one concept of culture: adopt either the idiographic or nomothetic view. To be sure, this may be difficult in practice, but theoretically it is fairly straightforward.

O'Brien's second manifestation of the 'make a choice' problem raises an important question: is it possible for cultural criminology to host two constructs of culture, or must the intellectual endeavour choose one construct at the expense of the other? Alternatively, one might wonder if it is possible for some cultural criminologists to utilise the idiographic view while others use the nomothetic view? It seems that most disciplines routinely host contradictory logics. Anthropology, for example, obviously hosts the idiographic and nomothetic views that O'Brien discusses. Cultural criminology, however, claims to offer a distinct lens for theorising crime, punishment, social control and so on. Given this, 'cultural criminology' is not equivalent to 'anthropology' or 'sociology' (or any other comparable discipline). As such, it would seem that cultural criminology – if it is to meaningfully operate as a distinct perspective – does require that culture be understood in a logically consistent manner.

In this sense, cultural criminology is currently in trouble. O'Brien is correct to posit that the field utilises culture in ways that are inconsistent – it is 'all over the map' as one might say. But even here, there is a simple solution. The field needs to settle on a construct of culture. To be sure, this is very basic 'in theory'; whether it will ever happen in practice is another story. If I were to hazard a guess, though, I doubt cultural criminologists will ever agree to working with a singular construct of culture. This would seem to betray their anarchist tendencies.

In any case, we can turn to the second, arguably more complicated (some may say convoluted), strategy. This was identified above as the 'develop a dialectical sensibility' approach. Instead of choosing a concept of culture, the cultural criminologist may respond by asking who, or what body of scholarly work, has ever managed to transcend or 'move beyond' contradictions of the type described by O'Brien? In some respects, O'Brien is demanding that cultural criminology choose between humans as creative or determined, capable of exercising agency or constrained by structure.

Many have rejected this kind of binary logic, often attempting to overcome it by 'synthesising' the elements that are held to be oppositional. Marx (1998, p. 15) transcends the dilemma by positing that 'men make their own history, but they do not make it … under circumstances chosen by themselves'; Bourdieu (1984) suggests that the 'habitus' (or the subject and its dispositions) is both 'structured and structuring'; the Frankfurt school turns to dialectics to suggest that neither the 'subject' (agency) nor the 'object' (structure) can be privileged in analysis. Objective conditions inevitably leave their mark on the subject; at the same time, however, the subject is congealed within objective conditions (Adorno 1973).

It might be said that a similar approach is available to cultural criminology, and it seems that some have endorsed it, if not effectively utilised it in the course of producing their accounts. Endorsing a dialectical logic is perhaps most evident in Ferrell's (2013) discussion of 'meaning' as central to cultural criminology. In fact, one may well argue that meaning is *the* analytic category for exploring the cultural. In defining meaning, Ferrell (2013, p. 258) writes that it 'refers to the contested social and cultural processes by which situations are defined, individuals and groups are categorized, and human consequences are understood'. Most salient within this definition, arguably, are the notions of 'contestation' and 'process'. They indicate that meaning suffuses social life; it is fought over and gets 'transferred' across groups, institutions and practices. In this sense, it becomes problematic to think of 'meaning' as either a consequence of material conditions or an autonomous force.

Perhaps the best way to illustrate this approach to meaning is by providing an example of how Ferrell actually puts it to use in the course of responding to critiques of cultural criminology. Distinctions have often been drawn between critical Marxist criminology and cultural criminology. The former is routinely understood as an 'economic critique of crime and its causes, with issues of culture, ideology, and meaning relegated to a secondary, superstructural position' (Ferrell 2013, p. 262). However, it is hard to see how culture could really be weeded out and accorded a 'secondary position' by Marxist scholars. To argue, for example, that a ruling capitalist class generally determines how the field of human behaviour will be carved up into acts that are 'criminal' and 'not criminal' is all well and good, but it cannot make much sense without assuming that the state and much of the public will actually accept (or have accepted) particular definitions of crime. In other words, any efforts of the capitalist class to draw distinctions between criminal and non-criminal behaviour may be driven by material interests, but any such process assumes certain definitions of reality, and seeks to impose certain definitions upon the social body. That, however, is surely a cultural process entailing the imposition of meaning.

Given the complexity of this dialectical approach, perhaps a second illustration will be useful. Let's imagine the large-scale manufacturing of a commodity that is hard to construe as a 'real need', such as luxury cars. The manufacture of such cars is obviously a material process, one that requires factories (with machines that make other machines), car parts, designs, labour power and so on. However, this material reality is embedded within, but also embeds, cultural logics, or some specific range of meanings.

In terms of the first part of this formulation – being embedded within culture – manufacturing luxury cars would make little sense outside of our consumerist frameworks. Alternatively, and to draw from Bataille (1991), it could be said that making such cars would not be feasible in the absence of a particular set of perceptions and beliefs regarding the utilisation of resources, technology and so on. Many of us, so it would seem, have come to accept that it is culturally acceptable to divert natural resources and human ingenuity into the production of impractical commodities while many people starve.

Concerning the second 'clause' in our formulation – material realities embed culture – the luxury car inevitably communicates more than its

simple, material presence. One may 'read into' it an encouragement to internalise certain desires and value orientations; a set of myths concerning what
we ought to regard as important to a meaningful life; an imparting of moral
lessons about the pursuit of individual interests over the collective good; an
inducement to abandon the 'protestant work ethic' and focus on pleasure; an
imperative that the individual construct their sense of self via commodities
that just so happen to be profitable to capitalism.

At this point, it may be worth returning to O'Brien's (2005) demand that
cultural criminology specify whether it subscribes to an idiographic or
nomothetic concept of culture. In light of the dialectical sensibility described
above, it should be clear why such a demand might be rejected. Because they
represent the polarities of a dichotomous logic – a logic that one is not compelled to accept – it is nonsensical to adopt *either* an idiographic *or* a nomothetic model. Whether one ought to be satisfied with this attempt at
resolution is, of course, open to debate. Such a debate, however, has been a
staple of many intellectual cultures for a long time now and appears destined
to remain on the agenda for a long time to come.

Conclusion

This chapter has covered three broad critiques of cultural criminology's
attempts to theorise crime. Feminist critics have called cultural criminology
into question for operating with a limited sense of power. Cultural criminology claims that it understands power as operative along multiple axes, such
as class, gender, 'race', age and so on. For the most part, however, it often
emphasises how young men are subordinated for their lifestyle choices,
thereby paying scant attention to 'race', gender, sexuality, or how these power
asymmetries often overlap. To be sure, these dimensions are not entirely
absent from cultural criminology. As can be seen in Chapter 3, for example,
they do appear in the work of Nightingale (1993) and Young (2003),
amongst others. As Naegler and Salman (2016) point out, however, oftentimes it seems that power dynamics associated with sex/gender, sexuality and
so on, are necessary for adequately interpreting observations, but do not
appear in the analysis. This leads to androcentric theories, interpretations
that are partial and limited.

Others have explored the ideological implications of the 'resistance thesis', a staple of cultural criminological thought (Hall and Winlow 2007;
Webber 2007). Along these lines, critics have argued that reading the indis-
cretions of youth as resistant or transgressive is to produce a distorted image
of resistance. To construe something which is actually apolitical as political
resistance becomes ideological because it encourages the misperception that
individuals or groups are countering asymmetrical power relations when
they are not. To provide one possible analogy, claiming that subcultures resist
political domination is akin to claiming that buying eco-friendly dish soap

will address the problem of global warming. Somewhat obviously perhaps, if we are serious about global warming we need to address the problems of over-production and over-consumption. It is an ideological delusion to think otherwise. Likewise, if we are serious about the major political problems and power asymmetries that organise contemporary social relations, a well-organised movement is indispensable.

In a final critique, we drew from O'Brien (2005) to explore how cultural criminology operates with irreconcilable definitions of culture. On the one hand, culture is seen as a site of creativity that allows us to organise social life (the idiographic view); on the other hand, it is read as a response to the constraints of material life (the nomothetic view). The contradiction at the centre of cultural criminology appears resolvable in some respects. It seems all would be well if scholars operated with a logically coherent notion of culture, or if the field settled on a singular concept and used it consistently. Alternatively, perhaps the field can work with a more dialectical view of culture. In reality, however, it does not seem like the issues spawned by the concept of culture will be resolved any time soon. Instead, cultural criminology seems destined to remain locked within the ambiguities of culture that were identified in the Introduction.

As with earlier chapters, it appears we are once again stranded in a land of unresolved problems. How should the idea of power asymmetries be incorporated into analysis? Recalling Figure 0.2 from the Introduction, we could choose between an intersectional approach (where the axes of power are understood to overlap) or emphasise some power asymmetries over others. If the latter, what is the basis for according priority to, say, for example, class rather than sex/gender? Are such decisions dependent on specific research problems and contexts, or can they be worked out at the theoretical level? Is crime well understood if interpreted as a mode of resistance, or is it more feasible to read crime as evidence of how individuals and groups are so thoroughly interpellated by socio-cultural relations? What is the political import of claiming that crime is resistance? Are such claims ideological in the sense that they produce a distorted image of what 'real resistance' looks like, or is it more ideological (and elitist) to dismiss subcultural activities out of hand? Must one choose between culture as idiographic or nomothetic? Does the possibility of dialectical approach allow us to escape the dilemma identified by O'Brien (2005)?

5 THE FRAMING OF CRIME AND SOCIAL CONTROL EFFORTS

Introduction

This chapter considers theoretical possibilities for demystifying cultural constructions and representations, and how they exert a profound influence over criminalised behaviours, public perceptions of those behaviours and/or the strategies of control that a society will entertain. I use the term 'representation' to encompass a range of particular concepts that elucidate how understandings of the world are created and communicated, thereby shaping practices. To represent is to re-present, usually via images, text, language, narrative and so on. Those who focus on representation are not necessarily interested in the extent to which depictions correspond to reality. That is, it is not simply a matter of examining the extent to which a way of portraying the world actually corresponds to the world. This is a difficult notion to grasp because we are typically encouraged to think of any given representation as either true or false in light of what our senses or logical faculties tell us is real.

When cultural criminologists – and other critically inclined scholars – interrogate depictions of reality they typically regard representation as having a relatively independent existence. This implies that the cultural criminologist essentially adopts a constructivist standpoint when examining portrayals of reality (see Chapter 1). You may sense that this is at odds with much of the content covered in the two previous chapters, where the theories discussed tended to assume the existence of a reality 'out there', one that can be mapped via language. It would be fair to say that there is certainly a contradiction or tension here: it is difficult to simultaneously maintain that the world exists independently of us, and that it is constructed via language. Nevertheless, cultural criminology often adopts a 'realist' standpoint on some occasions and a constructivist position on others. When the latter stance is adopted, representation is understood as a force that plays an active role in determining the social world (Hall 1997). This understanding opens the door to a series of critical questions. Two of the most obvious would be:

what kinds of interests drive the production of any given representation and what are the consequences of how the world is represented?

A quick example can, hopefully, make this rather abstract sense of representation a little more concrete. Consider the following statement: 'People who commit sins will be sent to hell where their soul will burn for eternity'. You may not have heard such a sentiment expressed in this exact way, but it is safe to assume that this idea is not alien to you. It may be controversial to say, but it is not possible to empirically demonstrate the truthfulness (or falsity) of this statement. From a 'scientific' viewpoint, we do not know if hell exists and we do not know if your soul will be set alight there. Indeed, whether we can be said to possess a soul is not entirely clear. No one has successfully made the journey to hell, managed to measure the intensity of Satan's hellfire, and returned to provide a detailed report. But for the scholar interested in representation, this is not necessarily all that important. What matters is whether people accept as true a statement such as this. It is not hard to imagine how acceptance of this idea might influence a person's behaviour and attitudes. It might also be relatively easy to develop a sense of which individuals or social groups are likely to promote such an idea and their reasons for doing so.

This chapter revolves around four concepts which, summarised in Table 5.1, can serve as starting points in the analysis and critical interrogation of discernible strategies within the realm of cultural representation: ideology, discourse, moral panics, and loops and spirals.

Not all of these have been developed by cultural criminologists, but those who work within the field effectively operate with a thorough understanding of these concepts when they analyse representations. As such, an appreciation of their subtle differences is important to the cultural analysis of crime and punishment. The four concepts may overlap in some respects, but they are also quite distinct and thus likely to generate different styles of analysis, interpretation, and argument.

Ideology

The concept of ideology is often associated with the work of Karl Marx and, more specifically, his critical analyses of capitalism. Insofar as it is in general use, ideology can refer to any organised, systematic way of thinking about the social world (Hall 1986). In this broad sense, one can speak of 'neoliberal ideology', 'free-market ideology', 'communist ideology', 'environmental ideology' and so on. Marx, however, used the term in a much more restricted way and one must take a little detour into some of his major arguments about the capitalist mode of production in order to appreciate the significance of ideology as a conceptual tool.

Marx showed that the capitalist mode of production was by no means natural, but a particular historical moment within the history of economic

Table 5.1 Summary of core concepts concerning 'representational practices'

Concept	Basic definition	Social origins	Social effect
Ideology	Ruling class ideas that serve the interests of the capitalist class	Capitalism and/ or class relations	Naturalise capitalism by 'concealing' inequality and its root causes
			Constructions of 'crime' and 'punishment' that serve the interests of capitalist classes
Discourse	Statements that cohere to produce understandings of any given topic	Threat of social disorder, or need to regulate populations Discernible via 'experts' and their statements (Foucault)	Instantiate particular practices
			Produce specific forms of subjectivity
			Construct which behaviours will be 'criminal', 'deviant'
			Legitimise particular punitive practices
Moral panic	An over-reaction to a behaviour or event that is relatively inconsequential	Multiple sources are possible: journalists, authority figures, public officials, concerned citizens	Multiple consequences are possible: new legislation, new symbols, intensified policing of a certain behaviour, spike in deviance/crime ('amplification')
Loops/ spirals	Collapsing of real events with their representation, and subsequent recurrence throughout the media scape	Grounded in power arrangements New media technologies or capabilities intensify the blurring of reality and representation	Multiple consequences are possible: reinforce or alter deviant practices, create new practices, harm to those that are drawn into media production processes

development. In a fairly advanced state by the 18th and 19th centuries, the rise of capitalism was made possible by certain technological advancements, such as the discovery of steam power, the development of machinery and new modes of communication (Engels 1999). Capitalism may have rendered previous modes of production obsolete, but it did not put an end to social inequalities. If anything, capitalism instituted new power arrangements and introduced a new way to hierarchically order society.

According to Marx, one of the defining features of capitalism was its tendency to increasingly divide the population into a small group of capitalists on the one hand, and a large group of labourers on the other (Marx 1906, 1994b). The capitalist class consists of those who own the factories and machinery, which Marx referred to as the 'means of production', necessary for producing commodities. The labouring class consists of those who do not own the means of production and are therefore compelled to sell their ability to work to the capitalist class if they wish to survive. As this description intimates, the capitalist class has all the power in this arrangement. It is they who get to make employment decisions and, to the extent that this is the case, exercise considerable sway over the lives of workers.

One of the problems raised by this structural arrangement is why workers allow a relatively small group of capitalists to exercise so much control over their lives. Marx suggested that capitalist economies were ultimately created and maintained by force, but that ideology was also important. As Marx (1994b, p. 174) famously put it, 'The ruling ideas of each age have ever been the ideas of its ruling class'. In other words, ideology suggests that capitalists produce ideas, or common ways of perceiving the world, in order to preserve their powerful position. These ruling ideas 'distort' reality, or misrepresent it. Nevertheless, insofar as society generally accepts such ideas as true, they allow contemporary social relations to escape challenge or critique.

To be sure, it is not simply the case that ideologies are created by the ruling classes, publicly announced, and then blindly accepted by society. The subsequent work of Antonio Gramsci showed that ideologies are subject to contestation and struggle. Ruling classes need to fight for their conceptions of the world to be accepted by others and, moreover, they need to maintain this public acceptance. Gramsci suggested that insofar as ruling classes successfully implement their ideological framings of the world, and thereby 'lead' a society, they achieve a state of hegemony (Gramsci 1971; Hall 1986).

Understood in this way, ideological struggles and quests for hegemony obviously involve processes that occur at a cultural level. Both notions suggest that there are disputes over the meaning of reality and how the world ought to be understood. It may seem as though all this Marxist theorising has little to do with cultural criminology, but there are many ways that familiarity with ideology and/or hegemony may be important to a cultural analysis of crime and punishment.

Consider, for example, what crimes immediately spring to mind when you hear the term 'serious crime'. Most people would probably use this term to group murder, rape, robbery, assault and burglary. This is not surprising given that the mass media routinely uses the term in this way and thus works to forge these sorts of associations. Furthermore, many governments embrace this understanding of 'serious crime' and use it in the course of gathering statistics that purport to map crime rates, which often become publicly available knowledge.

To be sure, these could be construed as serious crimes, but notice how things like fraud, tax evasion or environmental crimes committed by corporations are absent from the list? These types of crimes tend to be committed by those in powerful positions and can involve incredibly severe social costs. To give but two brief examples: it is well known that Ponzi schemes, which can rob many people of their entire life savings, are devastating; and massive oil spills that result from corporate blunders or carelessness can devastate eco-systems. Thought of in this way, we can get a sense of how the notion of 'serious crime' becomes ideological. By excluding crimes of the powerful from this rubric, we fail to see these crimes as a social problem and are less likely to devote police resources to apprehend such offenders.

Any number of examples could be chosen to show how ideology might be useful for making sense of the cultural logics that accompany strategies of punishment and social control. Perhaps more pronounced in academic debates, but certainly appearing in mainstream media, there is an ongoing tension between those who support the use of rehabilitative approaches in responding to those who commit criminal offences and those who see deterrence or incapacitation as the primary goal of punishment.

Those who endorse rehabilitation often see value in providing offenders with skillsets that will facilitate their reintegration into society. Arguments around deterrence and incapacitation generally stress the importance of using punishment as a communicative device to warn other would-be offenders of the risks of criminal activity, and as a way to 'protect society' from those who break the law. In such debates, rehabilitation may be framed as an approach that is 'too soft on criminals', whereas deterrence and incapacitation may be framed as 'ineffective' and as being of little long-term benefit to society.

When thought through with the concepts of ideology and hegemony, our attention would be drawn to the fact that there is a struggle between two possible positions here, which are not easily reconciled. We would also sense that the significance of the debate cannot be reduced to a matter of determining which view is 'correct'. What needs to be considered is who, or which social groups, advocate for these different positions and why do they do so? Whose interests are served by advocating a particular position? What consequences and implications follow from embracing either view? The concept of ideology might also lead you to ask if there are shared assumptions across those who advocate for rehabilitation and those who prioritise deterrence?

There are numerous possible resolutions to these questions. Perhaps those who advocate for rehabilitation are trained in psychology, psychiatry, social work and so on. If their policy suggestions were embraced, they would stand to gain as the public money that goes into criminal justice would support their employment. On the other hand, those who promote deterrence and incapacitation may work in politics and, operating under the impression that public opinion supports harsh punishment (see Chapter 8), may be seeking popular approval. If their policies were implemented, offenders may be liable to longer sentences and more people may be sent to prison. Those who work in the prison industry would stand to benefit from this and so they may also support such positions.

And, to give one further example of how ideology may facilitate a reading of this debate, it could be said that the tension between rehabilitation and deterrence essentially revolves around how to punish those found guilty of a crime. But this does not necessarily stop to question the behaviours for which the state is criminalising people, the policing and legal processes that lead to conviction, whether the state's use of punishment is legitimate and so on. Insofar as this is the case, both sides are 'within ideology' in that they fail to encourage a critical interrogation of criminal justice systems more broadly conceived, especially the extent to which they are shaped by the class structures in which they operate. In other words, the 'rehabilitation or deterrence' question gives off the appearance of debate, but it actually excludes many important questions. In doing so, it keeps us locked within a limited set of options, and thus locked within a limited ideological terrain.

Discourse

As a concept that can facilitate thinking culturally about crime and punishment, discourse is certainly important. However, making sense of discourse is complicated by the fact that it has been used in a variety of ways by scholars. In some accounts, discourse and ideology appear to overlap, but the concepts are generally perceived as outlining distinct theories of what constitutes power and how it operates through language. In Norman Fairclough's (1989) account, for example, discourse is used to suggest that speaking or writing always constitute social processes, and are therefore inevitably linked to broader structural arrangements, such as those grounded in class, gender and/or race disparities. Whereas Fairclough's use retains considerable overlap with Marxist thought, Michel Foucault utilises discourse to move away from some of the core assumptions about power that underpin Marx's notion of ideology. Given that Foucault's use has some important breaks with Marxist thought, and given the intellectual standing of Foucault within contemporary scholarship, it is his notion that will be discussed in more detail here.

Evidenced by his thorough examinations of contemporary institutions, it would not be unfair to say that Foucault was fascinated by the onset of modernity in the western world. Modernity can be understood as a fundamental shift in the organisation of everyday life. It represents a break with earlier social arrangements, such as feudalism, and is characterised by the emergence of capitalism, bureaucracy (or the rationalised administration of public life) and the displacement of religious authority by scientific reason (Weber 1979). Modernity also saw massive growth in population numbers and increases in average life expectancy (Foucault 1980, p. 151).

It is difficult to imagine, but a society that confronts the emergence of capitalism must somehow adapt to this new mode of producing commodities. Likewise, a society must address shifts in population numbers, bureaucratisation and so on. In short, populations must adjust attitudes and practices given the changes wrought by modernity. Herein lay something of a riddle for Foucault. How, for example, did society manage to accustom a very large portion of the population to suddenly work in a factory instead of on the land? How to regulate people in a way that ensures population numbers remain manageable? How to ensure that people will behave in accordance with social and cultural arrangements, and within the parameters established by modern law? In short, how does a society produce conformity in its members?

Foucault recognises that the capitalist class possesses power due to control and ownership of the means of production. However, he does not accept that the contradiction between the capitalist and labouring classes can be construed as the fundamental social contradiction. Relatedly, he does not accept that the power of the capitalist class accounts for the maintenance of social relations. Instead, the core social relation is constituted by conflict between the state/government and the population. A particular type of power – one that calibrates populations to modern social structures – corresponds to this social relation (Foucault 1977). 'Discourse' is used to designate this mode of power. If, according to Marx, it is capitalism that generates ideology, it is 'governmentality' that engenders discourse according to Foucault.

The concern with population control led Foucault (1973, 1977, 1978) to focus on how particular problems, such as sexuality, madness and punishment, were put into discourse. These areas were important to Foucault because he saw them as strategic sites in which the individual and the social body were linked. For example, the power to regulate the sexuality of individuals via discourse will have implications for practical efforts to regulate the population. As Foucault (1978, p. 146) put it:

> Sex was a means of access both to the life of the body and the life of the species ... Spread out from one pole to the other of this technology of sex was a whole series of different tactics that combined in varying proportions the objective of disciplining the body and that of regulating populations.

Likewise, how 'madness' is put into discourse will have implications for regulatory practices. We might, for example, construe madness as an underlying condition from which an individual suffers. Such a condition may appear evident in light of the behaviours or attitudes that one displays. If one were to go about claiming that they were God's chosen son (or daughter), sent to earth in order to absolve humanity for all its sins yet again, we may exclaim 'that person is mad'. You can probably identify places in which this kind of understanding has been promoted. Some version of it can be said to appear in a variety of academic journals, popular culture, news reporting and in everyday conversations. But framing this individual as 'mad' is not the only option at our disposal: we might believe them, we might ignore them, we might read the situation as comical, or as a form of sin. In some times and places, perhaps it was not unusual for numerous individuals to make such claims and so we waited for further evidence before passing judgement.

These variable ways of conceptualising the person who claims to be 'God's child' have different implications. If we think of this person as 'mad', we may also accept that they should be placed in a mental hospital and overseen by a psychiatrist until they are 'better'. This entails that a mental hospital be built, that 'expert' psychiatrists be trained within educational settings, that drugs capable of regulating behaviour are produced, that the state has a right to institutionalise some people, and so on. Here, madness works to regulate individuals and the social body. If, however, we see the 'mad' person as comical or relatively common, it is unlikely that we would support mental hospitals and all that they entail. Indeed, it is conceivable that 'madness' may not exist as a possible label. It is not, then, reality that generates the notion of madness, but discourses on madness that produce the reality of the 'mad man'. If we did not have a discourse on madness, we could not use it as a basis to frame what we can observe and we could not act accordingly.

This example can be used to draw attention to some additional corollaries of discourse. We have already noted that discourses cannot simply be attributed to a society's capitalist class and their function cannot be reduced to naturalising capitalism. Certainly, the capitalist class may channel discourses (on madness, productivity, sexuality, etc.) to its advantage, but it does not produce them. A much more obvious source for their production is the human sciences, such as psychiatry, psychology, medicine and so on. For Foucault, this suggested that discourse often worked by constructing distinctions between 'normal' and 'abnormal' human behaviour. To shed further light on this point, consider the discourses that are produced on things like criminality, intelligence or desirable forms of employment. Do not all of these somehow play a role in carving up populations, and indicating what kinds of behaviours and subject positions are 'normal', 'desirable' or even 'to be expected'? Moreover, these kinds of discourses seem to appear, circulate throughout a society, and then exert their effects. Foucault leveraged these aspects of discourse to suggest that power was not simply possessed by dominant groups and then exerted over others in a 'top-down' manner. Instead, the effects of discourse and new knowledges suggest that power is everywhere, that it infuses all of our social relations and saturates society. Indeed,

Foucault (1977, p. 27) posited that power and knowledge are not distinct concepts.

A second corollary is that discourses are likely to be in competition with one another and vie for dominance. It is likely that a particular discourse, which will support specific institutional practices and arrangements, will establish itself as an authority. Alongside this, however, one is likely to find critical discourses that challenge or offer counter-framings to more authoritative discourses. The former is often referred to as a dominant discourse, the latter as subjugated discourses (Foucault 1980, pp. 81–83). A subjugated discourse can be understood as a way of speaking about a topic that commands less attention. It is likely to be articulated less often and, when it is heard, it will often be dismissed. As such, a subjugated discourse will struggle to (re)configure practice. In our example of 'madness', it would be fair to say that psychiatry and/or psychology occupy dominant positions in crafting our contemporary understandings of mental illness, but these are subject to challenge. There is, for instance, a range of subjugated discourses surrounding the asylum and the use of psychological labels to classify individuals (Goffman 1961; Cohen 2008, 2016).

Third, discourses on any given topic are likely to be found across a range of sources and they will change over time. The notion of madness is discussed in multiple places. To name only a few academic disciplines, sociology, criminology, biology, psychiatry, psychology and medicine have all contributed to our understanding of madness. So too have a wide variety of commercial and readily available media sources. Indeed, the notion of madness would not exist in the absence of all these discourses on the topic. Foucault suggested that a discourse that gets repeated in multiple texts and in various guises could be understood as a 'discursive formation' (Foucault 1972). This notion might be important for those wishing to use Foucault's ideas of discourse, power, and knowledge for analysing language use and representations.

One can describe Foucault's notion of discourse without going into his analysis of punishment, but given that this is a book within criminology, it would be strange were the latter to be omitted. And so, in closing this section, a brief overview of *Discipline and Punish: The Birth of the Prison* will be provided. In *Discipline and Punish* (1977), Foucault utilises discourse to understand how and why state-orchestrated punishment systems changed in much of the western world around the late 18th century. Around this time, corporal punishment that physically attacked the body was replaced by confinement and efforts to 'correct' the perceptions, attitudes, and dispositions of offenders.

Corporal punishment was based on 'sovereign power', or the power possessed by the king to exterminate the life of his subjects. It was very public, often gruesome, and highly symbolic. But, with the shift to modernity, such demonstrations could not guarantee the preservation of state authority and the disciplining of a growing population. Corporal punishment was enacted in something of an ad hoc manner, it tended to condemn the most serious of crimes and its public aspect opened up opportunities for people to question how the state deployed its power (Foucault 1977, p. 59).

According to Foucault, modernity signalled the need for new strategies that could discipline the social body and, in light of this need, new discourses arose. Most notably in this case, Foucault charts the rise of 'reformist' discourses that articulated what a more rational, effective system of punishment would supposedly look like. This discourse could be found in the writings of influential figures such as Cesare Beccaria and Jeremy Bentham. Beccaria, for instance, argued that a more effective system of justice would be one that identified every criminal offence, no matter how minor, and exacted a punishment based on offence severity. Accordingly, minor crimes ought to be met with light punishments and severe crimes ought to be met with harsher punishments (Beccaria 1963; see also Chapter 1). The important point for Beccaria was that punishment needs to be certain in the event of criminal offending. If a justice system could accomplish this, then punishment would deter and control crime.

In Foucault's hands, discourses such as this are not about developing more humane systems of punishment, but systems that 'punish better' by inserting 'the power to punish more deeply into the social body' (1977, p. 82). They are about spreading power relations throughout society such that individuals self-regulate their behaviour. And, we can sense how the kind of logic advocated by Beccaria legitimates many current practices in the areas of crime control and punishment. Contemporary forms of surveillance increase; most states produce legislation that imposes rules upon every aspect of our daily existence; strategies of punishment are hierarchically organised and then matched to offence seriousness.

New discourses on how to punish do not only produce changes in criminal justice systems. They are also productive in that they imply new understandings of individuals and, more specifically, subjectivity. In order to deter people from crime, for example, we may also need knowledges about the extent to which individuals exercise rational judgment, what kinds of punishments people would find intimidating, and how to compel people to reflect on their behaviour. We may also need new techniques that are capable of generating knowledge about specific individuals, what drives them to crime, and what strategies may be effective in getting an individual to desist from criminal behaviour.

As Foucault (1977) suggests, a range of discourses quickly stepped in to fill such voids and we can discern how new practices have followed. To give but one example, in the course of many criminal trials it is not uncommon to find a range of 'experts' that assess the psychological condition of the defendant. We are no longer concerned solely with whether a crime was committed, but with the problem of who committed it. Is the offender before us a recidivist? Do they have psychological issues? Are they 'insane' or 'normal'? Did specific circumstances drive an otherwise rational person to an irrational act? Such practices would make little sense without a series of corresponding discourses and new knowledge formations concerning criminal behaviour.

Moral panics

Ideology and discourse offer distinct approaches to thinking about representations of crime and punishment, what drives such representations and the ends towards which representation is directed. Both concepts, however share the view that portrayals of reality are constantly made and remade, that they saturate our daily existence to such an extent that we may not be able to recognise their presence. In short, ideology and discourse treat representation as an ever-present strategy that works to make our contemporary social relations and practices appear as though they are 'natural' rather than historically specific.

The notion of moral panic offers a slightly different take on the nature of representation and therefore moves us into slightly different theoretical territory. The 'moral panic' concept was intimated in the work of Jock Young (1971), but it was Stan Cohen (2011 [1972]) who developed it in his study of the Mods and the Rockers, two subcultures that emerged around the 1960s in Britain. The Mods were known for riding scooters and being tidy in their appearance and clothing styles; the Rockers were associated with the riding of motor-bikes and a relatively unkempt look. In the early 1960s, members of these subcultures would travel to beach towns on public holidays, as would a variety of other young people and adults. It was how the media portrayed the behaviour of these youthful groups that led Cohen to develop the moral panic concept.

In what has become an often-cited passage, Cohen (2011, p. 1) defines a moral panic in the following manner:

> Societies appear to be subject, every now and then, to periods of moral panic. A condition, episode, person or group of persons emerges to become defined as a threat to societal values and interests; its nature is presented in a stylized and stereotypical fashion by the mass media; the moral barricades are manned by editors, bishops, politicians and other right-thinking people; socially accredited experts pronounce their diagnosis and solutions; ways of coping are evolved or (more often) resorted to; the condition then disappears, submerges or deteriorates and becomes more visible. Sometimes the object of the panic is quite novel and at other times it is something which has been in existence long enough, but suddenly appears in the limelight. Sometimes the panic passes over and is forgotten, expect in folklore and collective memory; at other times it has more serious

and long-lasting repercussions and might produce such changes as those in legal and social policy or even in the way the society conceives itself.

I have cited Cohen at some length because this passage draws our attention to the major aspects of a moral panic. Unlike ideology or discourse, moral panics can be thought of as discrete moments. That is to say, panics tend to 'erupt' within the sphere of cultural representation and then subside.

A moral panic can be said to occur when the reaction to a behaviour that is seen to violate accepted norms or laws is disproportional to the threat posed by the behaviour in question. As the term panic implies, it is an 'over-reaction'. Central to Cohen's analysis is the role played by the mass media, and he suggests that how a behaviour, practice or event is represented amounts to a moral panic if three patterns are evident. First, the media will exaggerate and distort the importance of events or their consequences. Second, they will assure the public that things will get much worse unless something is done about the allegedly problematic behaviour, an aspect that Cohen referred to as prediction. Third, designated as symbolisation by Cohen, the media will construct specific individuals or groups as 'folk devils'. They may also construe specific objects, such as clothing items or commodities that appear central to a group, as signs of 'evil' (Cohen 2011).

The moral panic concept has been utilised in many studies over the years and so concrete illustrations are not hard to find. By no means an exhaustive list, panics around crime, drugs, alcohol, sex, music, popular culture, new technologies and the behaviours of young people are not uncommon in mainstream media. Robert Wright (2000) has discussed how the music of Marilyn Manson (and, by extension, much rock and heavy metal music) has spawned what could easily be construed as a series of moral panics over the years. In terms of exaggeration and distortion, Wright draws attention to unfounded claims that listening to Marilyn Manson and/or heavy metal will cause young people to commit suicide. Concerning prediction, those fanning these moral panics often suggest that more rigorous censorship of popular culture would be required to keep in check the supposed dangers of music. Finally, Marilyn Manson and others have been transformed into 'folk devils', viable threats to the social order, and parents are encouraged to be concerned about their children listening to certain forms of music or adorning themselves in the clothing styles associated with 'goth' (Wright 2000).

What is interesting about the moral panic concept is its relative open-endedness in terms of what, or who, drives them and what the consequences may be. As the passage above indicates, Cohen (2011) does emphasise that mass media will be central, but that reporters, religious figures and/or 'right-thinking' people or social groups can drive a panic. In these respects, the concept may not be very specific, but it should sensitise us to the fact that social power relations will inevitably fuel moral panics. These power relations, however, may take any number of forms and they cannot be reduced to class relations as in Marx. Likewise, the consequences of a panic cannot necessarily be determined by the fact that one transpires. Some panics are inconsequential, but some may lead to the creation of new legal codes or social policies. In the wake of some moral panics, our normative or cultural frameworks – the way we broadly conceive and think about things – may be reconfigured. And, finally, instead of putting an end to a criminal practice, panics may actually amplify and produce more interest in whatever is portrayed as a 'social evil' (see Chapter 1).

Despite its theoretically open-ended nature, the moral panic concept tends to illuminate how media reporting often pushes relatively inconsequential behaviours beyond thresholds of cultural tolerance, and how this leads to new efforts in terms of social control. The work of Stuart Hall et al. (1978, pp. 223–227; 2006) can help clarify these aspects of media reporting and moral panics. Hall and colleagues refer to 'signification spirals', which rely on convergence, thresholds and escalation. Convergence is relatively straightforward and involves conflating distinct activities. The meaning of any given convergence is always crystallised against a backdrop of thresholds of social tolerance ranging from the 'permissive' to the 'extremely violent'. For example, erroneously linking 'student political protest' to 'hooliganism' or 'violence' pushes a legitimate activity (political protest) into the realm of criminality (violence), thereby making it appear 'unacceptable'. Convergence and the use of thresholds combine to escalate the sense of threat that an otherwise benign practice poses to society. Having made a practice appear more threatening or criminal than it actually is, escalation creates for agents of social control the legitimacy presupposed in the exercise of repressive measures.

Not long after Cohen, who appears to have developed the moral panic concept via an empirical examination of how subcultural groups were portrayed in the media, Erich Goode and Nachman Ben-Yehuda (1994) sought to develop a theoretical-diagnostic account. The approach of Goode and Ben-Yehuda (1994) is worth exploring insofar as it does more to specify the possible sources of a moral panic and provides clearly defined criteria for establishing whether a series of representations amount to a panic. In terms of sources, Goode and Ben-Yehuda (1994) suggests that panics may be driven by (a) the general public, (b) specific interest groups, such as police departments, state agencies and professional associations or (c) powerful elites, such as those who exercise most control within the economy or within political spheres. As in Cohen (2011), this typology of sources should help us identify what kinds of interests and power dynamics may be the driving engine of a particular moral panic, and the ends towards which it may be directed.

Arguably of more interest are the criteria they develop to help 'diagnose' a moral panic. Goode and Ben-Yehuda (1994) identify four symptoms along these lines: concern, consensus, hostility and disproportionality. 'Concern' suggests that the behaviour of a group of people, and the possible conse-quences of that behaviour, will generate public anxiety. This may be measur-able through opinion polls, increased public commentary and sudden activity that attempts to regulate behaviour. 'Consensus' implies that at least some portion of the community thinks that a problem exists and that it constitutes a threat. This is a tricky criterion and Goode and Ben-Yehuda (1994, p. 34) emphasise that its importance resides in helping us think about the size of a moral panic. 'Hostility' echoes Cohen's idea that moral panics will involve the creation of 'folk devils' that need to be controlled. Another way to think about this is to note that hostility will often manifest as a binary logic involving the drawing of distinctions between 'us' and 'them', 'good' and 'evil', 'order' and 'disorder'.

Of the four criteria, 'disproportionality' would seem to be of the greatest importance. Indeed, Goode and Ben-Yehuda (1994, p. 38) suggest that the concept of moral panics hinges on this criterion. They provide four ways to establish disproportionality, and note that if any can be demonstrated, then a moral panic can be said to exist. The first and second measures are 'exagger-ated figures' and 'fabricated figures'. The former refers to exaggerating the scope of a problem, in terms of either the number of people involved in the troubling activity or the harm it causes. The latter measure assesses whether a moral panic is actually based on empirical research. The other two mea-sures are relational. On the one hand, we need to test for the 'over-representation' of an issue. In such cases, an issue will become the subject of intense debate while another issue that is of far more significance will be neglected. On the other hand, we may test for changes over time in the ways in which an issue is debated. For example, where an activity remains consis-tent but media interest in the activity intensifies and wanes over time, that is, when concern over a certain behaviour is incongruent with actual patterns in behaviour, the criterion of disproportionality has been met. Many forms of criminalised behaviour are likely to have this quality of remaining relatively constant over time while media interest in it is likely to intensify and dissipate.

Loops and spirals

The concepts discussed thus far generally encourage the cultural criminolo-gist to anticipate particular sources and consequences of cultural portrayals of crime and/or punishment. We saw that the notion of moral panic is more theoretically open in these respects, but that it is often utilised to show how panics steer new strategies of social control. With the notions of 'loops' and 'spirals', however, we step into a realm of theory that is very open-ended or non-linear.

Developed by Jeff Ferrell, Keith Hayward and Jock Young (2008), loops and spirals encourage the cultural criminologist to focus on the dynamic interplay that occurs between representation and reality, or how the realm of images and the real often collapse into one another. In this view, it is not necessarily the case that there exists a reality, which is subsequently distorted by an ideology, but that reality and representation suffuse one another. Although the collapsing of representation and reality may have reproductive effects, it is just as likely to generate bizarre circumstances and new practices. In this sense, loops and spirals emphasise the relatively unpredictable nature of representation, the possibility of 'unintended consequences'.

Ferrell et al. (2008) begin with the premise that there is an urgent need to expand our theoretical understanding of representation in light of the contemporary media technologies that characterise late-modernity. With the rise of the internet and mobile devices, alongside the perseverance of television, information and imagery can be produced and disseminated with increasingly rapid speed. Moreover, we have become wedded to new technological gadgets and devices in ways that were impossible in the past, and this can easily ensure our constant entanglement with portrayals of crime and punishment. One need only think of how much time is devoted to online worlds and social networks, phone apps, video streaming, viral popular culture and so on, to recognise how contemporary life is saturated with new media.

Most of these media absorb real aspects of the world in one way or another, but they simultaneously transform that reality into an image that lends itself to consumption. 'Loops' and 'spirals' can be thought of as concepts that seek to capture how meaning is made via this process and the innumerable consequences it may have. Although related, there is a subtle distinction between loops and spirals, which intimates that there are distinct layers to how crime and punishment is culturally absorbed.

According to Ferrell et al. (2008, p. 130), a 'loop' can be understood as a moment in which an aspect of everyday life is recast as an image. A loop may operate in a 'relatively self-contained' manner, as if constituted by moments that circle round and round, or it may be the first stage of analysing more complicated spirals. To demonstrate the former aspect of loops, one can think of the US television show *Cops* (an example used by Ferrell et al. 2008). As is well known, *Cops* films police officers as they go about their daily work, often arresting people suspected of crimes, and edits this footage to produce 20 or so minutes of 'entertainment'. Obviously, the cameras are generating recorded images of real suspects who have, somehow, come to warrant police attention. But the presence of a video camera turns the external world into a series of images ripe for consumption. The process of producing such a show may lead to shifts in practices, such as officers who play up the dramatic elements of everyday policing for the cameras, but the loop is fairly contained: the realities of crime are constantly transformed into entertainment, with the two becoming dependent on one another. Over time, the show becomes fairly predictable and formulaic with each of its iterations.

Bearing this in mind, the notion of spiral is used to apprehend and analyse the ways in which looping effects may transpire within broader sociocultural contexts and escalate, thereby opening up new practices and perceptions (Ferrell et al. 2008, p. 133). Loops, then, do not simply continue to conflate a particular reality with its representation, but may play an active role in spurring shifts in crime, crime control, and/or representational practices.

Ferrell et al. (2008, p. 136) provide several examples of spiralling, one of which is the 'drug war' that has been playing out in the United States for some time now. Although the drug war can be dated to at least the 1930s, when prohibitions on alcohol were lifted, it surged in the 1980s and 1990s. And, although it may have been overshadowed by 'terrorism', by no means has it ended. Opposition to drugs may have started out as a strategy of political candidates to appear 'tough on crime', and thus devoted to public security, but it quickly meant that large sums of public money were poured into law enforcement. Drug arrests and prosecutions led to rapid increases in prison populations. Given that the portrayal of drugs often hinges on racist stereotypes – consider all those television shows now focused on drug production in South American countries (*Narcos, Queen of the South*), not to mention popular shows like *The Wire* – it is perhaps not surprising to find that those from racially marginalised social groups are grossly over-represented in the prison population (Alexander 2012; Wacquant 2009a).

'Terrorism' can serve as a second illustration of spiralling. The events of 9/11 were rapidly reproduced as images and repeatedly broadcast throughout much of the world. Such images played an important role in establishing the presence of 'evil' in 'our' midst, and led the US government and its allies to invade Iraq and Afghanistan. These invasions continued to occupy media attention over the subsequent years, their successes and failures securing or threatening the tenure of politicians. But broadcasting the invasion, alongside its material consequences, did not end terrorism. If anything, these forces had spiralling effects in relation to terrorism. Images of terrorist attacks, and the bombings of subsequent invasions, often served as recruiting tools for terrorist organisations. Similarly, as domestic anti-terrorism strategies emerged – in the United States, for example, things like increased airport security, random bag searches in subway stations, not to mention the Patriot Act – terrorists pursued 'innovations' in practice, such as bombing the buildings of newspapers, holiday destinations, public events. Terrorism, then, as a phenomenon that is simultaneously real and broadcast, does not 'stand still'. Instead, it leads governments and terrorist organisations into specific courses of action, some of which are likely to be quite novel.

Obviously, much more could be said about things like the 'war on drugs' and 'terrorism'. Hopefully, though, these brief examples provide a sense of what is meant by loops and spirals, and how they can be used to analyse the ways in which practices and representations intersect and produce new effects.

Conclusion

This chapter has explored four concepts – ideology, discourse, moral panics and loops and spirals – that belong within different traditions of thought or what one might call paradigms. Despite their distinct theoretical lineages, they share common ground in that they all offer a way to think about important cultural dynamics and how such dynamics may work to construct our worldviews of crime and social control. Furthermore, the concepts discussed here all encourage scepticism, inviting us to examine the representations made of crime and punishment through a critical lens. This is because cultural representations are not simply about capturing reality or creating a text that perfectly summarises the real world. Instead, cultural representations are more likely to be a product of the power arrangements that characterise a society, and it is likely that they will have some important connection to these power arrangements.

The concepts stand in tension with one another insofar as they accentuate different kinds of power asymmetries and therefore dispute the ultimate ends towards which cultural constructions of reality are directed. In Marx's ideology, it is the class relations and class inequalities associated with capitalism that constitute the essential backdrop, with representation operating to conceal this social reality from those who are most adversely affected by it. For Foucault, societies routinely confront the problem of adjusting populations to social demands, and so discourses emerge to articulate 'norms' and 'expectations'. Typically developed within circles of professionals or experts, these norms often possess a scientific veneer and act as standards according to which recalcitrant individuals can be disciplined. With moral panics, Cohen suggests a number of possible sources that may govern how a specific set of behaviours or practices comes to be framed, and a number of possible consequences. More often than not, however, the concept of moral panic is used to show how particular social groups construct some form of behaviour as problematic because they stand to benefit, either economically or ideologically, from doing so. Finally, with loops and spirals the problem of cultural representation becomes much more open-ended, and the distinction between reality and representation is called into question. In light of our current mediated age, what is real and what is image? What happens when reality can instantly become an image that rapidly circulates, possibly feeding straight back into practice?

Instead of trying to decipher which of these concepts is 'correct', it is perhaps more important to emphasise how they are suited to particular types of projects, and how their use should be determined in accordance with the assumptions by which any given project is underpinned.

Marx's ideology, for example, assumes that an underlying reality – the conflict between class groups – is distorted via representation. The task of the scholar is to demystify ideology, to reveal its distortions such that a 'true' picture emerges, or to reveal how ideology keeps us locked within limited modes of thought. In the Introduction (see Figure 0.2), we saw that power operates along multiple axes – class, gender, 'race', sexuality, age, disability and so on. For the scholar who accepts an underlying social reality, ideology could be appropriated to make sense of how any of these power asymmetries are distorted, thus naturalised. Marx may have reduced ideology and social conflict to class relations, but subsequent scholars are not obligated to follow suit. If, however, ideology is used, one is probably assuming that representations distort some underlying reality.

Cohen's moral panic concept makes similar 'realist' assumptions. But, it is distinct from ideology in at least two broad respects. First, whereas ideology typically assumes that representation is continuous – that is, ideology operates as a constant force in everyday life; it saturates existence – the moral panic concept is better attuned to episodic moments, or sudden, volatile ruptures in representation. Second, the moral panic concept does not provide clear directions concerning the drivers and consequences of representation. Ideology has as its corollaries 'social contradictions' and their 'naturalisation'. In this sense, it provides the scholar with direction. The moral panic concept is much more open-ended, perhaps one should say that it has too many theoretical links to origins and effects, and these are often contradictory. We saw, for instance, that a moral panic may swell from the ground up or be orchestrated by society's most powerful groups. Similarly, it may lead to new legal codes and cultural frameworks, or have no discernible effect. In any case, those interested in sudden outbursts of media interest in a topic may find this notion useful.

With Foucault and discourse, the realist underpinnings of ideology and moral panic are called into question. At the risk of oversimplifying, discourse typically encourages the scholar to disregard the search for underlying social realities in the Marxist sense. Rather, one is directed to seek out competing discourses, discern their fundamental categories or boundaries and consider their effects. Of course, one may concentrate on a particular discourse, but, even so, one would still theorise its boundaries and effects. 'Effects' is often understood quite broadly: discourses may engender institutional practices, imply the production of certain forms of subjectivity and, inter alia, impact other concepts or conceptual frameworks.

Finally, 'loops and spirals' is an idea advanced by those who identify as cultural criminologists, and so it would be problematic not to reference it here. Its connections to the moral panic concept are fairly obvious, but how it goes beyond this is not immediately clear. Its novelty might be said to reside in the fact that it is well-attuned to how reality and representation can become so immediately fused because of new media technologies. The emphasis placed on the rapidity of communication might also give loops and spirals an interpretive power in some contexts. But, it seems ill-equipped to provide clear directions for analysis given its open-ended nature. One might say that it is so open-ended that it provides a set of tools for describing, but not for analysing and developing theory.

Moreover, the way in which reality and representation are 'collapsed' invites confusion. Certainly, technology enables any given event to be caught on video and simultaneously broadcast, for images to reverberate throughout the realm of representation, and so on. But the speed at which reality can be turned into an image does not provide a rationale for suddenly construing the image as something other than a representation. Similarly, that these representations feed back into reality at a rapid rate does not represent a fundamental break from the notions of ideology, discourse, or moral panic – all of which assume that representations can impact practice. In these respects, it is not clear how loops and spirals advance the conceptual tools that are already available to us. This may explain why the notion does not appear to have been picked up by scholars, or why loops/spirals have not disrupted the use of ideology, discourse or moral panics. Nevertheless, for those interested in phenomena that are profoundly mediated by new communicative technologies, loops and spirals may provide a useful framework.

6 CONSUMING CRIME AND PUNISHMENT

Introduction

Whereas the previous chapter explored representational practices, this chapter revolves around a related, but distinct problem. Namely, the consumption of crime and punishment. Of all the forces that transform these aspects of social life into a consumable experience, it is the media that stands out the most. Transforming crime and punishment into items for consumption entails that they be treated as commodities (perhaps one should say 'cultural commodities'). Like radios, televisions, computers, clothing or any other mass-produced object, television shows, news stories, films, music, video games and so on, presuppose a relatively invisible production process driven by the pursuit of profit. To draw attention to this production process is to intimate that the media are not necessarily interested in 'informing the public', or providing people with the 'truth about crime and punishment'. Instead, they are primarily interested in manufacturing representations that, if consumed, secure economic rewards.

And, to be sure, this is big business. Ever since the development of media technologies, crime and punishment have provided much content and fodder. One could proffer a barrage of numbers detailing how much media space is devoted to crime, but it is somewhat unnecessary. All one needs to do is engage in a brief, reflexive moment: of the last five movies you watched, how many were about crime, or included scenes in which crime occurred? Think of your five favourite television shows. How many feature or revolve around criminalised behaviour or policing? Of the news stories that have recently caught your attention, or have appeared on your social media pages, how many have involved crime and/or punishment as thematic content? If you listen to podcasts, how many of these are based on crime, criminal justice and so on?

It has been said that the spectacles of crime and punishment become less visible in modernity (Foucault 1977). This is often supported by noting that state-orchestrated punishments are no longer performed in the public square, that the days of corporal punishment are long behind us, and that deviants are now sent to prisons that are relatively secluded and thus invisible to most. But crime and punishment certainly remain a spectacle if we are talking about mediated images and representations. Not surprisingly, a range of competing theories concerning the social consequences of a symbolic environment saturated with images of crime and punishment have emerged.

Four theoretical models concerning the significance of consuming crime and punishment narratives will be discussed here. First, we take a look at 'conservative' views, in which the media is construed as a cause of crime and corrosive of social order. Second, we will look at arguments in which media portrayals are seen as promoting an irrational fear of crime and thus punitive attitudes amongst audiences. A third way of deciphering the social function of media portrayals of crime and punishment treats anxiety and reassurance as central concepts. In this view, there exists very profound social forces that produce anxiety in individuals (e.g., lack of job security), but mediated images of social control swoop in to provide the public with reassurances that order and stability will be restored. Finally, the chapter will discuss arguments in which the media is understood as malicious in its effects. Not only do depictions of crime and punishment reproduce a social order that is deeply problematic, but the production processes upon which media content is unavoidably dependent entail specific forms of victimisation and exploitation.

Before discussing these four arguments in some detail, it might be worthwhile to make several general points about the media in contemporary society. It is important to acknowledge that (a) there are several types of media and media content, (b) it is difficult to maintain a distinction between representations of reality and fiction and (c) insofar as it exists as a social institution, there are numerous theories concerning the overall performance and role of the media.

Making sense of the media: Types, the factual and the fictional, a powerful socio-cultural institution

Media types and forms of content

Ray Surette (2015, pp. 6–27) has discussed media types and the forms of content that they host at some length. Table 6.1 provides a visual summary of the typology that Surette effectively outlines.

Surette (2015) suggests that print, sound and visual forms can be understood as 'legacy' media. They were all developed prior to the internet and, generally speaking, worked on the assumption that media companies produced content that was subsequently consumed by audiences. With the arrival of 'new media', the distinction between produces and consumers is undermined. The interactive qualities of new media afford the 'audience' some space to produce content. To be sure, the power of individuals and the

Table 6.1 Media types and content types (based on Surette 2015, pp. 6–27)

Media types			
Print	Sound	Visual	Interactive/new media
Newspapers	Radio	Film	Internet
Magazines	Music	Television	Video games
Novels	Podcasts		Smart phones
Comic books			Two core features:
			• Provides enhanced access to print, sound and visual media
			• Allows 'consumers' to become 'producers' of content

Content types (recurrent across all forms of media listed above)
Advertising
News
Entertainment
Infotainment

public to manufacture and disseminate content remains dwarfed by corporate media interests and officials who represent social institutions (Herman and McChesney 2001), but it is probably greater now than it was in the age of 'legacy media'. Arguably, the more important aspect of new media is its ability to provide individuals with rapid access to all types of legacy media and forms of content, and allow them to share such content with others on various platforms.

It is probably obvious, but all of these media forms – newspapers, magazines, literature, radio, film, television, internet streaming, video games, news, entertainment, infotainment and, albeit to a lesser extent perhaps, advertising – may disseminate images and narratives in which crime and punishment is a prominent theme. In fact, crime and punishment have been, and remain, amongst the most recurrent themes in media since its technological development. James Oleson (2015, pp. 600–603; citations omitted) paints a fairly vivid picture of how criminal justice saturates our mediated existence when he writes:

Many members of the public ... think that they know something about the justice system because they watch television and films. They think they know about organized crime because they have seen films like *The Godfather* ... They know drug abuse because they have seen films like *Rush* ... And because they are familiar with Anthony Hopkins in *The Silence of the Lambs* ... even serial murder seems to lie within their ken. Similarly, although most people have never worn the uniform, members of the public believe they know what it is like to be a detective, all because they have seen films like *Fargo*, *Dirty Harry* ... Because they have seen Kelly McGillis stand up for Jodie Foster in *The Accused*, they know what it is to prosecute a case ... Corrections, too, seems familiar. Even people who have never been arrested, much less spent any time in jail, often think they know what it is like to 'do time' in general population (... *The Shawshank Redemption*, *Oz*, or *Orange is the New Black*), to be thrown into 'the hole' ...

The question, of course, is what are the implications of residing within, and thus being socialised by, a cultural environment in which crime commands so much of our attention? Individuals from privileged social groups will have very limited, direct experience with criminal justice systems. Surette (2015, p. 25) posits that being issued an infringement notice for violating any given road rule will be, for many people, their most direct encounter with criminal justice. In his view, receiving a ticket for driving infractions is not a very robust basis on which to understand the complexities of crime and punishment. Given how distant the middle classes and privileged social groups are from criminal justice, the media comes to fill an important void in dominant understandings of crime, deviance and law enforcement (Brown 2009). We will return to competing claims about how the media fills that void shortly.

'Fact and fiction' or 'fact/fiction'?

It is reasonable to suspect that much of the public might be inclined to draw a distinction between media types that depict reality and those that are purely fictional. In terms of the former, any given individual may well suspect that the 'news' (and, perhaps to some extent, advertising) is premised upon an objective portrayal of reality; concerning the latter, most people would construe 'entertainment' as a form of storytelling and thus fictional. For critical scholars, however, distinguishing media types that deal with fact from those that deal in fiction is difficult, if not implausible (Ferrell et al. 2008; Fishman and Cavender 1998; Greer and Reiner 2012; Sparks 1992).

News media may often be perceived as interested in objectively portraying real events for its audience, but it is difficult to square this view with the nature of news production and presentation (Jewkes 2007). Journalists and news producers must make decisions about what stories to include and exclude from print and broadcast media. Moreover, from all the possible information about any particular event that they could pass on to the public, they must once again make selective choices. Such choices are often filtered according to assumptions about 'what audiences want' or 'need to know', and what news producers think will attract an audience, thereby generating profits/economic rewards (Chermak 1995). Furthermore, news reporting generally adopts a narrative form to engage audiences. This form demands that stories be built with thematic tropes that possess some degree of cultural resonance. Oftentimes, a symbolic evil emerges (the 'criminal') and disrupts the social order ('crime'), only to be overcome through some symbolic good ('law enforcement' and 'punishment').

To be sure, even media that appears to deal in fiction is not so straightforward. Most works of fiction inevitably refer to and draw inspiration from real events or social facts. The criminals, detectives, courtrooms, prisons and so on that appear within entertainment 'make sense' to audiences because they understand that such reference points have a real counterpart in social life. Once the difficulty of maintaining a distinction between fact and fiction is acknowledged, it is perhaps best to regard the media as a cultural force, perhaps somewhat akin to organised religion, a land of myth and narrative that is inseparable from the structures of everyday life.

Media performance debates: Serving the public or adjuncts of power and authority?

Numerous models for understanding the media as a socio-cultural institution have been developed and debated. For the most part, these models emerge from the specific context of analysing news media. Nevertheless, theories concerning news media performance might be useful for thinking about the consumption of crime and punishment in more general terms.

The 'watchdog press' perspective constitutes the common-sense view of the media. This is most true, perhaps, in the United States and other Anglophone countries. It is also the view that is most likely to be advanced by journalists and those who work within the field of news production. Those who subscribe to the 'watchdog press' perspective hold that the media are best understood as an independent social institution that critically evaluates the activities of government. In widely disseminating information, the media expose governmental processes, thereby holding officials accountable to citizens. Given such qualities, media can be thought of as a 'fourth' branch of political power that operates in tension with the state's 'legislative', 'executive' and 'judicial' functions. Assisted by an open media, public opinion is 'well-informed' and thus able to exercise rational control over government policy and practice (Bennett and Klockner 1996; Cook 2005; Donovan and Scherer 1992; Ferree et al. 2002; Schudson 2005).

According to the notion of 'liberal bias', the mass media are governed by a liberal and – often amounting to the same thing – a 'left-leaning' political agenda. For proponents of liberal bias, the major deficiencies of media stem from journalists, who are construed as exercising unmitigated control over the content of the news (Coulter 2002; Goldberg 2003; McGowan 2003). In this view, the media has a corrosive effect on social order.

A third view of the media revolves around the notion of 'indexing' (Bennett et al. 2007). In this perspective, the mass media (i.e., journalists) track public officials who are perceived to be in positions of power and therefore able to shape the course of historical events and policy outcomes. At least two important implications follow from the indexing model. First, given that journalists essentially transcribe the activities and statements of whoever is perceived to be an influential figure, it makes little sense to speak of either 'left-wing' or 'right-wing' biases in media (Bennett et al. 2007; Bennett 2009). What matters more than political ideology is who is in a position of institutional power such that they can influence others. Second, and closely related, indexing suggests that any perspective or worldview – on any given issue – has the same chance of receiving sustained coverage in the mass media provided it is championed by a powerful voice.

Finally, one can speak of the 'propaganda' model. This view is typically associated with the work of Herman and Chomsky (1988), who argue that mainstream news is 'filtered' according to five key principles before it reaches the public for consumption. These filters include: monopoly ownership of the major mass media firms; the financial support of the advertising industry, itself backed by other large corporations; relations of dependence amongst journalists and government officials; the regulation of critical opinions through 'flak'; and an anti-communist ideology or, to formulate this in positive terms, a pro-capitalist standpoint (Bagdikian 2000; McChesney 2004). In short, there is a readily identifiable political economy to mass media news content: the interests of 'big' economic players and government officials are closely intertwined and these effectively determine media content. This leads to a system of propaganda in which the interests of political and economic elites are supported (Herman and Chomsky 1988, p. 298).

As noted, these views have been developed in the course of analysing the production and dissemination of news, but it is not hard to see how they have important implications for debates about media content broadly conceived. The core issue concerns how the media sit in relation to social order: does media protect individual liberties and push for progressive change when necessary, or does it work to reinforce structural inequalities? Does the widespread consumption of images and narratives of crime and punishment foster well-informed public decision making, or does it generate non-rational worldviews and counterproductive practices within the criminal justice system?

Bearing this in mind, we can turn to some of the most prominent positions concerning the relationship between mediated images of crime and punishment, audience perceptions and behaviours, criminal justice, and social order. In what follows, four broad approaches for making sense of media consumption will be discussed. Table 6.2 offers a schematic overview of these approaches.

Table 6.2 Perspectives on consuming media portrayals of crime and punishment

	Image of media (may be implicit)	Consequences of consumption	Manifestations/locus
'Conservative'	'Liberal bias' 'Too permissive'	Encourage crime and/or aggressive behaviour Undermine social order	'Moral panics' over media Media effects (esp. video games experiments) 'CSI effect'
Irrational fear and punitiveness	Approximates a 'propaganda' model Severely distorts the 'realities' of crime and punishment	Irrational concern with crime (as chances of victimisation small) Punitive attitudes Promotes 'law and order' policy	Media effects Cultivation approach Analyses of media content
'Collective realities'	Approximates a 'propaganda' model Media narratives 'speak to' socially induced anxieties, but distort sources of anxiety	Displaces rational, socially produced anxieties onto crime Transcend 'guilt' Manage 'late-modern' anxieties	Sparks (1992) Cheliotis (2010) Hollway and Jefferson (1997)
Malicious media	Approximates a 'propaganda' model	Normalises a variety of power asymmetries Exploitation (of those who appear in media) Resistance	Ferrell et al. (2008) Presdee (2000) 'Creative crimes' Barak and 'newsmaking criminology' (1988, 2011)

The conservative view: Media as corrosive of social order

In conservative views, the media is understood as promoting a 'liberal agenda' that undermines what is presumed to otherwise be a desirable social order. The media is seen as failing to adopt 'appropriate standards' concerning the content and messages that it puts into circulation. Without such standards in place, the media will wreak havoc on the 'moral fabric' of society. Claims that concern the undermining of social order take a fairly predictable form: overexposure to mediated crime and violence will cause consumers to perceive deviant behaviours as non-problematic.

The most obvious manifestations of this view are found in certain 'moral panics' (see Chapter 5) surrounding media and experimental research in which playing video games is examined as a driver of increased aggression in players. Concerning the former, it is often posited that the media are criminogenic: they create in some viewers the propensity to copy the crimes that they see portrayed, or 'teach' individuals how to commit certain crimes, or construe crime as an appropriate course of action in various circumstances (see Surette 2015, pp. 74–98; see also Sparks 1992, pp. 66–72). Concerning the latter, there is no shortage of studies that examine the supposed effects of playing violent video games. Such studies typically ask an experimental group to play video games for an allotted amount of time, and then observe their later behaviour or assess their attitudes. Not surprisingly, many studies report that those exposed to violent video games subsequently adopt behaviour or thinking patterns that are problematic (see for example Anderson and Bushman 2001; Greitemeyer and Mügge 2014; Shaw et al. 2014; Sherry 2001).

Despite the amount of studies conducted along these lines, it is not clear that they are well equipped to adequately theorise the relationship between media consumption, behaviour, attitudes and so on. It is, for example, very hard to measure and identify a causal relationship between media exposure and behaviour. Is it the exposure to crime and violence in the media that drives behaviour, or are motivations to deviance simply encouraged by media? In terms of video game studies, it is difficult to gauge whether observable behavioural effects will endure over time or carry over to other social settings. From a more sociological viewpoint, such studies tend to downplay the broader social, economic and political contexts in which motivations to behaviour are formed. And, of course, constructivist positions would accuse such studies of according categories like crime and aggression an ontological status that cannot be justified. In other words, behavioural effects type studies fail to interrogate the constructed nature of its central concepts.

A relatively recent manifestation of the conservative view can be discerned in claims of a 'CSI effect'. *CSI: Crime Scene Investigation* is a television series in which a team of crime scene investigators gather and analyse evidence, often with the aid of technologies that do not exist, and invariably identify those responsible for violent crimes. As Simon Cole and Rachel Dioso-Villa (2011) note, the notion that *CSI* has an adverse effect on the criminal justice system initially surfaced in the mainstream media. Cole and Dioso-Villa (2011, p. 22) posit that the 'CSI effect' entails six specific possibilities, which can be paraphrased as follows:

- That jurors will increasingly find defendants not guilty (because forensic evidence in actual cases does not parallel that seen on *CSI* and other similar television shows).

- That prosecutors will feel compelled to explain to juries any absences in forensic evidence.

- That juries will perceive forensic expert witnesses to be infallible.

- That the public's understanding of science will be improved.

- That more individuals will be attracted to careers in forensic science.

- That criminals will learn how to evade detection.

It is the first of these claims – juries will demand that the guilt of defendants is proved 'beyond a CSI standard' – that has been met with most concern (Cole and Dioso-Villa 2007; see also Huey 2010; Mopas 2007). That this seems to be the primary concern says more about current perceptions concerning criminal justice than it does *CSI*: the threat that *CSI* supposedly entails is its potential to weaken the resolve of juries to find defendants guilty, thus interfering with the punitive capacities of the state! Somewhat ironically, available evidence suggests that conservatives need not worry about this. Cole and Dioso-Villa (2007, p. 462) show that the acquittal rate in the United States has steadily declined since 1945, possibly indicating that juries are becoming more punitive and inclined to see defendants as guilty (see also Cavender and Deutsch 2007).

Irrational fear and punitiveness

This leads us nicely into our second model for understanding the consequences of consuming media portrayals of crime and punishment. Many have come to argue that the media promote a 'fear of crime' and this, in turn, encourages the public to see punitiveness as the most viable method for controlling crime (Carlson 1985; Lowry et al. 2003). In most accounts along these lines, the fear of crime is assumed to be irrational given that serious crime is relatively rare, thus rendering one's chances of victimisation statistically unlikely.

Within this view, the media is generally understood as a propaganda machine of sorts: the media severely distort the realities of crime and deviance, and this leads the public to adopt specific ideologies concerning punishment. As Surette (2015, p. 59) puts it, the media can be understood as governed by a 'backwards law' when it comes to crime and punishment:

> In every subject category – crimes, criminals, crime fighters, attorneys, correctional officers, and inmates; the investigation of crimes and making of arrests; the processing and disposition of cases; and the experience of incarceration – the media construct and present a crime-and-justice world that is the opposite of the real world.

To elaborate upon this point, violent and extreme interpersonal crimes amongst strangers are grossly over-represented in media portrayals. Actual crime rates are, by and largely, constituted by property offences that do not typically entail direct victimisation (Oleson 2015, p. 614). Criminals are routinely depicted as demonic, evil masterminds, their crimes as manifestations of defective personalities (Jewkes 2007). Very rarely are criminals and their crimes understood as the product of social circumstances and contexts (Chermak 1995, p. 176). In mediated representations, those who fight crime are construed as 'heroes'. One way or another, they will 'solve' the crimes they are tasked with investigating (Greer and Reiner 2012, p. 255). Resolving crime may follow when the hero operates within officially sanctioned practices of law enforcement or, perhaps more common, be the product of extreme violence that, in all likelihood, would be met with severe reprimanding were it to actually occur (Chermak 1995, p. 177; Surette 2015, pp. 100–121). In any case, the resolution rate of crime-fighting heroes is remarkable – it almost approaches 100%. In the real world, a significant number of crimes elude resolution (Taylor 1996).

Taken together, these misrepresentations of crime and punishment intimate why media portrayals promote irrational fears and punitive sentiments. Crime is seen as randomly distributed, committed by 'defective individuals' who target innocent strangers for reasons that are more or less unfathomable (hence, 'fear'). However, the crime-controlling hero inevitably comes along and, through violence that often exceeds that of the criminal, order and harmony are restored (hence, the desire for 'punitiveness'). In such a scenario, social solutions that control crime by pre-empting and addressing its fundamental causes are never entertained. The media diet is an extremely limited one, consisting primarily of atrocious criminal events. These criminal events, obviously enough, transgress moral boundaries, but cohesion will soon be restored through action that is violent, forceful, extralegal and retrospective.

The 'fear and punitiveness' argument owes a profound debt to the work of George Gerbner and colleagues (Gerbner 1970; Gerbner and Gross 1976). Gerbner was interested in understanding 'media effects' by determining the prevalence of violence on television and how, if it all, this was absorbed by audiences, thereby fostering certain worldviews. Not surprisingly, violence was found to be a common component of television programming: around 80–90% of television shows portrayed violence and about eight incidents of violence occurred per hour (Gerbner and Gross 1976, p. 187).

To gauge the effects of this upon audiences, surveys were conducted to ascertain if different worldviews could be correlated with 'light' and 'heavy' television viewers. Gerbner and Gross (1976, pp. 191–193) found that 'heavy' television viewers were more distrustful of people and exaggerated their chances of experiencing violent victimisation. In short, rather than proffer 'rational' responses to survey questions, as 'light' viewers veered towards, 'heavy' viewers responded with 'television answers'. From this, Gerbner and Gross (1976) conclude that television 'cultivates' particular understandings of the world. In the specific context of crime, violence and social control, they posit that television viewing ultimately fosters a 'heightened sense of risk and insecurity' and that this is 'likely to increase acquiescence to and dependence upon established authority, and to legitimize its use of force' (Gerbner and Gross 1976, p. 194).

The 'fear and punitiveness' approach has been criticised for implying that there is a reality about crime and justice that can be known (say, for example, through official statistics) and that this should govern perceptions. But it is hard to maintain that a general, 'rational' level of fear can be determined. As Steven Box (1981) pointed out long ago, official statistics concerning crime are not necessarily an accurate reflection of reality. Moreover, social groups are differentially positioned throughout social space, and so what may be an 'irrational' level of fear for some might be 'rational' for others. For example, women's fear of violent victimisation, although some forms may be statistically unlikely, might be entirely rational given hegemonic constructions of masculinity that sanction men's violence (on this point, see also Dobash et al. 1998, pp. 52–56).

Another limitation of 'fear and punitiveness' stems from its tendency to privilege media distortions, and subsequently assess their effects upon perceptions. In doing so, the problem of why audiences are attracted to crime and punishment narratives eludes analysis. What is it that audiences find so appealing about the media's penchant for saturating our lives with crime and social control? Why are we attracted to representations that we are likely to find unsettling? What meanings are conveyed within media texts and what meaning do we derive from them? Why do we find pleasure in consuming media?

'Collective realities': The 'rational' kernel within media distortion

This line of questioning is central to the 'collective realities' approach. Those who claim that some form of 'collective reality' helps to account for the investments that are made in media depictions of crime and punishment posit that social relations are real, and that they are a genuine source of anxiety. Hence, audience fears cannot be dismissed as, or assumed to be, irrational. Instead, the mediated nature of crime and punishment works to displace real social anxieties onto particular objects (i.e., 'crime' and/or 'criminals'). It is in this sense that the media, although tapping into something real, works in ideological ways. However, given the complex, multifaceted nature of social relations – and how individuals are positioned within such relations – the particular anxieties that they induce is open to debate. As a result, distinct ways of resolving why audiences are attracted to depictions of crime and punishment, even though they may find such depictions disconcerting, have been proffered. In what follows, three variations on this theme will be discussed.

In his account of television crime dramas, Richard Sparks (1992) begins by noting that viewers are not 'dupes' who simply consume whatever the media makes available. Media content must be produced according to some sense of its presumed audience, and it must 'speak to' those that it addresses if it is to be successful. As such, crime dramas will necessarily entail some degree of shared ground amongst producers and consumers/audiences (Sparks 1992, p. 117). This view allows Sparks to examine the most characteristic and general features of mediated forms of crime and punishment in order to explain their appeal.

Sparks (1992, p. 131) suggests that crime fiction plays with the tension between anxiety and reassurance. Viewer satisfaction comes from having anxieties provoked, albeit with the reassurance that order and coherence will soon be re-imposed upon the external world. When it comes to the socially induced anxieties that concern audiences, and that are assuaged by media representations of crime and punishment, Sparks' account is somewhat ambiguous. On the one hand, he suggests that 'an indefinitely large range of anxieties' may be displaced through the consumption of crime narratives, some of which may be related to crime and law enforcement (Sparks 1992, p. 120; see also Lupton and Tulloch 1999). On the other hand, his analysis of media themes and tropes indicate that more particular anxieties are in play.

Sparks notes, for instance, that most crime dramas are set in cities, and that most villains are 'rich, male, white and outwardly respectable. They are businessmen, corrupt policemen and politicians' (1992, p. 143). Their criminality is usually portrayed as motivated by an unrestrained quest for riches upon riches. And, insofar as crime is carried out by individuals from impoverished backgrounds, it is often depicted as being orchestrated by privileged, powerful characters. All of which indicates that the social anxieties addressed by crime narratives stem from urbanism, class relations and economic inequality (for a variation that also entertains anxieties around urbanism and inequalities, see Taylor 1996).

Importantly, however, crime fiction does not necessarily spawn resistance to inequality, but manages it. After all, it is not excessive wealth that is the problem within crime drama: it is the combination of excessive wealth and irresponsibility, eccentricity, ruthlessness, psychological deficiency and so on. Crime fiction thus suggests that economic inequality is not a structural problem that requires a structural solution. Rather, the problem is framed as one of irresponsible individuals who happen to possess an unhealthy obsession with wealth. Within crime narratives – and herein lies the solace they provide to audiences – such individuals can be identified and, through the use of force, brought into line by the morally upright super-hero. As Sparks (1992, p. 156) concludes, the ultimate effect of this is to move us 'more towards distraction from rather than confrontation with the sources of our social sentiments, more towards consolation than transcendence'.

For Leonidas Cheliotis (2010), crises that follow from contemporary economic relations are also central to anxiety, but audiences get something other than distraction from consuming crime and punishment. For Cheliotis, media representations of crime and the prison allow audiences to transcend, albeit symbolically, their sense of unconscious 'guilt'.

At first glance, this interpretation may appear surreal: why do audiences feel 'guilt'? Cheliotis (2010, p. 174) notes that the media construe crime as a product of 'individual and group pathologies, and thereby divert attention away from such structural crises as deindustrialisation, economic deregulation and the collapse of the welfare state'. Audience anxiety, however, does not stem from denying the social causes of crime. Rather, it arises because significant portions of the audience effectively sanction the economic conditions that are intimately connected to crime.

Much of the public in recent times have supported, and continue to support, neoliberal governments that dismantle public welfare and pander to market interests, thereby intensifying social inequalities. As such, the consuming audience is complicit in creating the social and economic conditions that, in reality, underpin the crime and punishment practices that appear in sublimated form 'on screen'. In this context, when media representations posit that individual pathologies are the fundamental cause of crime, and that harsh prison conditions are essential to the control of crime, the public is afforded a 'scapegoat' (criminals and deviants) that can alleviate any sense of their responsibility for promoting social conditions that engender human suffering.

The work of Wendy Hollway and Tony Jefferson (1997) moves us away from theory in which anxiety is tied to economic inequalities, and suggests that 'late-modernity' unleashes a range of anxieties.

Drawing from Ulrich Beck (1992), Hollway and Jefferson (1997, p. 258) note that scientific and industrial developments associated with the late-modern period introduce threats and hazards that are not restricted to specific times and places, relatively unpredictable and, when things do go wrong, finding who is responsible is increasingly difficult. As a result, the effort to calculate and assess risk has emerged as a fundamental leitmotif of late-modernity. The possibility of misfortune is now discussed in terms of probabilities, chances, the likelihood of events, and so on. Individuals are expected to calculate the most rational course of action in light of estimates, forecasts, and patterns in actuarial tables.

All of which might be feasible if we were 'rational' subjects. The problem, however, is that we are also moral and political beings; when things go wrong we want to see that someone is held accountable. Moreover, rather than rational calculations that may make it possible for danger to be eluded, we often demand order and prefer certainty over ambivalence and chaos. In the absence of such certainty, the subject will soon be saddled with a profound sense of anxiety concerning their existence and place in the world. It is in this context that the popularity of crime and punishment narratives begins to make sense: such representations essentially partake in the ritual endeavour of promising that order and control are possible in a world that is otherwise plagued by uncertainty. As Hollway and Jefferson (1997, p. 260) put it, 'people will be drawn to discourses and practices which appear to offer the hope of order and control'.

They illustrate this position by drawing from in-depth interview material that pries open how individuals are invested in fear of crime discourses. One respondent, Bob, is a middle-aged man, who is unemployed due to an accident in the workplace. He is married to a woman who is also unemployed. They live in public housing and their apartment has been burgled once. Both Bob and his partner remain preoccupied with this burglary, even though it was an isolated incident in which a handful of electronic items were stolen.

Hollway and Jefferson (1997, p. 263) suggest that an external observer of Bob's situation would conclude that his fear of crime is largely irrational. However, it begins to make a lot more sense if it is situated relative to his overall social position and experience. Bob's ongoing concern with crime displaces fears that are 'far more intractable' and thus escape the possibility of being brought under control. These 'other fears' would appear to have a more rational – perhaps one should say 'social' or 'real' – foundation. As they put it, Bob's fears may well stem from 'fear of physical incapacity and ageing; fear of the meaninglessness of his current existence; fear of an unfamiliar and potentially hostile world outside the home' (Hollway and Jefferson 1997, p. 263). Bearing this possibility in mind, rather than exacerbate Bob's sense of fear, media representations of crime may play an important role in alleviating his anxieties.

The 'collective realities' approach is not without its limits. While it certainly generates a range of fascinating interpretive readings of crime in the media, it tends to neglect verifying its interpretations by detailed examination of audience responses. Perhaps more important, analyses in this style do not dismiss those who consume representations of crime and punishment and subsequently fear crime as 'irrational', but they can appear somewhat elitist in claiming that audiences 'displace' anxieties. This could be construed as elitist to the extent that audiences are seen as shifting their anxiety to what is presumed to be a 'wrong', or 'inappropriate', object (such as crime). Such claims may assume that the interpretive scholar knows individuals better than they know themselves.

Malicious media: The reproduction of power asymmetries

In Chapter 5, the notion of 'loops and spirals' developed by Ferrell et al. (2008) was discussed in some detail. In that context, 'loops and spirals' was described insofar as it can be understood as an analytical concept. That is, it is a notion that promises to facilitate the analysis of how media representations and 'real life' are mutually constitutive, and how this symbiotic relationship has implications for social life. However, 'loops and spirals' also entails a theoretical stance concerning how media, especially its depictions of crime and punishment, relates to social order and power asymmetries. In a remark that is perhaps worth accenting, Ferrell et al. (2008, p. 130) note that 'when it comes to crime, transgression, and control, this looping circularity offers up dynamics that interweave the ludicrous with the malicious'.

The use of the term 'malicious' provides a particular frame for theorising the social significance of a media obsessed with crime and punishment narratives. The media can be thought of as malicious in at least two senses. First, it is malicious in its capacity to absorb and thus reproduce the power asymmetries that define contemporary social orders. Second, the production processes that must transpire if media images of crime and punishment are to be available for consumption often involves suffering and exploitation.

Those who recognise the malicious nature of the media often stop to consider how this might engender resistance. Holding fast to the view that where there is power there is resistance, scholars within this camp emphasise that dissent and critique of the media can be discerned. This dissent may manifest in the form of 'creative crimes' or subcultural formations (e.g., 'culture jamming'), but it has also emerged as a scholarly pursuit ('newsmaking criminology'). The remainder of this section begins by exploring the two senses in which media might be understood as malicious. Following this, it outlines some forms of resistance that have emerged in response to contemporary media.

Media and power

To understand how media reproduces social order it might be worth recalling that power can operate along multiple axes for the cultural criminologist (see Introduction, Figure 0.2). These include, but by no means are limited to, class, status, race, gender, age, 'ability' and sexuality. It is, of course, also possible for the dynamic lines along which power operates to intersect, thereby compounding the problems endured by those with relatively little power. Although much cultural criminology focuses on tensions between young people and adults, argument concerning malicious media have led to a focus on power relations grounded by race, class, and urban location.

The discussion of 'gangsta rap' provided by Ferrell et al. (2008) can serve as an illustration. As they point out, gangsta rap is often criticised for its salacious content, and the supposedly negative effects that it has on the behaviour of individuals who consume such cultural products. According to Ferrell and colleagues, however, the defining quality of gangsta rap (alongside numerous other media products) is that it markets criminal transgression as a lifestyle choice, especially to young men from marginalised social locations. But in a cruel twist of socio-cultural fate, the adoption of deviant symbols and lifestyles quickly comes to operate as a basis for policing, criminalisation and social control (Ferrell et al. 2008, pp. 137–144. See also Hayward and Yar 2006; Kramer et al. 2016). As such, one powerful segment of the social order (mainstream cultural media) encourages 'deviant styles', and possibly fosters criminal behaviour, that other social institutions (e.g., the criminal justice system) curtail through criminalisation. Via such processes, the propensity for criminal justice systems to operate in racially discriminatory ways – by disproportionality focusing on poor, racially marginalised youth within inner cities, for example – is reproduced and normalised.

Sometimes the mediated nature of transgression and violence works to reproduce certain aspects of the broader social order in more straightforward ways: video games that glorify and normalise war are an apt example. Of particular concern are video games that compel players to situate themselves as US military personnel engaged in aggressive wars involving racialised 'others'. Games such as *America's Army* and *Kuma War* invite players to shoot and kill 'enemy' combatants (Ferrell et al. 2008, p. 146). When games compel players to carry out the kinds of behaviours demanded of US soldiers in real combat situations, the effects on the psyche and libidinal investments of individuals are likely to be quite profound. Such games effectively demand that players identify with the interests of the US 'war machine' and its allies. In securing 'consent' to the dominant order, such games disqualify narratives in which the geopolitical relations and foreign policies that currently produce tensions between the 'west' and the 'east' are critically evaluated (for a detailed discussion of how video games invite players to invest in contemporary geopolitical power relations that are heavily racialised, see Cremin 2016).

Because those who focus on the malicious effects of the media emphasise its problematic content, analyses along these lines may appear to parallel conservative approaches. However, conservative and malicious readings of the media are opposed. In the former approach, it is assumed that contemporary social arrangements are desirable, but threatened by media content and messaging; in the latter, contemporary social arrangements are seen as deeply problematic, but nevertheless reproduced via media content and its adverse effects on the subject.

Media as commodity: Production processes, victimisation, exploitation

In Chapter 3, we saw Mike Presdee suggest that crime is a pleasurable carnival for those who directly engage in it. Related to this argument is the claim that it is also pleasurable to consume crime and punishment. Insofar as it can be consumed, crime and punishment become commodities that secure profit for their producers. It is a strange thing to consume transgression: we find it enticing, but also disturbing. We love it when Jerry Springer's guests start fighting on stage and security guards appear to pry the combatants apart, even if we think the show is morally bankrupt (Presdee 2000, p. 73). Consuming transgression is a 'guilty pleasure', like listening to popular music hits that you secretly love even though they are 'uncool'.

Much of the guilty pleasures that stem from the consumption of crime are problematic according to Presdee. Following the notion that crime and punishment are a media commodity, Presdee (2000) notes that all such media texts necessitate a production process. The production process that lurks behind our consumption of crime and punishment is disturbing to say the least, especially because it involves real people. To produce and televise youthful forms of offending, such as joyriding, young people must engage in such activities and they may be criminalised, convicted and sent to prison for doing so (Presdee 2000, pp. 65–66).

But all this becomes immaterial when transformed into images for consumption governed by the pursuit of personal pleasure. The reality that goes into representations, the relations between real people, are rendered invisible, and we cease to concern ourselves with what actually happens during the manufacturing of media content. What constitutes a real, oftentimes costly experience for those who are central to the production of media, becomes enjoyment for those who are privileged enough to consume.

Even more problematic, by consuming crime and punishment we play an active role in reproducing the logic of commodifying crime and transgression. Like any other commodity, the media requires that a consumer exist in order to complete the cycle of production that makes profit possible. As Presdee (2000, p. 65) explains:

> If the [criminal, transgressive] event is not filmed there can be no product. If the product is not communicated there can be no distribution. If we don't watch there is no consumption and the process of production is incomplete. So when we do watch, we consume and become willing partners in the creation of crime itself and willing consumers of the excitement it produces.

In completing the circuits of media production through consumption, we ensure more victims and more humiliation for individuals (Presdee 2000,

p. 72). We enlist ourselves as allies in the production of crime, processes of criminalisation and victimisation.

Modes of resistance: 'Creative crimes' and 'newsmaking criminology'

While reproduction of the dominant social order and 'indirect victimisation' are core tenets of those who see the media as malicious, this is not to say that resistance is impossible or does not transpire. Resistance can emerge in various ways, but I will discuss two forms here. The first, 'creative crimes', can be understood as something of a 'grassroots' form; the latter, 'newsmaking criminology', emerges from within a well-established social institution, the university.

The notion of 'creative crimes' has been elucidated by Avi Brisman. In Brisman's (2010, p. 205) account, creative crimes are seen as a response to 'socially injurious acts' which nevertheless elude being classified as 'civil or criminal violations'. This notion of 'socially injurious acts' is quite broad, but many of the malicious aspects of the media discussed above would easily fall within this frame. Brisman identifies three kinds of 'creative crimes': culture jamming, interventionism and sabotage.

Culture jamming involves playing with 'sign systems' such that new meanings are produced. The most obvious manifestation of culture jamming involves playing with advertisements to subvert their intended meaning. For example, the New York Police Department once orchestrated an advertisement campaign to attract new recruits in which the text 'MYNYPD' was featured. Culture jammers 'embellished' many of these advertisements so that they read 'MYNYPD killed Sean Bell', thereby drawing attention to the problem of state-sanctioned murder (Brisman 2010, p. 208). 'Interventionists' go a little further than culture jammers by seeking to disrupt actual moments in which power and capital flow, or circulate through social life. An example of this might be something like 'reclaim the streets', a movement which hosts spontaneous street parties in busy areas of the city in order to momentarily disrupt everyday patterns in which the flow of capital is privileged and to reassert the importance of public, communal space. 'Sabotage' is constituted by actions that seek to bring the everyday workings of capitalist society to a grinding halt. It may take a variety of forms, ranging from the disruption of animal research to throwing food at famous and powerful people. Perhaps the most relevant example in the present context is the well-known 'pieing' of Bill Gates, the chairperson of Microsoft, a company that has been pivotal to the development of 'new media' (Brisman 2010, p. 211).

What unites these manifestations of 'creative crime' is their ability to express dissent, draw attention to power inequalities, and compel those in positions of power to pay greater attention to the social problems for which they are, at least to some degree, responsible. Creative crimes have the potential to call disreputable, objectionable behaviour into question, thereby promoting social change (Brisman 2010, pp. 215–219). As the examples noted above intimate – particularly the case of culture jamming – creative crimes are often inspired by media content and messaging, or the pervasiveness of media throughout everyday social life.

Whereas 'creative crimes' tend to have 'grassroots' origins, 'newsmaking criminology' is an idea and practice that has emerged amongst some critical and cultural criminologists. The basic idea is to insert critical narratives within media discussions of crime and social control (Barak 1988, 2011). Given that such criminologists typically work within university settings – institutions that possess some degree of power and authority – their perspectives are likely to be consecrated or venerated, at least to some extent, when and if appearing in the media.

Newsmaking criminology appears viable due to how the mass media tends to function. On the one hand, newsmaking criminology generally construes the mass media in a way that is broadly consistent with the propaganda model. That is, mass media promotes the agendas of those with the most economic and political power, and seeks to 'win the consent' of the powerless to such agendas. The agenda of society's most powerful has important implications for how crime and punishment is portrayed and discussed in the media: stories will focus on a very narrow range of crimes (i.e., interpersonal and property crimes committed by the powerless); criminalised behaviour will be construed as a problem that stems from individual deficiencies (rather than social inequalities); instead of rehabilitation and social reform, harsher punishment will be promoted as the best way to resolve the 'crime problem' (Barak 1988, 569–576).

On the other hand, however, newsmaking criminology recognises that journalists are exposed to 'occupational norms of fairness and objectivity' during their training and whilst on the job (Barak 1988, p. 581). Moreover, some may take these principles of journalism seriously, thereby opening up cracks in what might otherwise amount to a simple propaganda machine. It is these cracks and fissures that one needs to identify and take advantage of. To the extent that they can do so, newsmaking criminologists may be able to smuggle critical accounts of crime and punishment into the mass media. As Barak (1988, p. 566) suggests, such accounts should (or could) attempt to:

> ... demystify images of crime and punishment by locating ... 'serious' crimes in the context of all illegal and harmful activities ... [A]ffect public attitudes, thoughts, and discourses about crime and justice so as to facilitate a public policy of 'crime control' based on structural and historical analyses of institutional development; [allow] criminologists to come forth with their knowledge and to establish themselves as credible voices in the mass-mediated arena of policy formation.

There are, then, possibilities for resistance to the mass media and its problematic, ideological content. Perhaps the most obvious question this raises, though, is one we have already seen in Chapter 4. Arguments about challenging media messaging through criminal practices (or practices that run some risk of criminalisation) parallel the 'resistance thesis'. Critical Marxists would find this unconvincing. In such a view, these kinds of petty crimes are not comparable to large-scale movements that fundamentally call the power of the state and capital into question. And so, it is ideological to read resistance into such practices; the cultural criminologist effectively distorts the meaning of resistance by doing so. To be fair, Brisman (2010, p. 220) does acknowledge this problem in noting that whether such resistances will develop into broader social movements of any significance is open to debate.

A parallel critique can be made of 'newsmaking criminology'. It is not necessarily problematic for academics to do media interviews and insert critical narratives into the media, but working this up into some kind of resistance thesis might be stretching an already thin idea too far. It seems unlikely that a handful of critical voices will make much difference, especially given media tendencies to prioritise official perspectives and remain locked within ideological boundaries. Moreover, critical criminologists may work for universities, but there is also a very strong chance that they will occupy relatively marginalised positions within such institutional settings. And, the 'late-modern', neoliberal logics that currently dominate much of the Anglophone world are marked by a certain 'anti-intellectualism', which often dismisses critical thought in order to propound moral-political sentiments and convictions (see Chapter 8).

Conclusion

This chapter has provided a general overview of media forms and types, and emphasised that media is inevitably embedded within social relations. In this latter respect, the media can be thought of as an 'effect' and a 'cause': broad power relations overwhelmingly determine media content and messaging, but the circulation of such content and messaging also operates as a force in the reproduction of power relations. This basic dynamic is not altered when representations of crime and punishment are utilised to provide media forms with content. If anything, power asymmetries and inequalities are normalised and intensified by such practices.

With the exception of the conservative approach, it is noteworthy that all of the other theoretical accounts considered in this chapter operate with some notion of propaganda to demystify media content.

To be sure, there is disagreement on precisely how media operates as an ideological force. In the 'irrational fear and punitiveness' approach, the focus is on a particular strand of ideology, that which promotes punitive logics and practices in the promise of delivering social control. Such an ideology fore-closes the possibility that developing structural solutions to the problems of crime and punishment would be far more rational and beneficial. In an age of mass incarceration that has witnessed unprecedented levels of imprison-ment, it is not surprising to see numerous scholars develop this line of thought.

In the collective realities approach, the ideological functions of crime and punishment narratives are a little more diffuse. Such narratives are said to displace rationally grounded anxieties, which can stem from an array of structural contradictions. Anxiety can be kindled by a recognition of one's general insecurity, health concerns, possibilities of victimisation, uncertainty around the environment and its capacity to sustain life on earth, the sense that the future cannot be predicted, and so on.

Finally, in what I have referred to as the malicious media perspective, the consumption of crime and punishment narratives is not sustained by the need to displace justifiable anxieties, but to fabricate consent to the multi-plicity of power relations that undergird contemporary social orders. There are possibilities of resistance and, arguably, resistant moments and narratives can be found even within mainstream media, but the odds do seem stacked against those invested in dissent and fighting for social change.

This is to close on quite the pessimistic note. Given the overwhelming tendency of media to operate in ways that are ideological, propagandistic and driven by profit motives, it would seem a lost cause to hope for 'better' content. Before becoming completely jaded, however, it might be worth revisiting Presdee's (2000, p. 65) notion that the circuit of media production needs to be completed by consumption. Seen this way, perhaps we should 'do nothing', if by this one means it is best to 'tune out' of our mediated existence when and where possible.

7 CULTURE AND PUNISHMENT

Introduction

Punishment is a major theme within the field of criminology. Not surprisingly, it is an area saturated by controversies and intense debate. In discussing punishment within a cultural criminology context, one should probably begin by noting two important problems. The first centres on what is meant by 'punishment'? Amongst cultural (and critical) criminologies punishment is typically regarded as a broad field, albeit one constituted by particular or concrete punitive techniques. Such techniques may include fines, good behaviour bonds, compliance with court-mandated treatment programmes, community work, imprisonment, corporal punishment and so on. As this list intimates, the concern with punishment often amounts to focusing on punitive strategies that are imposed by the state and thus surrounded with an aura of legitimacy. In any case, it is important to emphasise that scholars generally attempt to develop theories that account for punishment as a field of related practices, even though this will most likely entail analyses of particular punitive techniques and strategies.

The second problem stems from how the relationship between crime and punishment ought to be understood. Within positivist or 'administrative' strands of criminology, punishment is often perceived as a legitimate state response to crime. As such, crime and punishment are often construed as intimately connected. When punishment is understood as something that follows from crime, debate often comes to focus on whether punitive techniques are effective in terms of deterrence, retribution, rehabilitation, or some other goal associated with criminal justice (for an in-depth analysis of punishment and its relationship to deterrence, retribution, and rehabilitation, see Canton 2017; see also Chapter 1).

Cultural criminologists are very likely to adopt a different view of the crime–punishment relationship. Indeed, most of those who work with cultural concepts and frameworks regard the field of punishment as one that operates independently of crime or criminalised behaviour. That is to say, cultural criminologists begin with the premise that there is no relationship between crime and punishment. From here, the problem becomes one of explaining what governs the field of punishment if not crime? Why, for example, do new systems of punishment emerge every now and then? Why do systems of punishment evolve or mutate within a given set of social relations? How do systems of punishment actually operate in practice and do they work in ways that can be described as fair or impartial?

These kinds of questions have given rise to a variety of theories concerning punishment, some of which will be explored in this chapter. Four theoretical ideas will be discussed. The chapter will begin with Georg Rusche and Otto Kirchheimer's *Punishment and Social Structure* (2005), which is often recognised as the text that theoretically distinguished punishment from crime. Following this, we take a look at David Garland's *The Culture of Control* (2001), a work that builds upon Foucault (see Chapter 5) to make sense of the punitive regimes that characterise late-modernity.

The chapter's third strand of thought concerns punishment theories that owe a debt to the work of Emile Durkheim. Here we will start with Kai Erikson's *Wayward Puritans* (1966), a major reference point, which essentially claims that the need to maintain cultural boundaries explains much that happens in the realm of punishment. Turning Durkheim in a surprising direction, Philip Smith (2008) suggests that punishment techniques must abide by cultural norms surrounding 'order' and 'decorum' if they are to be socially accepted. Finally, we take a look at feminist scholarship that has made several important contributions to thinking culturally about punishment. This section begins with *Women's Imprisonment* by Pat Carlen (1983), a work that suggests women are primarily punished for their refusal, or inability, to follow cultural scripts surrounding 'motherhood', 'domesticity' and 'femininity'. The chapter closes with Alison Young's *Femininity in Dissent* (1990). Young dissects the ways in which cultural understandings of femininity are inherently prescriptive, and thus imply the possibility of punishment for those who are seen as departing from behaviours that are socially construed as 'appropriate' for women.

The chapter, then, has a particular arc. It begins with a text that is well-known for turning punishment into a problem, and subsequently delves into some landmark attempts to explain the punitive field through a cultural lens. With feminist theory, the chapter ends with the notion that culture may not be reducible to something that 'explains' punishment. Rather, it may be the case that culture operates in ways that are inherently punitive. In this sense, perhaps the problem of 'culture *and* punishment' should be reformulated as one of 'culture/punishment'.

Freeing punishment from crime: Georg Rusche and Otto Kirchheimer

The work of Georg Rusche and Otto Kirchheimer is often credited with dissociating punishment from crime, thereby turning the former into an independent area of scholarly concern (see Foucault 1977). It makes sense, therefore, to devote some attention to their ground-breaking text *Punishment and Social Structure*. Initially published in 1939, the text is premised upon a comparative analysis of various European countries in terms of their economic conditions, crime patterns and penal practices. Although heavily indebted to Marx's view that economic conditions play a pivotal role in shaping social life, Rusche and Kirchheimer's text does have important cultural dimensions that are worth teasing out.

Rusche and Kirchheimer suggest that punishment needs to be thought independently of crime in at least two senses. First, punishment should not be understood as a response to crime. As they put it:

> The bond, transparent or not, that is supposed to exist between crime and punishment prevents any insight into the independent significance of the history of penal systems. It must be broken. Punishment is neither a simple consequence of crime, nor the reverse side of crime, nor a mere means which is determined by the end to be achieved. Punishment must be understood as a social phenomenon freed from both its juristic concept and its social ends. (Rusche and Kirchheimer 1939/2005, p. 5)

Much of Rusche and Kirchheimer's text goes on to demonstrate how shifts in underlying economic conditions, fiscal concerns and profit motives best explain developments in punishment practices. Some of the arguments along these lines are not all that surprising and would appear to be fairly obvious. For example, it is only possible for a criminal justice system to make heavy use of fines as a mode of punishment in a money-based economy (Rusche and Kirchheimer 2005, p. 6). Other ways of demonstrating the connection between social structure and punishment, however, are not so straightforward. But, to provide one illustration, Rusche and Kirchheimer (2005, pp. 84–113) show how prison conditions will fluctuate according to labour market trends: prison conditions will improve in times of full employment, but they will deteriorate in periods marked by high levels of unemployment. We will return to this point below.

The second way in which Rusche and Kirchheimer dissociate punishment from crime is by showing that crime rates are not affected by penal policies. If crime rates and punishment were connected we should observe high crime rates when penal policies are lenient, but also the flipside to this: crime rates should be 'driven downward by intensifying punishment' (Rusche and Kirchheimer 2005, p. 193). Examining available statistics for a variety of crime types across multiple countries (i.e., England, France, Germany and Italy), Rusche and Kirchheimer (2005, pp. 193–205) observe a number of patterns. They find instances of harsh punitive policies combined with high crime rates, lenient policies paired with low crime rates, uneven punitive policy but stability in crime rates, consistent punitive policy matched with fluctuations in crime rates, stable crime rates despite intensified punitive policies and so on. In short, many patterns can be observed, but none of them support the view that crime rates are influenced by the punitive practices that constitute a penal field. One may suspect that such an argument is now well past its use by date, but similar disjunctures between punitive practices and crime rates are still observable today (Wacquant 2009b; Western 2006).

Divorcing punishment from crime was a decisive step forward for thinking critically about punitive strategies. But Rusche and Kirchheimer manage to go further than this. Arguably of more significance for those interested in cultural dimensions, they intimate how the relationship between social structure and punishment requires specific ideologies surrounding punitive practices. This need for ideology follows because if social structure determines punishment, and if that social structure is fundamentally unfair, then punitive practices are likely to replicate or embody broader social injustices. To recall from Chapter 5, Marx's concept of ideology refers to powerful ideas that are called forth by socio-economic arrangements and work to reproduce the class relations that hierarchically order capitalist society. In this sense, ideology denotes a cultural process. Whether in the form of arguments, discourses, rhetoric, public opinion, moral sentiments and so on, a set of ideas comes to circulate and shape the contours of social consciousness.

Although Rusche and Kirchheimer make little direct reference to the cultural layers associated with punishment, they effectively identify several ideologies that come to surround and legitimate the punitive field.

The first such cultural layer is discernible in what is often referred to as the principle of 'less eligibility'. Less eligibility posits that punishment must subject individuals to conditions that are worse than the basic living standards of the lowest free working classes if it is to have any deterrent effect. The core logic underpinning 'less eligibility' is that the lowest free working classes would have little reason to follow society's legal codes if the living conditions and life chances of criminals were improved by the punishments they receive (Rusche and Kirchheimer 2005, pp. 94, 104). Consistent with Marxist thought that sees ideas as a product of economic conditions, it is not hard to understand why less eligibility arises as a powerful governing principle in capitalist economies.

The notion of less eligibility implies a deep, cultural resentment and hatred for those deemed criminal and thus subject to state punishment. This resentment is likely to surface amongst all free members of a society, but it will be especially pronounced amongst those who are compelled to work long hours in order to maintain a bare minimum existence (Rusche and Kirchheimer 2005, pp. 95–98, 111. One might want to compare this with the discussion of Young 1999, 2003 from Chapter 4). It is this kind of cultural resentment that insists, for example, that prisons should not provide prisoners with work or educational opportunities even if doing so facilitates reintegration into the community upon release. For those who hold such resentment and animosity, any 'assistance' that the state provides to prisoners is likely to be perceived as far too generous. Likewise, food provisions should be as basic or minimal as possible, cells should not be too comfortable, any 'luxuries' should be forbidden and so on (Rusche and Kirchheimer 2005, pp. 106–108). In short, less eligibility promotes a cultural worldview in which harsh punishment is seen as desirable, if not absolutely necessary.

Second, and on a somewhat related note, less eligibility creates an irreconcilable contradiction between the ideals of rehabilitation and deterrence. That is to say, to the extent that capitalist societies promote the principle of less eligibility, it will be impossible to focus on rehabilitating *and* deterring individual offenders. According to Rusche and Kirchheimer (2005, pp. 158–159), a choice between these options must be made and, given the entrenched class antagonisms upon which it is premised, capitalism will inevitably gravitate towards deterrence or harsh punishments that militate against the reintegration of offenders.

It is difficult to see, however, what social good can come from such an arrangement. The insistence on deterrence is entirely irrational if we take the goal of punishment to be crime reduction or the reintegration of offenders. Yet, spawned by class dynamics, less eligibility places a cultural premium upon making sure that 'benefits' do not follow from criminal offending. This would help to explain why efforts to rehabilitate offenders often get reframed as being 'soft on criminals', if not taken as evidence that the state provides services to those who are 'unworthy' or 'undeserving'.

The third cultural sentiment that escapes a punitive field governed by structural-economic forces concerns the inability to recognise and critique the ways in which social inequalities are the root cause of crime and punishment techniques. The failure to acknowledge the role played by social structure ensures a 'social consciousness' (Rusche and Kirchheimer 2005, p. 207) that attributes any failures in reform to individual wickedness and thus calls for further repressive, punitive measures. In short, the 'default logic' of the punitive field comes to be a cultural worldview in which 'easy solutions', such as repression or containment of deviants, are repeatedly advocated even though it is well-known that such strategies are ineffective. Rusche and Kirchheimer (2005, p. 207) express the problem with more elegance than I can muster:

> The futility of severe punishment and cruel punishment may be proven a thousand times, but so long as society is unable to solve its social problems, repression, the easy way out, will always be accepted. It provides the illusion of security by covering the symptoms of social disease with a system of legal and moral value judgments.

It is remarkable to think that this was written in the 1930s, but appears as though it could have been written yesterday. The fact that such a statement continues to make sense could be construed as evidence that Rusche and Kirchheimer's argument concerning the bond between social structures and punishment remains viable. If anything, much of Rusche and Kirchheimer's work is validated by recent trends in punishment and the further entrenchment of capitalist social relations (see Chapter 8). For example, countries that have seen economic inequalities grow since the 1970s, such as United Kingdom, Australia, New Zealand and United States, are also the regions with the most alarming rates of incarceration. In the United States, the incarceration rate is 750 people per 100,000 of the population, which affords it the dubious honour of being a world-leader in terms of imprisonment.

There are, of course, several limits to the Rusche and Kirchheimer thesis. One of the critiques that is often levelled against Marxist approaches is that they reduce problems to economic and class dimensions. Such a critique certainly applies here. Rusche and Kirchheimer pay very little attention to how other sociological factors, such as race/ethnicity and gender, may shape the field of punishment. This is especially problematic given that social groups marginalised on the basis of race are routinely over-represented in criminal justice data, such as imprisonment rates and police–citizen interactions.

Likewise, the problem of crime is also reduced to one of economics. While factors such as economic marginalisation, unemployment and poverty may play some role in determining criminal behaviour, the causes of crime are likely to be much more complicated. In Chapter 3, we saw several competing theories about criminalised behaviour that stemmed from differential understandings of culture. Such theories drew attention to links between criminalised behaviour and peer-group influences (Anderson 1999; Miller 1958), culturally induced desires (Nightingale 1993; Young 2003), the situational dynamics to crime (Katz 1988), political resistance (Ferrell 1996) and the quest for escape (Lyng 1990). Some might be sympathetic to Rusche and Kirchheimer's efforts to locate the causes of crime in social structure, but this does not mean that their conception of social structure is very robust.

Capital versus discourse: Cultures of control

In Chapter 5, Foucault's notion of discourse was discussed in some detail. As we saw, Foucault used discourse to explain a variety of institutional practices, but paid particular attention to the relationship between new discursive formations and the rise of modern punishment systems. Foucault (1977) essentially sought to understand the transition from 'sovereign' power and its preferred tactics of punishment (i.e., extreme forms of corporal punishment that were typically very public) to 'disciplinary' power and its preferred strategies (i.e., imprisonment, psychological and psychiatric treatments, training, etc.). Such changes were found to occur during the 18th century in various parts of the world and could be attributed to major social developments (e.g., population growth, industrialisation).

Given that Foucault has already received much of our attention, here we can focus on the use of his thought to make sense of why places like United States and United Kingdom have abandoned punishment strategies premised upon 'reform' and moved towards tactics that emphasise 'control'. According to David Garland (2001), this transition occurred not long after World War Two, and it can be understood to entail the rise of 'late-modern penality' or a 'culture of control' at the expense of 'penal welfarism' or 'correctionalism'.

Like Rusche and Kirchheimer and Foucault, Garland accepts the proposition that punishment systems are best understood as intimately connected to general social conditions. In this sense, one could say that punishment systems and social conditions are always related, and therefore need to be thought of together. It is the general stage of social development that not only generates penal strategies, but strategies that seem to make sense to most members of a society. We have, then, two fields of punishment that correspond to distinct forms of social organisation according to Garland. It makes sense to start with 'penal welfare' given that it precedes 'cultures of control'.

Penal welfare, which has its origins in the 1890s, came to dominate the punitive field for much of the early 20th century, and was at its height until the late 1960s (Garland 2001, p. 34). The fundamental principle underpinning penal welfare is that punishments should concentrate on rehabilitating individual offenders rather than simply enacting revenge. In terms of concrete penal practices, welfare-oriented punishment incorporated things like indeterminate sentences linked to the possibility of parole for 'good behaviour', consulting reports from social workers and psychiatrists during the sentencing process, individualised courses of treatment for offenders and, amongst other things, an emphasis on providing offenders with educational or work-related experiences that could facilitate community reintegration upon release from prison (Garland 2001, p. 34).

This punitive field appears to make sense when considered in light of the conditions – economic, social, cultural and epistemic (i.e., available knowledges/conceptual frameworks) – in which it emerged. For much of the 20th century, as Garland tells the story, economic conditions generally improved in ways that benefitted much of the population. By the 1950s, labour was in demand and this ensured job stability, high employment rates and wages that allowed one to support a family whilst maintaining a good standard of living. The role of the state included regulating the economy in order to protect and maintain basic living standards. Such economic conditions ensured a society that was relatively cohesive with low crime rates. Most of society's members could be provided with incentives and rewards that encouraged acceptance of social rules and expectations (Garland 2001, p. 79).

Culturally speaking, the Protestant ethic was a powerful force, encouraging individuals to value work and enjoy a modest life. Given the relative comfort of the period, a sense of concern and duty could be extended towards others, even those who were less fortunate and turned to crime. In terms of epistemic regimes, or dominant knowledges of the time, psychological and sociological understandings of crime and punishment were in vogue. Both disciplines encouraged the view that engaging in criminal behaviours was somewhat beyond the control of individuals, but that the underlying causes of crime could be addressed through rehabilitative interventions. If the cause of crime was some kind of emotional disturbance, for example, then this could be addressed through treatment. Likewise, if low levels of education and poverty were drivers of crime, the solution lay in devising punishments that equipped individuals with skillsets that would allow them to become socially productive. Such courses of action were perceived as worthwhile, at least in part, because the labour market was in a position to absorb workers.

By the late 1960s and early 1970s, penal welfare and, more importantly, the social order that underpinned it, were in crisis. The core driver of penal change was, arguably, globalisation or the intensification of communication. Large companies that effectively organised industry and manufacturing were able to reap the most benefit by communication technologies that compressed space and time. Around the early 1970s, many companies began to relocate their manufacturing capacity to the so-called third world for the sake of exploiting cheaper labour power. Often referred to as deindustrialisation, this process meant that many manufacturing jobs in the United States and the United Kingdom simply vanished within a very short time frame.

With the eradication of stable working opportunities, the basic living standards of large swaths of the population deteriorated. Work went from being relatively stable to very precarious, wages and buying power diminished, unemployment rates increased and economic inequality grew (Garland 2001, p. 81). Such changes were possible because globalisation weakened the power of organised labour (i.e., workers' unions) and of the state. The balance of power was tipped to the advantage of large companies via globalisation: if workers pushed for better working conditions, or if the state attempted to implement (or even preserve) economic policies that protected workers, companies could relocate or at least threaten to do so.

These economic shifts inevitably altered social relations, thereby (re)creating a series of problems. The 1970s and 1980s saw increased levels of family breakdown, higher crime rates and greater animosity between the poor and those who were relatively well off (Garland 2001, pp. 82–90). The power of the state was surpassed by large economic players in the globalised world, and this usurping of authority, according to Garland, had implications for social life: the state's ability to regulate social problems, especially that of crime, was greatly diminished. The growing power of capitalism implies the presence of an increasingly weakened, 'limited sovereign state' (Garland 2001, p. 110).

By no means did the cultural sphere manage to escape unscathed from the social and economic upheavals that characterised the 1970s and 1980s. Instead of adherence to the Protestant ethic, capitalism now suggested that reckless spending and endless consumption were the ultimate source of happiness (Garland 2001, pp. 80, 86). Although pegged to one's disposable income, 'happiness' was now regarded as something of a personal lifestyle choice. Those who were unable to spend and produce their own happiness were somehow to blame for landing themselves in such a predicament. This new cultural sensibility weakened the sense that the state should aid those in less fortunate circumstances (Garland 2001, pp. 97–102). Indeed, the faith that once surrounded the state's ability to maintain social order has more or less eroded.

Finally, in the realm of knowledge, discourses that were very different from those associated with the era of penal welfarism, but quite well-attuned to the new social order, gathered ground. Garland draws attention to various discourses, but three are probably of greater significance for explaining shifts in penal practice. First, there arose the 'nothing works' approach to punishment (Garland 2001, pp. 61–63). In this view, rehabilitation efforts are seen as ineffective and thus futile. As such, there is little point investing in them, and there is little reason to hope that criminal justice systems will produce individuals who refrain from breaking the law. Second, and closely related, the idea that some people are 'simply evil' experienced a resurgence during the 1970s and 1980s (Garland 2001, pp. 131, 184). Most famously articulated in the late 19th-century writings of Cesare Lombroso, this view posits that criminal justice should focus on physically preventing individuals from offending rather than 'fixing' them.

Third, a range of discourses that emphasise how crime can be inhibited emerged. For example, 'routine activities theory' and 'situational crime prevention' suggest that criminal offending is a product of opportunities that are available within everyday routines and the nature of physical space (see also Chapter 1). From here it follows that preventing crime can be achieved by subtle shifts in the organisation of everyday life and 'target hardening'. As Garland (2001, p. 129) puts it:

A thousand small adjustments are required. Replace cash with credit cards. Build locks into the steering columns of automobiles. Employ attendants in parking lots and use close circuit TV cameras to monitor city centre streets.

As this description intimates, such strategies are not concerned with what motivates offending behaviour and how the attitudes and dispositions that drive criminal behaviour might be changed. Instead, the emphasis is on containing problematic behaviours or making it impossible for certain behaviours to be enacted due to the organisation of social and physical space.

This brings us, at long last, to the penal field that corresponds to these developments in social structure. As noted above, Garland's account of the new field of punishment amounts to what could be labelled 'late-modern penality' or a 'culture of control'. Whatever label is preferred, the new punitive field is characterised by two major dynamics: preventative partnership and punitive segregation (Garland 2001, pp. 140, 167–192).

Preventative partnership refers to the recent ways in which the state has increasingly outsourced its responsibilities for crime control to a series of non-state or quasi-state actors. Throughout the 1970s and 1980s, and continuing up until the present, the United States and United Kingdom saw the private security industry expand to take on what were previously state-managed policing functions. Alongside this development, the period also witnessed growing expectations that private and public actors take more responsibility for their safety, evidenced by the proliferation of business improvement districts (BIDs) and community watch groups (Garland 2001, p. 141). This aspect of the penal field can be attributed, for the most part, to the limited ability of states to control the social problems that accompany a 'deregulated' capitalist economy.

By punitive segregation, Garland (2001, p. 144) is suggesting that punishment has increasingly come to focus on incapacitation strategies that exclude individuals from society for prolonged time periods, if not permanently. This component of the penal field is evident in 'three-strikes' laws, restrictive sentencing guidelines, the abolishment of parole and so on (see Chapter 8). Such measures are often rationalised by claiming that they are intended to keep the public safe, and are often a response to popular sentiment, especially the rise of victim rights movements that demand the state create punishments that satisfy victims of crime. Garland suggests that punitive segregation is partly driven by the state recognising its impotence and reacting against this. It can also be regarded as a consequence of a shifting cultural climate in which sympathy for less fortunate individuals has been replaced by animosity and fear.

Garland covers a lot of territory in showing that a transformation has occurred in the logic by which punishment in the United States and United Kingdom is underpinned. But this does not mean his account is without problems. Garland takes much inspiration from Foucault, especially his view that discourses emerge against a backdrop of structural developments, and instantiate practices that adjust individuals to social demands. In focusing on reformist discourses, which promised to 'rehabilitate' offenders or 'correct their souls', Foucault revealed how these constructions were damaging to freedom. Such discourses promised that some greater good would follow from rehabilitative interventions – for the individual offender and the social order – but they ended up instantiating penal systems that saturate everyday life.

In Garland's account, the perniciousness that Foucault saw in 'rehabilitation' appears to fall by the wayside. And, this leads to a dichotomous logic in which 'penal welfarism' is equated with 'good' while the 'culture of control' is equated with 'evil'. This is probably most obvious in Garland's description of the industrial era, where people were employed, nuclear families prevailed, crime rates were low, common morality dictated that we should be concerned with one another's welfare and the state provided security. One may certainly speak of social changes over the period, but Garland's account of the penal welfare era tends to construe it as some kind of 'golden age' to which we ought to return. It is hard to square this with Foucault's critique of reformist discourses.

In summarising his overall approach, Garland (2001, p. 23) suggests that he is operating within a 'weak structuralism'. Presumably, this is to draw a contrast with structuralist arguments, which typically posit that underlying structural forces are causative of what are presumed to be observable, real problems. For example, the class inequalities that define capitalism may be said to explain particular types of crime and punishment practices. The work of Rusche and Kirchheimer described above could easily be read as a manifestation of structuralist logic and its 'strong determinism'. However, the radical constructivist is unlikely to be persuaded by the suggestion that 'weak structuralism' amounts to an alternative. Garland may be able to show how economic forces, discourses, social relations and so on, are mutually influential, but this does not lead him to call the category of crime into question. Instead, crime rates are said to fluctuate according to underlying conditions, and remain an effect of what is happening in the social order. This is peculiar given that 'discourse' plays an important role in the theory, yet its capacity to breach the self-evident nature of crime is not utilised.

Two Durkheimian models: Reinforcing moral boundaries and pollution crises

Inspired by the work of Emile Durkheim (1958, 1960, 2001), several scholars have advanced theories that concentrate on how cultural order and punishment are related. Along these lines, Kai Erikson's *Wayward Puritans* (1966) and Philip Smith's *Punishment and Culture* (2008) stand out as important texts in the field. These texts are interesting because, although adopting Durkheim as a point of departure, they end up developing quite distinct ideas concerning the culture–punishment nexus. We will look at these two texts in turn.

Kai Erikson and the reinforcement of cultural order

Erikson's *Wayward Puritans* starts by suggesting that communities are underpinned by a shared recognition of their moral boundaries, and that these moral boundaries regulate a society's individual members. As Erikson (1966, p. 130) notes, Durkheim referred to this as:

> The 'collective conscious' of the group – that sense of firm ideological commitment, that willingness to participate fully in the rhythms of group life, that feeling of common heritage and common destiny which gives every society its underlying cohesion.

This collective conscious – which can be thought of as a deeply engrained set of norms, sentiments, values, behavioural expectations and so on – is not necessarily visible or explicitly acknowledged by a society or its individual members. In this sense, it is vastly different from a society's laws, which can usually be observed in books, statutes or online as the case may be.

Despite its 'infra existence', the collective conscious nevertheless retains a significant degree of force in holding a group together. Consistent with Durkheim (1958, 1960), Erikson (1966, p. 103) suggests that specific moments of social life become more understandable if we assume they are a product of, and thus embody, moral sentiments. As such, a society's moral contours can be indirectly observed, or perhaps one should say inferred, from individual and group behaviour. If one wanted a metaphor, the collective conscious can be inferred from social practice much in the same way that Freud 'observed' the unconscious in slips of the tongue.

Wayward Puritans examines the Puritan settlements of the mid to late 17th century in the Northeast of the United States to show how crime and punishment are inevitably connected to a society's collective conscious. Crime is an area of social concern because, by definition, it plays with boundaries. To engage in crime or deviance, or to be perceived as doing so, is to transgress a border, to cross a line. From this observation alone, Erikson identifies several important features of crime.

First, the particular acts that come to be regarded as criminal will hinge upon a society's moral boundaries (Erikson 1966, pp. 19–23). A society that values private property, for example, will most certainly place prohibitions on behaviours that threaten this value orientation, such as rules that legitimise the punishment of theft. Likewise, a society that values adherence to particular religious doctrines will feel threatened by the emergence of new theological worldviews.

A second important implication of construing moral boundaries and crime as deeply interwoven is that society will be invested in producing criminal acts and classifying some portion of individuals as deviant. In other words, Erikson (1966, pp. 27–29) suggests that crime is an important social resource and that its presence fulfils necessary functions within a society. This may sound odd at first because we are routinely encouraged to think of society as heavily invested in the eradication of crime. However, Erikson's point makes sense when we think of crime as a range of behaviours that 'summon', or call forth, the right to punish.

The presence of prohibitions and their associated transgressions enables some to be labelled criminal, but they also legitimise a punitive social response to that criminality. This is one of the crucial moments in which Durkheimian thought links culture and punishment. For it is the imposition of punishment that allows a society to rearticulate its fundamental moral codes, thereby preserving and reinvigorating their centrality to social cohesion. Punishment may exclude and stigmatise the individual offender, but it also announces group values and asserts the power of those values over the individual. In this, social cohesion may be fostered by the threat of punishment, but its more important function is to forge consent to group norms.

The ritual aspects of punishment would appear to lend support to this view. Most punishment rituals involve a reading out of the offence, or the accusation being made against an individual. A process of establishing guilt then follows. Once guilt is established, not only will a sentence be imposed, but it is very likely that the reasoning for the sentence will also be articulated. Throughout the process, but particularly at sentencing, the defendant will likely be given a chance to speak. When defendants are given such opportunities, it is often expected that a display of remorse will be forthcoming, or that the individual offender will acknowledge the fairness and just nature of their punishment (Erikson 1966, pp. 190–195). As Erikson (1966, p. 195) suggests, the confessional moments associated with punishment render the whole affair 'a little like ritual sacrifice' rather than a simple effort to repress crime.

The reference to sacrifice is interesting. In its more conventional use, sacrifice suggests that a living being is slaughtered to appease a deity; the sacrificed individual is like a 'payment' to the gods for some greater good, such as a plentiful harvest. Something similar occurs in punishment for Erikson. An individual's punishment may entail slaughter, physical harm, branding and, amongst many other possibilities, imprisonment. In these ways, they are made to pay and can be thought of as saddled with the costs of punishment. However, there is a 'deity' in all of this for Erikson, a 'higher authority' that needs to be appeased in order for a greater good to be realised. That deity is the collective conscious, the moral-cultural boundaries that ensure social cohesion and order will prevail over community disintegration.

Philip Smith and the cultural regulation of punishment techniques

Whereas Erikson uses Durkheim to explore the cultural significance of punishing individuals, Philip Smith draws from cultural theory to explain why societies adopt and reject particular technologies of punishment over time. If Erikson is concerned with individualised punishment, Smith focuses on the social control side of the equation, or how the use of concrete punishment strategies is also determined by underlying cultural forces.

In *Punishment and Culture*, Smith (2008) analyses specific historical transitions, such as those from public hangings to electric chairs, and from electric chairs to lethal injections. Akin to Foucault, Smith accepts that theorising the rise of new systems of punishment requires the notion of discourse. However, Smith holds that Foucault was far too obsessed with 'expert discourses', or those ideas that would appear to carry weight because they emerge from scientific and intellectual communities (see Chapter 5). Alongside such expert discourses, seemingly grounded by reason, Smith posits that there exists a wide range of popular opinion and debate. This realm of discourse is not dependent on the rhetorical conventions associated with science, but nevertheless plays an important role in determining which techniques of punishment will be adopted or, conversely, rejected.

Drawing from Durkheim (2001) and Mary Douglas (1984), Smith begins with some propositions concerning the cultural order that underpins social relations. According to Douglas (1984), one of the fundamental aspects of our shared cultural order is an obsession with 'dirt'. This is not dirt in the conventional sense. Rather, the term refers to 'matter out of place'. Douglas is suggesting that cultural orders essentially ensure the creation and maintenance of boundaries. Things that cross over or exceed those boundaries are framed as 'pollution', offences against 'good order', and may stir up strong emotional feelings such as disgust. In this respect, our cultural order dictates that 'matter out of place' must be returned to its proper location, or somehow controlled.

The idea of cultural order proposed by Douglas may seem very abstract. Douglas is describing something that is so taken for granted, and simply assumed as we go about our everyday lives, that we are unlikely to be consciously aware of how cultural orders exist and shape our perception. But a somewhat trivial example should demonstrate the point Douglas is making. Imagine you are in a supermarket at the fruit and produce section. You notice that a stray apple has somehow found its way into the banana section. Do you buy that apple? My guess is that your response to this question is 'no'. As it is not with the other apples, it is effectively 'matter out of place' and inspires a series of questions: what is it doing in the banana section? How did it get there? Is something 'wrong' with it? Who 'touched' the apple in the course of its emigration to the banana section? The apple now seems 'suspicious' and it is probably creeping you out a little. This kind of mental process and judgement is likely to occur even though it is not necessarily rational. The out of place apple is probably no different than the other apples in the store and, in all likelihood, an employee will return it to its 'rightful' place in due course, whereupon order will be restored and another customer will purchase it.

What Smith demonstrates is how this kind of culturally induced thought process influences particular forms of punishment. Given this conceptualisation of culture, Smith reasons that any specific method of punishment must be consistent with our deeply ingrained sensibilities regarding order.

Punishments that involve disorder will trigger emotional disgust and outrage and will soon be cast aside.

Historical shifts in punishment are used to develop this proposition. Public hanging, for example, was initially acceptable to many people because it promised to be a 'clean' and quick way to execute an offender. But, once the process of hanging was observed, and as soon as there were a few 'failed performances', the technique quickly evoked public criticism. Some bodies twitched for several minutes while dangling at the end of some rope; there were individuals that did not die soon enough and could be seen gasping for air or making strange facial contortions. This kind of visual experience does not sit very well with the public's culturally engrained sense of order (Smith 2008, p. 143).

The electric chair came next, and it was also ushered in with the promise to be a clean, efficient, orderly way of conducting executions. It was soon apparent, however, that the electric chair was an even greater failure than hanging: individuals literally 'fried' in the chair, giving off a smell of burnt chicken; urine and faeces involuntarily exited the body; eyeballs popped out of heads (Smith 2008, pp. 150–166). Efforts were made to correct these signs of disorder, such as covering the head of the individual to be executed and placing a barrier between the execution stage and audience. As with hanging, however, cultural sensibilities were offended, criticism of the procedure emerged and the electric chair was soon phased out of existence.

While it may appear as though these kinds of cultural processes are driven by empathy or humane concerns, this is not really what is at stake. As noted, it is *order* that is central, and it is therefore breaches of this order that we find offensive. We are perfectly happy to execute citizens provided this is done in ways that do not offend our sensibilities; we do not worry about the extensive use of prisons and prison conditions as long as everything appears to be running in an orderly manner. However, when we hear of disorders in prison settings, such as correctional officers organising fights between prisoners, our moral indignation is likely to be triggered.

In concluding his account, Smith returns to his initial dialogue with Foucault. Here, he emphasises that populating the concept of discourse with public sentiments, emotive arguments and so on, is not antithetical to the accent that Foucault supposedly places on scientific statements. What it does suggest is that the field of discourse cannot be reduced to 'rational', 'scientific' narratives or forms of debate. Our cultural universe, the way we represent and speak about issues, is much broader than this. It incorporates beliefs, fallacies, mythologies, non-rational claims, value judgments and so on (Smith 2008, pp. 169–183). These discursive forms may not be 'rational', but this does not mean they can be written off as inconsequential. Furthermore, these different ways of speaking about issues may interact in a variety of ways: sometimes ideas from scientific fields will gel with public opinion, but at other times they may operate at cross-purposes. For the analyst interested in the problem of how culture and punishment intersect, it is important to be aware of diverse types of discourse. Of course, while Smith's point is well taken, one may reject his notion that Foucault was somehow unaware of such diversity!

Durkheimian approaches are often criticised for their circular, or tautological nature, and the tendency to gloss over the problem of power. To accuse an argument of being tautological is to suggest that it effectively treats the effects associated with a social activity as the cause of that activity. This circular reasoning is perhaps embedded within Erikson's view that punishment arises *because* it re-energises and protects the collective conscious. This raises the question of why a society would develop systems of punishment to achieve the goal of social cohesion? Are there not more efficient ways to articulate the cultural contours that keep a society together? Why utilise such an 'indirect' route to accomplish what would appear to be a fairly important social function?

A second critique often levelled against Durkheimian arguments is their tendency to gloss over power asymmetries and/or the conflictual relations amongst social groups within a society. This critique could be applied, at least to some extent, to Smith's account. For example, there is a tendency in *Punishment and Culture* (2008) to construe society's members as though they were all plugged into the same cultural grid and thus shared an obsession with 'pollution' or 'matter out of place'. This may well be the case, but it is also reasonable to suspect that what constitutes 'disorder' for one person or social group may well amount to 'order' for others. The fact that there is likely to be debate about whether a practice involves too much 'pollution', or transgresses boundaries of what is appropriate, indicates that the adoption (or rejection) of punitive techniques is a political outcome as much as it is a cultural one.

Furthermore, Smith does not pay much attention to the fact that punishment techniques are utilised in socially patterned ways. Power relations, especially those grounded in class and 'race', play an important role in governing which social groups tend to find themselves on the receiving end of punitive techniques and which groups will get to orchestrate the punishment process (Brown 2009). Whether any given punitive technique can be constructed as 'too disorderly' may hinge on the social groups towards which it is overwhelmingly directed. Would we, for example, continue to perceive mass incarceration as 'orderly enough' if it ceased targeting social groups marginalised on the basis of race?

Feminist interventions: From 'culture and punishment' to 'culture/punishment'

Thus far we have discussed a handful of theories that work on the assumption that culture and punishment are separate entities. But, as some feminist scholarship suggests, it may be useful to break with that assumption and focus on the points of overlap, or how culture can be inherently punitive. In order to arrive at this point, it makes sense to begin with the problem of culture, women and state-sanctioned punishment before moving on to culture as an 'extra-legal' force. Two important texts will be used to anchor a discussion that moves from state-orchestrated punishment to culture as a force that exceeds formalised strategies of control: Pat Carlen's *Women's Imprisonment* (1983) and Alison Young's *Femininity in Dissent* (1990).

In *Women's Imprisonment* (1983), Pat Carlen offers an ethnographic account of Cornton Vale, Scotland's only prison for women during the early 1980s. Carlen's analysis is based on interviews with 20 prisoners and, in addition to this, interviews with a range of criminal justice officials, including police officers, judges, correctional officers and social workers. The theoretical insights found in *Women's Imprisonment* (1983) render it a ground-breaking text. Carlen's study covers a lot of ground, such as the economic, political and institutional arrangements that structure the lives of women and severely limit their life chances. We will focus, however, on some of the cultural dimensions that help illuminate women's prison experiences.

Carlen acknowledges that those imprisoned at Cornton Vale have engaged in offending behaviours, but argues that the punishments imposed upon them – typically short terms of imprisonment for not being able to pay fines and alcohol-related offending – cannot be explained on this basis alone. Rather, those who end up held at Cornton Vale are perceived as having 'stepped outwith' domestic discipline or family life, sociability, femininity and adulthood (Carlen 1983, pp. 16–24, 59, 155).

In using the term 'outwith' Carlen strives to capture the peculiar way in which imprisoned women are connected to cultural expectations. The women have somehow stepped beyond what is culturally expected of them ('out') and yet they are construed as irrevocably connected to those expectations ('with') (Carlen 1983, p. 233, fn 4). Constructing women as 'beyond' but still within the orbit of expectations renders their imprisonment a strange, contradictory enterprise. While some effort may be made to realign imprisoned women with normative behavioural patterns and codes that they have rejected, or simply cannot embody due to circumstances well beyond their control, they often come to be regarded as 'lost causes' and thus unworthy of rehabilitative resources (Carlen 1983, pp. 16–18, 155–194).

Of the cultural expectations that the women have stepped beyond, Carlen pays much attention to domesticity and shows how this shapes the sentencing process and the prison setting. At sentencing, women who have experienced family breakdown, who no longer have responsibilities towards children and so on, come to be seen as more eligible for a prison sentence (Carlen 1983, pp. 59, 63). In short, the further women move away from idealised images of domesticity and motherhood, the closer they move towards prison.

Once in Cornton Vale, women are organised into small groups and assigned to living quarters that seek to mimic the standard nuclear family model. The disciplinary goal of structuring prison life in this manner is to 'readjust' women to the gendered roles that underpin mainstream models of family organisation. This is all rather odd according to Carlen. After all, the women are in prison precisely because they do not occupy the kinds of social locations that would enable them to model their lives according to more conventional standards of family life (Carlen 1983, pp. 72–73). A theoretical insight of much importance is embedded in this analysis. Carlen essentially shows that it is incredibly difficult to divorce the process of punishment, and the specific punitive techniques utilised by the state, from culturally constructed notions of 'woman', gender and femininity.

Carlen was writing at a time when the experiences of women prisoners were generally ignored by scholars. This situation has changed to some extent, but it would not be inaccurate to say that the imprisonment of men still garners more attention. This imbalance of scholarly focus may reflect the fact that relatively few women are sent to prison if comparisons to men are drawn. To be sure, this is changing: scholars have shown that the rate of women's imprisonment has outpaced that of men in recent years, even though the absolute number of incarcerated women remains much lower than that of men (Davis 2003; Worrall 2002).

However, Carlen's key point that punishment and cultural understandings of gender are deeply interwoven has significance beyond the prison's walls. Indeed, there is a range of feminist scholarship that focuses on punitive mechanisms that operate independently of state-sanctioned punishment. One of the core ideas found within such scholarship – and an idea of obvious significance in the present context – is that women are less likely to find themselves formally punished by the state, or in prison, because they are tightly regulated and controlled throughout social space. Much of this regulatory work is accomplished through cultural codings of femininity (Bartky 1988; Bordo 1988; Summers 1975).

In a way that is somewhat comparable to Philip Smith (2008), Alison Young's *Femininity in Dissent* (1990) begins with some core claims about underlying cultural structures. According to Young, culture can be understood as entailing a dichotomous logic that generally operates well below the level of consciousness. The cultural realm encompasses a seemingly endless proliferation of dichotomies or binary pairs: rational/irrational; order/disorder; normal/abnormal; good/evil; peaceful/violent; good/evil; normal/deviant; man/woman; masculine/feminine.

The polarities that make up any given binary pair are not equivalent according to Young (1990). Instead, one side will typically be privileged or dominant. The imbalanced nature of a cultural binary may shift in different times and under particular circumstances, but one side will come to act as a censure that denigrates the other, or one side will be able to 'repress' the other (Young 1990, pp. 124, 142). For example, to successfully frame a particular behaviour as 'deviant' rather than 'normal' will intimate that something is 'wrong' with that behaviour and thus in need of 'correction'.

Consistent with some of the theory discussed above (Erikson 1966), Young construes culture as an invisible, 'infra' force, yet one that is discernible in particular moments or episodes of social life. One such moment, which constitutes the empirical substance of Young's text, is the Greenham Common Women's Peace Camp (GCWPC). The 'Greenham women' were a group that protested against nuclear weapons by setting up a camp outside a cruise missile base in Berkshire, England. The protest started in 1981 and initially included men and women. By February of 1982, however, men were excluded from the protest site/peace camp (Young 1990, p. 30). After 19 years of existence, the camp was disbanded in 2000 (Greenham Common Women's Peace Camp 2018).

It is not so much the material realities of the protest camp that allow for an analysis of cultural dynamics, but how the camp and its associated events were covered in mainstream media reporting. Analysing a large volume of media reports, Young (1990) shows how the mainstream press deployed five major motifs that censured the Greenham protests and transformed the women into objects of public ridicule, if not deviants in need of control.

Discernible across a wide spectrum of the press media, ranging from outlets typically regarded as epicentres for the production of 'serious news' to 'tabloids', the women were construed as (a) 'communist sympathisers' rather than 'proponents of democracy', (b) 'dirty' (as individuals and as a group) rather than 'clean', (c) 'emotional' (and thus unfit for the political sphere) rather than 'rational' (and thus suited to enter political decision-making processes), (d) 'homosexual' rather than 'heterosexual', and (e) 'hysterical' rather than 'normal' (Young 1990, pp. 41–88).

With the exception of the first of these binaries, it is not hard to discern how framing the Greenham women in these ways is likely to be effective in (re)casting public opinion. Each frame draws its power from culturally sedimented codes pertaining to womanhood and femininity: women have often been dismissed and disempowered by an idealised femininity in which appearance, an embracing of domesticity, and heterosexuality are regarded as 'appropriate' (Bartky 1988). To be sure, Young (1990, p. 99) does show how the communism/democracy binary is not without gendered dimensions. The media routinely portrayed the women as a 'red threat' which has well-known links to communism. However, 'red' also connotes menstrual blood, a bodily fluid that stands at odds with images of femininity as something 'pure' or 'clean'. Indeed, it could be argued that menstrual blood is one of the most feared and despised bodily fluids within a masculinist world.

To deviate from such cultural standards – or, more specifically, *to be discursively positioned on the denigrated side of cultural binaries* – is to invite censure and punishment. Young sees these kinds of portrayals as punitive in at least two senses. First, at the level of representation, they are harmful to the women involved in the protest and to women as a social group. For instance, such representations deny the political significance of the protest and they work to normalise a social order in which women are disadvantaged. Second, they legitimate material strategies of punishment and control. Despite exercising their political rights, many women were arrested and prosecuted for various activities during the course of the protest (Young 1990, pp. 19–29). More generally, many women will internalise and strive to embody the cultural expectations that surround 'desirable femininity' in order to avoid any negative repercussions due to perceived deviations.

The import of all of this should be fairly obvious: it may not be productive to limit analyses to the problem of how culture influences punishment, or vice versa. Arguably, room should also be made for the possibility that culture – its binary logics, its sedimented codes, its normative valencies – may well be punitive in itself. As Young (1990, pp. 151–152) concludes:

> The conception of censure to which I would adhere recognises that the very fact of existence within the category defined as femininity *implies* the potential for the generation of particular series of condemnatory discursive moves.

With this, we are quite removed from the tendency to accord state-sanctioned practices a central place in theorising punishment and construing these as effects of culture. Feminist theory draws attention to how culture is punitive. This is a rich premise for studying punishment, one that opens up many avenues of exploration. Because culture saturates social life, and because of its capacity to punish, the criminologist can extend a critical gaze to a variety of areas that, at first glance, may seem to lie beyond the realm of criminology. The cultural logics that underpin educational institutions, workplaces, much of everyday life, public space and so on, can be explored for their capacity to regulate.

Of course, this is not to suggest that how cultural logics saturate criminal justice is irrelevant. It does, however, suggest distinct problems if one wishes to retain a focus on criminal justice institutions. For example, it makes sense to assume that formal, state-orchestrated punishment is never simply a response to crime, or a finding of guilt, but is inflected by cultural scripts. In other words, one may ask for what is one formally punished? Is it the simple infraction of law (and being apprehended for this), or is it how well one can embody certain cultural expectations? As Carlen (1983) shows, the punishment of women is not simply governed by their infractions of law, but by how far they have departed from some idealised notion of 'femininity'. This insight is of broad applicability: how do things like employment status, educational levels, one's 'racialised' status, appearance and so on, infuse contexts of formal punishment? How do they shape police–citizen interactions? These can all be understood as factors that indicate the extent to which one embodies cultural expectations concerning 'normality', 'conformity' and so on, and they can easily operate as the fundamental basis for passing judgement.

Conclusion

Despite covering distinct ideas, this chapter ultimately makes several key points about punishment. First, it is important for the cultural criminologist to recognise that punishment needs to be regarded as a problem in its own right. Rather than simply following from crime, punishment can be imagined as a series of practices that are inevitably connected to social, economic, political and cultural forces. Furthermore, punishment may reinforce or naturalise these broader social relations.

Second, while punishment is an over-determined phenomenon it is safe to assume that cultural logics play a pivotal role in shaping punitive techniques and strategies. Given that everyday life is permeated by cultural forces, it makes sense to adopt the view that punishment and culture are inevitably related. That is, it is very unlikely that punishment could ever transpire in a cultural vacuum, or a space in which culture does not exert its influence. As to how we conceptualise 'culture' and thus theorise precisely how it shapes punishment, however, is open to much debate.

The third key point to take away is that culture can, and often does, intersect with practices that effectively constitute criminal justice systems, but it also operates in 'extra-legal' ways. In this sense, culture can be said to traverse informal mechanisms of social control and regulation. As noted above, cultural norms play an important role in family settings, educational institutions, workplaces and so on. In these contexts, culture provides a sense of what is 'normal', 'appropriate' or 'expected' (and, of course, what is 'abnormal', 'inappropriate' and 'unexpected'), and thus a mechanism for understanding behaviour or making it intelligible to us.

Finally, and very closely related to the preceding point, cultural norms can be thought of as inherently punitive. This is especially evident insofar as our cultural frameworks are often built from dichotomies in which one side is privileged or 'desirable' relative to the other. For example, we typically understand 'rational' behaviour through some notion of 'irrational' behaviour. But, in addition to this, we tend to be less concerned with behaviour that can be framed as 'rational'. Conversely, to say that some behaviours are 'irrational' is to denigrate them, thereby inviting some form of disapproval, if not regulation. To the extent that this holds, our shared cultural backdrop – all of those normative orientations, values, discourses, mental frameworks and so on – can be thought of as loaded with the capacity to punish.

8 CRIMINAL JUSTICE AND NEW POLICIES ON CRIME CONTROL

Introduction

Most of us would probably like to think that rational considerations and robust analyses inform the selection of possible public policy choices. In many areas, this may well be the case. When it comes to criminal justice and crime control strategies, however, it would seem as though policy is not crafted in a 'vacuum of rationality'. Instead, policy choices are inseparable from the broader cultural, economic, political and social contexts in which they emerge.

This chapter revolves around a series of crime control policies that several countries in the Anglophone world have implemented in recent years, such as 'mandatory sentencing', 'broken windows policing' and the 'war on drugs'. Such policies share in common a punitive undertow and, alongside comparable developments, are at least partially responsible for the contemporary problem of 'mass incarceration'. As the label implies, mass incarceration entails massive growths in prison populations, such that the experience of incarceration has become an expected part of the life course for many people. In places like the United States, the surge in incarceration rates is without historical precedent.

In what follows, some of the cultural forces and processes that have contributed to the normalisation of harsh, punitive policies and mass incarceration will be explored. We take a look at three broad theoretical arguments. First, we examine the role of the media in shaping policy choices. Here, we return to the work of Ray Surette (2015), which appeared in Chapter 6, and discuss Michelle Brown's (2009) account of culture and punishment. Surette argues that mediated representations of crime and punishment (within films, TV, news, infotainment and so on) are responsible for propagating misleading and false images of crime and punishment. Even though grossly inaccurate, media representations nevertheless encourage a general worldview in which punitive techniques, and oftentimes extra-legal strategies, are perceived as the only viable way to control crime. Policy makers are certainly not immune from such representations, and so the cultivation of such a worldview can come to operate as the basis for policy choices.

In Michelle Brown's (2009) account, prison tours, academic debates and media stories demonstrate how culture is saturated with images of punishment. These images and representations come to stand between much of the public and the reality that is central to punishment: the infliction of pain upon others. This amounts to a problem. The public think they know something about punishment via its representation, but they are actually distant from its fundamental realities. Interfacing with cultural portrayals of punishment turns individuals into 'penal spectators', subjects that view punishment from afar, but nevertheless develop moral standpoints concerning punitive strategies. In light of late-modern anxieties, this spectatorship easily leads into a generalised complacency with punitiveness. Brown, however, goes further by connecting penal spectatorship to the racism and classism of punishment in the United States. Penal spectators often occupy privileged social locations, but those subject to punishment overwhelmingly come from social groups that are marginalised on the basis of class and race. As such, penal spectatorship implies that the public effectively sanctions racist and classist policy by its dependence on cultural representations in which the pains of punishment are repressed.

Second, the chapter will take a look at 'penal populism' (Bottoms 1995; Pratt 2007), which has some overlap with the notion that media portrayals shape policy, but is distinct in some important respects. Penal populism recognises the importance of media, but posits that late-modernity has seen the rise of a punitive public that demands harsh crime control policies from elected officials. This punitive public often emerges in the form of 'victims' rights movements', typically spearheaded by an individual who has been victimised. Usually on a quest for revenge, such individuals and movements may attract media attention and win advocates. As they gather momentum and become more vocal, they command the attention of public officials. Such victims' rights movements are bolstered by two further trends. Late-modernity evinces a certain 'anti-intellectualism', which disparages expert and professional opinions, thereby allowing emotive discourses to win space in the public imagination. As a corollary to this, advances in social media have enabled the public to interact with public officials and policy makers in ways that are much more direct. This also works to denigrate or 'sidestep' expert opinions that historically provided a buffer zone between policy makers and the general public.

Finally, the chapter discusses arguments concerning the 'new penology' and 'neoliberal state-crafting'. Whereas penal populism posits that popular, emotive-laden discourses exert a powerful influence over elected officials and thus criminal justice policy, the 'new penology' suggests that one can readily discern a shift in expert discourses in the era of neoliberalism (Feeley and Simon 1992). Prior to deindustrialisation, when the economies of places like the United States and United Kingdom could absorb significant portions of their working populations, crime control policy prioritised the rehabilitation and reintegration of offenders. However, with the exodus of jobs, this rehabilitative ideal no longer makes much sense. In economies that ship manufacturing work overseas, there is less potential to reabsorb offenders into the working population. This is not because people refuse to work, but because so few jobs are available. As a result, expert discourses have come to focus on how best to control and manage aggregate populations and groups, especially those that are now more or less permanently excluded from mainstream social life.

Loïc Wacquant's (2010) notion of 'neoliberal state-crafting' complements Feeley and Simon's 'new penology' by connecting the rise of punitive management strategies that target the poor to fundamental shifts in the economy and state activity. The neoliberal state, which emerged after World War II and became entrenched throughout the 1970s and 1980s, essentially supports economic policies that produce social insecurity and precarity. In earlier modes of capitalism, the state recognised a duty to provide a basic social safety net for those that found themselves excluded from the legitimate economy. In the neoliberal era, however, the state has abdicated any such duties or obligations towards citizens. Instead, it pours exorbitant sums of cash into criminal justice in order to control society's most marginalised members via punitive control strategies, especially imprisonment.

This theory certainly moves us into explanations in which material forces, such as the state and the economy, play a central role. However, there are important cultural dimensions to neoliberal state-crafting. Most notably, the theory holds that ideologies of 'personal responsibility' operate as the cultural grease that smooths out the functioning of the neoliberal state. Notions of personal responsibility assert that individuals have the power to make choices – and have indeed made choices – that explain their lot in life. More importantly, perhaps, the ideology of personal responsibility is used to justify the state's disavowal of its historic social responsibilities. If individuals are responsible for themselves, it follows that the state does not have any obligations towards its citizens, no matter how destitute many of them may have become.

Before we can expand upon these theoretical ideas, it may be useful to provide a brief overview of the types of policies that have arisen in recent years and that signify the 'punitive turn' in criminal justice.

A general note on recent trends in criminal justice policy

Much policy development is mundane and passes by unnoticed. But, when it comes to crime control, there is a tendency for proposed policies to quickly be surrounded by public debate. The most noticeable trend over the last 40 years or so has been the development and implementation of criminal justice policies that are increasingly punitive in nature. In public debates, this punitive orientation is often evident in rhetoric emphasising the need to be 'tough on crime' (Altheide and Coyle 2006, p. 288; Newburn and Jones 2005). Such punitive policy can be difficult to reconcile with approaches that are oriented towards rehabilitation and reintegration. Indeed, punitive policies often displace and disqualify the very notions of rehabilitation, reintegration and proportionality – ideas that were historically regarded as fundamental cornerstones of criminal justice.

Although the particular details of local policies may vary (Jones and Newburn 2006), this 'punitive turn' is especially discernible in Anglophone countries, such as the United States, United Kingdom, Australia and New Zealand (of course, this is not to say that punitive criminal justice policy is only found in such places). While some scholars have approached punitive policy as a general trend, others have developed important theory via the analysis of particular manifestation of punitiveness. Despite nuanced approaches, however, there is general agreement on the types of policy developments that signify the punitive turn. Some of the most important policy moments that have been identified as evidence of the state turning to more draconian modes of social control are briefly summarised below.

'Mandatory sentencing' or 'sentencing guidelines', and 'truth in sentencing'

Policies along these lines are designed to calibrate offences to specific sentences, and ensure that those convicted actually serve prison sentences in full (or significant portions of imposed sentences). They curtail the discretion of judges during sentencing and parole boards when considering whether to release an individual from prison (Steen and Bandy 2007, p. 9). Proponents often claim that in the absence of such policies, judges will impose sentences that are 'too lenient' and parole boards will release dangerous individuals into the community. The well-known 'three-strikes-and-you're-out' legislation is probably the most obvious manifestation of mandatory sentencing. In places where some type of 'three-strikes' legislation has been enacted, judges are typically required by law to impose a life sentence for a third felony. This can easily lead to inconsistency in sentencing and punishments that are radically disproportionate to offending behaviours (Zimring 1996, p. 249). Sentencing guidelines, now enacted in some form in most (if not all) US states, essentially transform the sentencing process into an instrumental calculation of sorts. Judges are required to impose sentences that fall within upper and lower limits in light of specified criteria, typically 'offending history' and 'offence seriousness' (Feeley and Simon 1992, p. 461; Shichor 1997, p. 477; Zimring and Hawkins 1991).

'Preventive detention' and 'sexual predator laws'

Preventive detention can be thought of as a sentence option that exceeds imprisonment. Although preventive detention assumes various guises in criminal justice policy (e.g., predictions of future behaviour are often a consideration in bail decisions and cases involving psychopathy), some states have inflected it with quite specific meanings in recent history. Whereas a prison sentence explicitly states the period of time to be served for committing a criminal offence, preventive detention allows for the imposition of indefinite sentences. In New Zealand, for example, an individual given a sentence of preventive detention can be incarcerated until the state comes to accept that they no longer pose a threat to the community. This is fairly extreme: it effectively means that the state can imprison individuals who are thought to be dangerous, and thus may commit offences if released. It is incredibly problematic given that it allows the state to imprison individuals on the basis of their predicted or anticipated behaviour. Most sentences, of course, are premised upon specific punishments for acts that individuals have actually committed.

Preventive detention is typically rationalised by claiming that its primary function is to control 'predatory sex offenders', a population that is vehemently despised by much of the population. However, the policy can easily extend from beyond this group and become a sentence option for a wider variety of offending types. Moreover, it can also encourage punitive logics, thereby inspiring associated policies. Alongside preventive detention, many states have introduced sexual predator laws. These typically place restrictions on sex offenders who have been released after serving a term of imprisonment. Such laws may take the form of forbidding sex offenders to reside near schools and/or other public facilities, compelling them to register their whereabouts on public sex offender registries, and surgical/chemical castration (Spencer 2009). Such policies are hard to reconcile with important legal principles, such as rights to privacy and 'double jeopardy'.

The 'war on drugs' (and, more broadly, adopting a 'war mentality' in relation to crime)

The war on drugs was announced in the United States in 1982 during President Reagan's time in office. Since then, it has continually gathered momentum with both the Republican and Democratic parties supporting it. This support takes ideological and material forms. Concerning the former, there is no shortage of anti-drug rhetoric and discourse that demonises drug use in the media (Ayres and Jewkes 2012; Brown 2007; Linnemann and Wall 2013; Rosino and Hughey 2017). Concerning the latter, as Alexander (2012, p. 53) notes, in 1986 'the House passed legislation that allocated $2 billion to the antidrug crusade'. Subsequently, in 1994, President Clinton devoted a further $30 billion to the 'war on crime'. Much of that funding was used to support 'three-strikes-and-you're-out' legislation and enable prison expansion. Of course, portions of this were also devoted to the war on drugs (Alexander 2012, p. 56).

The war on drugs has been a major driving force of mass incarceration in the United States. Since the 1980s, the US prison population has gone from

300,000 people behind bars to over two million, with much of the increase constituted by those suddenly caught up in the criminal justice system for minor drug offences, such as simple possession (Alexander 2012, pp. 6–7; Wacquant 2009a, p. 61). As is quite true of many criminal justice systems throughout the world, anti-drug efforts are skewed by race/ethnicity, with much of the state's resources being used to target those from racially and economically marginalised communities.

More recently, there may be some evidence to suggest that something of a 'retreat' from the war on drugs has commenced. Some US states, for instance, have moved towards the decriminalisation of marijuana, or have at least begun rethinking some current anti-drug policies. Such moves, however, are most likely being driven by the massive and unsustainable costs of the drug war and mass incarceration (Altheide and Coyle 2006, p. 298). Moreover, it is not clear how large swaths of the population, now tainted with criminal records because of the drug war and thus socially excluded, will be reintegrated into society and the economy.

'Broken windows' and 'zero-tolerance policing'

Broken windows refers to a theory (I use the term very loosely) advanced by James Wilson and George Kelling in 1982. Wilson and Kelling (1982) speculated that minor signs of disorder, such as graffiti writing, public drunkenness and loitering, would invite serious crime if left unchecked. Although this argument lacks any robust empirical foundation, this has not stopped political elites from embracing broken windows as if it were an incontrovertible truth (Kramer 2012, 2017). From here, the theory has been translated into 'zero-tolerance policing' and/or 'order maintenance policing', which can be understood as concrete policing practices that criminalise those who are seen as symbolic of 'social disorder'.

In 'zero-tolerance' approaches, police officers are encouraged to use criminal sanctions against minor forms of offending and 'nuisance behaviours', such as loitering, fare evasion and public intoxication. Oftentimes, zero-tolerance policing violates due process requirements and the constitutional protections supposedly granted to individuals. Some have suggested that the broken windows theory has been abused by the state and its public officials insofar as its practical implementation often violates constitutionally protected rights (Fagan and Davies 2000). However, Wilson and Kelling (1982, p. 6) were adamant that reliance upon the discretionary power of police officers is necessary for the preservation of social order, even if such discretion will lead to practices that are discriminatory and antithetical to constitutional protections:

> [H]ow do we ensure that age or skin colour or national origin or harmless mannerisms will not also become the basis for distinguishing the undesirable from the desirable? How to ensure, in short, that the police do not become the agents of

neighbourhood bigotry? We can offer no wholly satisfactory answer to this important question. We are not confident that there is a satisfactory answer except to hope that ... the police will be inculcated with a clear sense of their discretionary authority.

In other words, Wilson and Kelling (1982) acknowledge that order maintenance policing is inherently problematic, and that very few steps are available to curtail the excesses associated with endowing police officers with too much discretionary authority. Instead of insisting upon the protection of legal rights, however, Wilson and Kelling simply 'hope' that police officers will 'do the right thing'.

The peculiarity of punitive policy

What is peculiar about the types of policies briefly outlined above is how they effectively target offending behaviours that range from those that are 'serious' to those that are 'trivial'. Many would agree that offences involving interpersonal violence and sexed crimes are 'serious', but personal drug use and disorder-type offences hardly seem to warrant state intrusions that entail punitive policing and control. What seems to unite punitive policies is their tendency to target and quarantine those who are perceived to depart from mainstream social norms, especially those who struggle to find a place within normative social institutions, such as education, family and community, and labour markets. In these respects, one might be inclined to say that punitive policies are directed towards those who have effectively been rendered 'unworthy', a 'surplus population' within late-modern societies (Feeley and Simon 1992; Pratt 2007; Shichor 1997).

As intimated, such policy developments have certainly facilitated, if not culminated in, 'mass incarceration'. The United States currently has the highest incarceration rate within the world, imprisoning around 750 people per 100,000 of its population (Alexander 2012). Places like New Zealand, Australia and the United Kingdom do not have incarceration rates this extreme, but relative to other social democratic countries, they are certainly 'world leaders' when it comes to rapidly expanding prison populations: New Zealand's incarceration rate stands at about 214 per 100,000 (Buttle 2017); Australia currently incarcerates 172 people per 100,000; and the United Kingdom incarcerates 140 individuals per 100,000 of its population (Wacquant 2009a, p. 309; World Prison Brief 2019).

While it is important to discuss mass incarceration in terms of rates, numbers and ratios do not necessarily convey why it is such a problem. In places where it now makes sense to speak of mass incarceration, the chances of some people ending up in prison are comparable to, if not greater than, their chances of going to college (Pettit and Western 2004; Western 2006). This essentially means that the prison, for many people, is an institution as fundamental to their existence as mainstream social institutions – an almost inevitable part of their 'life course' (Clear 1994). Historically, the prison was regarded as a marginal social institution, one that should play a minor role in everyday life. Today, it is effectively a mainstream institution, one that commands the life of many individuals.

Moreover, the prison does not operate in ways that are socially neutral or objective. In places where mass incarceration can be identified as a problem, one typically finds that those who are marginalised on the basis of race/ethnicity and class constitute a disproportionate number of those behind bars. African Americans and Hispanics constitute 32% of the general population in the United States, but 56% of its incarcerated population (NAACP 2019); in New Zealand, Maori constitute 15% of the general population but 51% of its prison population (Buttle 2017, p. 102); in Australia, Aboriginal and Torres Strait Islanders constitute 2.8% of the general population, but 28% of the prison population (Australian Productivity Services 2018).

In what follows, three influential ideas for making sense of punitive policies – especially those that seem directly connected to the problem of mass incarceration – will be discussed. Given that harsh punitive policies and mass incarceration are over-determined phenomena, these theories are not necessarily mutually exclusive, but they do tend to place different accents on the cultural, social and political forces that shape punitive policy.

Media and public policy

In Chapter 6, Ray Surette's concept of a 'backwards law' was discussed. According to this notion, media depictions of crimes, criminality and criminal justice are diametrically opposite to what tends to transpire in the real world. In the realm of mediated representations, crime is typically violent, random and occurs between strangers. Defective individuals, who are seen as irredeemable, are posited as the fundamental cause of crime. The police are usually cast as heroes who rely on violence and sophisticated technologies to identify, capture and punish criminals for their wrongdoings. Interestingly, courts are often portrayed as 'soft on crime' or overly sympathetic to the rights of offenders, and thus seen as contributing to the 'crime problem'.

According to Surette, the relationship between this type of media landscape and policy is complicated. The mediated realm is best understood as 'part of a larger social matrix that generates and preserves the dominant attitudes about crime and justice' (Surette 2015, p. 221. See also Green 2009, p. 533). Due to its ability to operate as a broad, powerful cultural force, the media can exert a direct influence over policy makers and policy, but it is more likely to work in subtle ways to influence the perceptions of policy makers and much of the public.

In such a context, the core problem becomes what kinds of criminal justice policy are rationalised by mediated representations of crime and punishment? Surette unpacks this question by drawing a distinction between the 'due process' model and the 'crime control' model (2015, p. 204). In the former approach, criminal justice is understood as a system in which the guilt of an accused person needs to be proven against a backdrop of inviolable procedural rules. Such procedural rules are important because they ensure that the rights of citizens are protected and that government authority is exercised fairly. By way of contrast, the crime control model demands that criminals be identified and rapidly processed by the criminal justice system. Doing so will supposedly ensure that criminal wrongdoers are punished and that future crimes are inhibited because swift punishment operates as a deterrent. In this latter model, due process and procedural rules are likely to be seen as a hindrance to effective crime control.

Notwithstanding the possibility of marshalling evidence to support either view, Surette (2015, p. 204) ultimately concludes that mediated portrayals of crime and punishment overwhelmingly encourage acceptance of the crime control model, and do so at the expense of due process. In other words, media representations not only support harsh and punitive policy, but also disparage concerns with legal rights, important principles of justice, and broader systemic changes that would foster the development of a more just society (Surette 2015, p. 221).

Much of this interpretation of the 'media–criminal justice policy' relationship can be substantiated by reference to contemporary policy choices and surveys of public attitudes. As noted above, much recent policy evidences a turn towards punitive and draconian strategies. Legislation that authorises the creation of sex offender registries, for example, could quite easily be understood as a consequence of media campaigns that emerged after the Megan Kanka case. Megan, a seven-year old girl, was abducted, raped and murdered by a recidivist sex offender. Having received much media attention, the case moved President Clinton to pass 'Megan's Law', which requires that communities be informed of sex offenders who reside within their neighbourhood (Surette 2015, p. 208). Such laws may be popular with the public, but their long-term effectiveness is questionable. Moreover, while the Megan Kanka case is certainly disturbing, it remains a relatively isolated incident. As such, it is probably not the best basis for determining general criminal justice policy (on these points, see also Pratt 2007, p. 112).

Surveys of public attitudes also seem to reflect broad patterns in media depictions of crime and punishment. Consistent with media portrayals, much of the public seem to think that criminal justice systems perform quite poorly, but that anti-crime policies should focus on enhancing the powers of law enforcement (Surette 2015, p. 207). This perception parallels a mediated world in which courts are construed as 'too lenient' and 'deferential' to the rights of suspects, while simultaneously portraying as heroic those police officers who sidestep procedural rules to apprehend and punish criminals.

Finally, it is perhaps worth noting how recurrent patterns in media depictions of crime and punishment broadly correspond to contemporary crime control logics and policy. Most notably, those in law enforcement usually figure as the main individuals capable of controlling criminals. Such figures are often facilitated in their work by a range of technological devices and gadgets. James Bond is, arguably, the most obvious manifestation of this 'hi-tech' law enforcement operative. But Inspector 'Dirty' Harry Callahan (Clint Eastwood), with his famed 44 Magnum hand gun, is also quite reliant on technology. And, of course, then there is the CSI franchise, which invariably features a team of scientists with remarkable technologies at their disposal.

The underlying message in all of this would appear to be fairly obvious: science and technology offer the most viable mechanism for curtailing crime problems. This kind of 'faith in technology' could certainly be said to char-acterise much recent criminal justice policy, whether it take the form of building more prisons, enhancing the powers of the police, passing more and more anti-crime legislation, lengthening prison sentences, investing in target hardening strategies/public surveillance and so on (Kramer and Oleson, 2021, forthcoming). There is an important flipside to this tendency to fetish-ise technology. It usually entails a profound denial of the structural inequali-ties and social problems that underpin the criminalisation of certain behaviours and their punishment. As will be explored in greater detail below, over the last 50 years or so, many Anglophone countries have embraced neoliberal policies that have intensified inequality while simultaneously eradicating provisions for welfare and social security. Instead of rethinking this kind of political economy, the state increasingly turns to technological strategies to manage the problems that emerge within a crumbling social order.

In such a context, it becomes difficult to read the fundamental tendencies in media portrayals of crime and punishment as anything other than a nor-malisation of contemporary social order and its associated orientations in criminal justice policy. Criminal justice is increasingly tasked not with addressing structural inequality, but with managing the behaviours that accompany the growth of profound structural inequalities; media portrayals of crime and punishment assure policy makers and much of the public that such a strategy is not only viable, but the only one available (Surette 2015, pp. 209–211).

In *The Culture of Punishment* (2009), Michelle Brown also explores the general 'attitudes about crime and justice', but does so through a nuanced repertoire of sites and concepts. Alongside movies and television, Brown analyses prison tourism, mediated scandals surrounding Abu Ghraib and Guantánamo, and expert discourses as sites in which punishment emerges as a cultural thematic.

The main idea that follows from these analyses is penal spectatorship. With this concept, Brown seeks to capture how punishment is encountered, albeit in cultural forms that filter its tangible realities in quite specific ways. Punishment saturates culture, and so we 'experience' it daily, but it is unlikely that many of us will ever endure the concrete realities of punishment.

We may see the prison portrayed in films, but most people will never set foot in an active prison, one with actual prisoners, correctional officers, slamming doors, bells and alarms, the odours that accompany human activity, the lack of freedom to leave at any time and so on. In this sense, penal spectatorship ensures that punishment is observed, but always from a distance (Brown 2009, p. 193).

In this distancing, something fundamental is filtered out or repressed: the fact that punishment always involves a relationship between the punisher and punished. In this relationship, it is the former that inflicts pain upon the latter. Prison tourism can serve as an illustration. When transformed into a tourist attraction, it is usually a vacated, defunct prison that is opened to the public, such as Alcatraz in California or Eastern State in Philadelphia (Brown 2009, pp. 85–121). As such, the tourist cannot learn anything about prison experiences directly from those who are incarcerated. And, any experience of imprisonment provided by prison tourism is superficial. One may enter a cell for a few minutes, but this is hardly comparable to being in a cell for 22 hours of the day for a prolonged time period.

Without an acknowledgement of the pain that accompanies punishment, one can easily become indifferent to it. For Brown, the problem is not so much that the public actively pushes for punitive policy (although they certainly may do this at times), but that they have come to embrace a passive, blasé attitude towards contemporary punishment logics – which are historically unprecedented and incredibly punitive in orientation. In other words, when the public is reduced to a penal spectator it will brush aside the pain of others.

Importantly, Brown emphasises that comprehending this culture of punishment, in which passive spectatorship reigns supreme, requires acknowledging the social relations in which it transpires. The penal spectator generally occupies a privileged social position, and therefore is unlikely to experience the pains of punishment. Those subject to punishment, conversely, come from social groups that are marginalised on the basis of class and race (Brown 2009, p. 7). When pain is brushed aside, then, it is the pain of quite specific social groups, those that are relatively powerless and socially marginalised. The penal spectator can adopt a cavalier attitude towards others because it is unlikely that they will ever experience the pains of punishment. (For accounts that draw attention to the possibility of counter-narratives to those that encourage spectatorship, see Brown 2014; Wilson and O'Sullivan 2005.)

Penal populism

Penal populism is a view often associated with the work of Anthony Bottoms (1995) and John Pratt (2007). Pratt (2007) provides one of the most concise summaries of penal populism and so it is worth exploring his account in some detail here. What distinguishes penal populism from those who posit a relationship between media content and policy is the emphasis that it places on the growing power of specific segments of the public to directly influence punitive policy. This 'specific public' is typically constituted by those who have been victimised (either directly or indirectly) by some form of extreme, albeit rare, violent crime, and who go on to attract media attention and mobilise the public to create new policy. Such figures often find a receptive audience for their 'moral crusades' against criminals, and this is what penal populism ultimately seeks to explain and understand.

Penal populism begins with the notion of globalisation and/or neoliberalism. While globalisation has some benefits, it also entails many social costs. People may have greater access to information and ideas from anywhere in the world, but the life chances of individuals are profoundly circumscribed within the global, neoliberal economy (Pratt 2007, p. 59). Due to the rapid modes of communication it makes possible, globalisation allows major companies to locate almost anywhere in the world to exploit cheap labour power. Of course, this means that labour is devalued everywhere and the power of workers to mobilise is severely limited. If workers become 'too demanding' in one country, multinational corporations can simply relocate production centres to other parts of the world where labour is poorly organised or politically suppressed.

For its part, the sovereign state has also lost much of its power to control corporations and economic activities. Comparable to organised labour, if a state pursues policies that protect workers and enforce fair wages, and if such policies are construed as undesirable from the perspective of powerful corporations, the latter can simply go elsewhere. This has encouraged neoliberal states to 'de-regulate' their local economies (Pratt 2007, pp. 53–57). Simply put, states are increasingly tasked with creating policies and conditions that are favourable to corporate interests in order to retain jobs and generate tax revenues. To be sure, the jobs that do remain are likely to be devalued, poorly paid and increasingly precarious.

Amongst the general public, such broad developments in political economy lead to a very real, and thus likely to be intuited (even if obliquely), sense of precarity. No matter how much one works and invests in mainstream social order, life is now experienced as plagued by vulnerability and insecurity. Due to its perceived weakness to provide a secure social existence, the state comes to be regarded with scepticism and distrust, especially amongst those who sense the precarity of their existence.

Rather than inviting a critique of neoliberalism, however, feelings of vulnerability and distrust amongst the public often generate demands for the state to reimpose order and social stability (Pratt 2007, pp. 37, 126. See also Brown 2009, p. 192; King and Maruna 2009). The state, in turn, satiates this demand by focusing on 'law and order' issues in which 'protection' and 'security' comes to be equated with 'cracking down on crime'. This is something the sovereign state can do or, to be more specific, it is something the state can appear to be doing. It is quite easy to pander to public anxiety and anger by promising (and sometimes imposing) tougher policies that will supposedly combat crime. In this sense, 'law and order' campaigning has an expressive potential, which allows for social anxieties – induced by the precarity spawned by a globalised economy – to be displaced onto 'criminal behaviour'. Although profoundly weak when assessed in light of its status within the globalised economy, the state can appear to be a strong protector of the public.

The media, and especially social media, do not help this situation. We have already noted that much of the mainstream media portray crime and punishment in ways that promote an irrational fear of victimisation and predatory behaviour. However, for those advancing the idea of penal populism, a more important quality of new media concerns its capacity to enable relatively direct communication between the public and political elites (Pratt 2007, pp. 80–82). To give a quick example, it is now relatively easy for Joe and Jane Smith to interact directly with political elites and public officials via Twitter accounts and/or through government webpages.

Because the public can interact more directly with political leaders, they are increasingly unlikely to show deference to experts and the specialised forms of knowledge that once dominated state institutions and policy development. Civil servants and academics, for instance, are no longer trusted or even perceived as necessary. Instead, they are now seen as 'elites' that are detached from reality and thus do not understand the experience of victimisation. This is an important dimension of the penal populism argument: expert civil servants and academics were historically asked to analyse the impact of proposed policies, the costs associated with possible policy options, and the likelihood of specific practices actually accomplishing their purported goals. In this sense, experts provided what Zimring (1996) refers to as a layer of 'insulation' between policy makers and an emotive, punitive public. Without this 'buffer zone' of expertise, however, politicians are increasingly susceptible to a vindictive public that does not concern itself with rational questions of cost and effectiveness.

Indeed, according to the penal populist position, the vindictive public has become so powerful a force that politicians can no longer afford to ignore it, no matter how irrational, ineffective or profoundly unjust its suggested policies may be. Any politician that strives to point out the excessive costs, irrationalities and overall ineffectiveness of punitive policy will simply fail to get elected and thus be forced out of office. This is perhaps most evident insofar as the vast majority of politicians affiliated with major political parties in neoliberalised economies overwhelmingly strive to present themselves to the public as *the* 'tough on crime' candidate or party member (Reiner 2012, p. 142).

The new penology and neoliberal state-crafting

In some respects, the penal populism argument is compelling. It is not too hard, for example, to find 'victims' rights movements' that are vocal when criminal justice policy is on the public agenda. Moreover, it seems fairly obvious that recent policy developments defy rationality. However, the notion that an emotionally driven public has come to dominate policy debates is not without its problems. As Michelle Brown's (2009) work indicates, the public may normalise punitiveness via their passivity, social distance and indifference rather than their emotional investments and vocal campaigning efforts. One may also wonder if politicians are as determined by their constituencies as penal populism intimates. Somewhat ironically, the argument seems to presuppose that the political realm operates according to democratic principles: public groups can voice their opinions and the state will listen.

Other scholarly accounts of punitive policy imply further critiques. For some, penal populism would be read as downplaying the ongoing importance of professional and expert discourses. It is not so much that all experts are now ignored, but that expert opinions are selectively utilised. For others, the claim that the sovereign state has lost much of its power in the neoliberal era has been called into question. Instead, the sovereign state can be understood as a massive apparatus when one considers the rapid expansion of its capacity to punish. The former argument has been advanced by Feeley and Simon (1992), whereas the latter has been developed by Loïc Wacquant (2009a, 2009b, 2010).

In 'The New Penology', which has become something of a classic, often-cited article, Feeley and Simon (1992) acknowledge that neoliberalism ushers in growing inequality, intensified social precarity and produces an ever-growing 'surplus population'. These shifts in society and political economy have rendered the idea of a penal system that focuses on the rehabilitation and reintegration of offenders obsolete. Punishments that focus on rehabilitation make little sense because the economic arrangements that define neoliberalism cannot actually absorb released prisoners, no matter how 'rehabilitated' they may be.

Akin to the structure of Foucault's (1977) argument that capitalism and the population growth associated with modernity necessitated new discourses and punishment strategies, Feeley and Simon (1992) posit that neoliberalism has compelled a need for distinct punitive logics and discourses. They refer to this recent discourse on crime and punishment as the 'new penology'. It is characterised by three dimensions: (a) new discourses, (b) new objectives and (c) new techniques.

These characteristics can be understood by juxtaposing them with the discourses, objectives and techniques of the 'rehabilitative ideal', which held sway over punitive policies from the late 19th century through to the 1960s/1970s. The *discourses* of the rehabilitative ideal assumed that individuals were responsive to, and thus the locus of, state-orchestrated interventions that would 'correct' their problematic dispositions and behaviours. In the 'new penology', the individual is no longer the central concern, and has been replaced by discourses in which the need to manage *groups* in light of risk categories and probabilities of future offending are prioritised (Feeley and Simon 1992, p. 453).

In terms of *objectives*, the era of rehabilitation certainly insisted upon punishment, but it was also about reducing crime by reintegrating individuals into society. In comparison, the new penology is geared towards the identification and management of groups that are extraneous to neoliberalism. Crime is no longer thought of as a social problem that can be eradicated. Instead, the new penology assumes that crime problems will inevitably persist and, as such, the best we can hope for is their management and containment (Feeley and Simon 1992, pp. 455, 465).

Finally, rehabilitation relied on *techniques* such as offering work, training and education programmes within prisons. Such techniques, it was held, would provide skillsets that facilitate community integration and law-abiding behaviour upon release from prison. Consistent with this logic, the failure of prisoners to reintegrate upon release was seen as evidence of a problem within the prison, and thus something that the state needed to correct.

Conversely, when the goal is to contain and manage crime, there is little need for techniques premised upon reintegration. Prisons become 'no frills' warehouses that simply incapacitate those who are thought to be dangerous. Assessing the dangerousness of individuals hinges on risk assessment instruments and actuarial judgment/prediction (Feeley and Simon 1992, p. 457). Risk prediction instruments typically assume that a series of variables (such as one's criminal record, seriousness of offending, alcohol and drug abuse and, amongst others, whether one is married) can be measured or counted, thereby generating a score that locates an individual somewhere within a risk classification scheme. These schemes typically include three possible categories: low risk, moderate risk and high risk. Such risk classification scores are often incorporated into the sentencing process and thus used to determine punitive outcomes. Rather than stemming from a punitive public, such techniques have been developed by statisticians and mathematicians, and have often been advocated within positivist, administrative criminological discourse (Kramer and Oleson, 2021, forthcoming). Furthermore, individuals who are released but end up returning to prison come to be read as evidence of effective penal policies: if people are returned to prison, then the institution is 'fulfilling' its obligations to contain crime problems and/or those from 'dangerous', 'high risk' groups (Feeley and Simon 1992, p. 455).

It probably goes without saying, but the emergence of risk discourses and their infiltration of punitive strategies heralds a rather sceptical, pessimistic turn in criminal justice policy. The rehabilitative approach, whatever its limits, at least retained a promise of trying to provide services that assist those in prison. In the new penology, there is little reason to provide those in prison with programmes that would assist their reintegration. The core problem is that such individuals cannot be absorbed back into society and the economy because there are so few jobs. Instead of striving to rethink political economy, however, the new penology focuses on developing technologies and strategies that can most effectively contain society's most marginalised individuals and groups (Feeley and Simon 1992).

If the work of Feeley and Simon challenges the notion that expert discourses have been brushed aside by popular sentiments, Wacquant's (2010) account of neoliberal state-crafting can be used to suggest that the sovereign state has not lost its power and authority. As noted above, those advancing the penal populist interpretation claim that the state's authority has diminished in late-modernity, thus creating a need for expressive displays of power. According to Wacquant, however, a 'smaller' state cannot be understood as a corollary of neoliberalism.

Rather than a simple diminishment of power, it would be more accurate to say that the state has reoriented itself given the triumph of neoliberal capitalism. During capitalism's industrial phase – that is, when places like the United States and United Kingdom housed industry and manufacturing jobs – governments were much more willing to invest in, and devote significant resources to, welfare and related public services. The basic idea was to provide social security and assistance to those who found themselves 'outside' or excluded from legitimate labour markets. The state thus intervened into individual lives, but it was to provide support during difficult times, often assuming that the economy would reabsorb unemployed persons in due time.

With the transition to neoliberalism, this orientation towards social security has certainly evaporated, and thus it may appear as though the state is 'smaller', 'weaker' or 'of diminished capacity'. However, corresponding to the decline of welfare there has been a pronounced investment in, and thus massive expansion of, the state's punitive capacities (Steen and Bandy 2007, p. 12). In short, the state is still a large enterprise, and it is still prepared to intervene into individual lives. What has changed are the types of intervention it is prepared to engage in. The state has replaced any obligation to shield individuals from the worst excesses of capitalism with punishment and exercising control over those who have been cast aside by contemporary labour markets (Wacquant 2009a; see also Simon 2000).

This transition to punitiveness and draconian social control is not surprising given the fundamental dynamics of neoliberalism: an increasing portion of poorly paid jobs, growing inequality and generalised social insecurity. Moreover, in the absence of industry, accepting the view that unemployed persons will soon be 'reabsorbed' into the economy appears to defy reason. In fact, Wacquant (2009b) claims that massive investments in the state's punitive capacities – especially its criminal justice system – need to be understood as an inevitable aspect of neoliberalism. The neoliberal state does not have many other options for managing the social precarity that its preferred economic policies invariably produce. As Wacquant (2010, p. 211; emphasis in original) puts it, neoliberalism:

> ... *entails the enlargement and exaltation of the penal sector* of the bureaucratic field, so that the state may check the social reverberations caused by the diffusion of social insecurity in the lower rungs of the class and ethnic hierarchy as well as assuage popular discontent over the dereliction of its traditional economic and social duties.

Furthermore, as it is social precarity that needs to be managed, it follows that neoliberalism's punitive strategies will be geared towards society's most marginalised individuals and groups. Wacquant (2010, p. 206) expresses it well when he notes that:

> ... penalization is not an all-encompassing master logic that blindly traverses the social order to bend and bind its various constituents. On the contrary: it is a skewed technique proceeding along sharp gradients of class, ethnicity, and place, and it operates to divide populations and to differentiate categories according to established conceptions of moral worth. At the dawn of the twenty-first century, America's urban (sub)proletariat lives in a 'punitive society', but its middle and upper classes certainly do not.

Thus far it may seem as though much of this theory revolves around economic and political realities. It does, however, have an important cultural layer, one that explains why such an unfair, unjust system is met with little resistance. At the cultural level, neoliberalism and its punitive control of the poor is normalised via an ideology of personal responsibility. According to this notion, individuals are seen as capable of choosing between possible courses of action. Because individuals determine courses of action, it follows that they are responsible for their life outcomes. As such, those who find themselves ensnared by the state's punitive institutions do so because they have made 'poor' or erroneous choices (on this point, see also Brown 2009).

Importantly, this ideology is not only central to accounting for individual life outcomes, but also operates to justify the social irresponsibility of the neoliberal state (Wacquant 2010, p. 214). More specifically, ideologies of personal responsibility allow the neoliberal state to dismantle social welfare and public assistance programmes that, prior to the era of neoliberalism, provided important forms of support for those excluded from the economy and society.

Conclusion

This chapter has provided a brief overview of recent policies that reveal a punitive turn in criminal justice. 'Mandatory sentencing' schemes, 'truth in sentencing', 'zero-tolerance policing' and so on, generally end up targeting society's most marginalised members and have contributed to mass incarceration. Punitive policies and mass incarceration are complicated phenomenon, and both are determined by a wide variety of factors. Many of the theories discussed above were prioritised because they draw attention to some of the cultural forces – mediated images of crime and punishment, emotive discourses, rational/expert discourses and dominant ideologies – that help to make sense of recent policy developments and the directing of criminal justice along a punitive rather than rehabilitative path.

One of the underlying assumptions throughout this chapter, and embedded within much of the theory that has been discussed, is that excessively punitive forms of crime control are largely irrational and/or ineffective. Of course, this last statement hinges on what we are to understand by 'effectiveness'. Many critical scholars would understand effective crime control policies as those that substantially reduce, if not eradicate, crime as a social problem. Arguably, the goal of criminal justice ought to revolve around fostering a social order in which motivations for crime do not develop. This would involve working to ensure that more equitable structural relations prevail within any given society.

With punitive policies, we are quite far removed from such an ideal. If anything, the punitive turn seems to entail the view that crime and criminalised behaviour will always be with us. As such, the best we can hope for is the management or 'containment' of criminalised individuals and/or groups. This, however, is not a viable, long-term solution. For one thing, trying to 'contain' society's most marginalised members is an incredibly expensive approach. States that have embraced punitive policies can easily come to spend exorbitantly on crime control, imprisonment, prison construction and so on. While this may satiate that portion of the public with a taste for vengeance, it does not necessarily keep society's members safe. If anything, the opposite is probably closer to the truth. The ultimate effect of excessive penalisation is to increase that portion of the population that will, in all likelihood, struggle to meaningfully reintegrate into society (Simon 2000, p. 1125). Crime may be contained to some extent, but criminality will lurk beneath the surface, waiting for opportune moments (Reiner 2012, p. 142). The question we ought to be asking ourselves, arguably, is who really wants to live in such a society? How have many come to evince a 'preference' for gross inequalities accompanied by growing fears of victimisation and excessive punitiveness, rather than greater social equality combined with actual safety? How has it come to pass that we appear happy to spend heavily on policies that exclude rather than include?

Somewhat ironically, perhaps, the irrational nature of crime control policy constitutes a cultural problem in itself. What much of the theory discussed above demonstrates is that we now have in place a range of mental frameworks, discourses and ideologies that render ineffective criminal justice policies as desirable. Getting out of this predicament is not going to be easy, and it will require radically rethinking the social, economic, political and cultural relations that characterise the neoliberal era.

CONCLUSION

The first two chapters of this book explored the theoretical ideas that have played an important role in informing cultural criminology, and the methodological and political orientations that are often seen as central to building a cultural criminological lens. Chapter 3 revolved around concepts of culture and how they have been utilised to make sense of criminalised behaviour, a problem that one might expect in a criminology text. How cultural criminologists theorise crime has been subject to much critique, some of which was explored in the fourth chapter. Chapter 5 focused on concepts that can be useful for making sense of how the world is represented, its mediated nature. This chapter served as a bridge into a side of cultural criminology that focuses on the effects of representation. In Chapter 6, the core problem entailed theorising the socio-cultural effects that follow from such a heavy 'media diet' of crime and punishment. Chapters 7 and 8 explored punishment and social control, which can be thought of as practices that are invariably informed by how they are refracted within culture. Whereas Chapter 7 focused on punishment in a broader sense – one might say punishment as a field – the eighth chapter examined the rise of particularly punitive policies in the post-World War II era, a trend that is pronounced in much of the Anglophone world.

In concluding, I want to return to the elements of Figure 0.1, which appeared in the Introduction. These elements were used to summarise cultural criminology as a perspective and included: culture/meaning; power asymmetries; methods; and political standpoints. Together, they provided a matrix for exploring criminalised behaviour (typically when it adopts subcultural form) and punishment or social control. We have seen these elements recur over the course of this book, but it might be useful to close by evaluating how they facilitate, but also hinder, the idea of a cultural criminological approach.

Throughout the architecture of cultural criminology, one finds a tension that manifests in various ways. One might formulate this tension in the following manner: there is a gap between what cultural criminology promises it can deliver and what it actually delivers when put into practice (i.e., when utilised to identify and analyse a research problem). In other words, cultural criminology's potential is seductive, but its practice can easily shatter our illusion that fulfilment will be forthcoming. In what remains, how this tension plays out across the building blocks of cultural criminology will be recanvassed. This sets the scene for one last problem: is cultural criminology possible despite its contradictions?

Culture, or that realm of *meaning*

Cultural criminology is correct in positing that the concept of culture should be central in efforts to theorise crime and punishment. Criminalised behaviours and punitive practices are loaded with meaning for their participants, and for the audiences who 'look on' in one way or another. With its tendency to reduce crime and punishment to means–ends calculations, positivist criminology seems ill-equipped to capture the excess of meaning that accompanies crime and punishment.

Culture, however, is a polysemic notion. As it is replete with multiple meanings, how to understand and use it raises problems. In Chapter 4, we saw how cultural criminology oscillates between various understandings of culture that are not reconcilable. In some cases, it adopts an idiographic view, in which culture is understood as a source of human creativity in organising social life; in others, it embraces a nomothetic view, where culture is construed as a response to material constraints (O'Brien 2005). According to O'Brien (2005), jumping between these conceptions leads cultural criminology into contradictions.

It may be possible to resolve the contradictory uses of culture in various ways. Individuals may just need to settle on a definition and use it consistently. In terms of cultural criminology as a perspective, the question becomes whether the field can host different concepts of culture or if it needs to choose a particular, coherent notion with which to work. Another alternative – as to whether it is convincing is open to much debate – is to adopt a dialectical understanding of culture. In this view, culture would be understood as 'relatively autonomous', or as circulating such that it does not make sense to frame it as either 'primary' or 'secondary'. In other words, can one understand culture and material forms as co-constituted?

Power asymmetries

To its credit, cultural criminology recognises that power operates along multiple axes, and that analyses should be sensitive to how power asymmetries shape criminalised behaviours and social control efforts. This allows the cultural criminologist to work with an expansive notion of power, one that could be applied in an endless array of research contexts. An awareness of power asymmetries does govern much of the work that cultural criminologists produce, but it often seems to be something that is expounded rhetorically rather than substantively. To be sure, the idea of power is complicated, and so it is not surprising that a perspective attuned to it will hit some stumbling blocks.

That cultural criminology undermines its rhetorical promise to centre power becomes most discernible when one looks at the power asymmetries it often selects in the course of analysing particular problems. In Chapters 3 and 4, we saw how cultural criminology tends to focus on group activities of relatively young men. In these respects, it is the axes of 'age' and 'lifestyle' (see Introduction, Figure 0.2) that are used to explore the relevance of power relations. For feminist scholars, emphasising such relations is problematic because doing so tends to exclude the axes of sex/gender and sexuality, which would appear to be of far more significance in general, and in the specific projects upon which cultural criminologists embark (Naegler and Salman 2016; Smart 1976).

Moreover, emphasising some axes of power at the expense of others will skew analysis and interpretations of phenomena in particular directions. As discussed in Chapter 4, if the axis of 'youth' is made central, criminalised behaviours may come to be interpreted as expressions of resistance directed against the hegemonic social order. Conversely, if sex/gender is centralised, youthful activities may come to be read as strategies to embody a type of 'hegemonic masculinity'. We have gone from seeing 'resistance' to finding 'conformity' (that is, conformity to dominant scripts concerning the performance of masculinity). It is hard to see how these disparate views could be reconciled, but both are possible according to the overarching logic that cultural criminology seeks to build and claims to operate within.

Methods

The preferred methods of cultural criminology include ethnography and textual analysis (see Chapter 2). Both of these methods can mean a variety of things, and can be put into practice in numerous ways. Despite all the variations they can produce, such methods are accorded priority in light of assumptions concerning the subject, social relations, common behaviours and institutional practices. For the cultural criminologist, all of these areas are saturated with meaning. Individuals operate in contexts that are somehow meaningful to them (often acting in accordance with 'value-rational' judgments); social relations cannot be reduced to mechanical, instrumental ties; institutions (e.g., criminal justice systems) are not akin to machines – they are governed by particular narratives, politically determined objectives, value judgements concerning social groups, and so on.

Given the inescapability of meaning, cultural criminology is on strong ground in advocating for methods that capture it, thereby revealing how it saturates our existence and plays a profound role in shaping most of what can be phenomenally apprehended. The cultural criminologist often pits ethnography and textual analysis against the methods that are favoured within positivist criminology, which tend to construe the world as a series of discrete variables that can be quantitatively measured and organised into correlations or cause–effect-type relationships. In my view, the methods of cultural criminology are preferable over quantification. Of course, some problems may have dimensions that are worth quantifying, but numbers should not be fetishised. When it comes to crime and punishment (and many other problems in social science), we find ourselves in deeply emotive, meaning-laden territory. Given this, it seems unlikely that we could depend upon positivist logics to develop rich understandings of crime and punishment.

Contradictions, however, certainly await us. For ethnography and textual analysis are, for the most part, underpinned by distinct epistemological standpoints. Ethnography typically embraces a 'realist' epistemology. That is, the method assumes that there is a real world 'out there'. This world consists of practices, interactions, human emotions, mental frameworks, moral sensibilities and so on. Moreover, the analyst can make discoveries about this reality through observation. One may accept this epistemological stance, but it is hard to reconcile it with textual analysis. Many of the methods that accord priority to texts assume that the world is constructed via the ways in which it is mediated through language. Hence, the importance assigned to texts! These are the observable moments in which we see the world being constructed. In this epistemological space, there does not exist a world 'out there' that waits for us to discover it, and then represent in writing.

We have, then, two broad methodological orientations that cultural criminology wishes to claim for itself. These methods, however, cannot always be located within the same epistemological standpoint.

Politics of research

Methods and the politics of research are bound together for the cultural criminologist. This is so much so that cultural criminology considers it impossible to produce knowledge 'outside of' political values and ethical commitments. It is this view that often leads cultural criminology to draw a hard line that separates it from the methods associated with positivist criminology. The cultural criminologist, however, goes further than this: because ethnography and textual analysis are understood to involve political and ethical choices, they are then presumed to ensure the production of scholarly accounts that are politically and ethically desirable. In other words, cultural criminology asserts that critical knowledge – or knowledge that speaks back to power – is assured by its methodological preferences.

Cultural criminology, at least in my view, is correct to posit that knowledge production cannot be divorced from political and ethical standpoints. Moreover, knowledge production always has political and ethical implications. As a result, it is appropriate for cultural criminology to promote reflexivity in research, to suggest that one should think carefully about the political and ethical dimensions of their research. What is construed as a problem? What assumptions is one importing into the analysis of any given problem? What political effects are likely to accompany the scholarly narrative that I produce?

This is all well and good 'in theory', or as a promise. However, by no means can it be assumed that specific methodological preferences will produce politically progressive knowledge by default. There are at least two problems that merit attention.

First, knowledge may always be political, but this does not necessarily inhere in the selection of methods. Methods are tools, strategies, ways of doing research. They can be marshalled in ways that support contemporary power asymmetries or disrupt them. We saw arguments along such lines advanced by Sandra Harding (1986, 2015) in Chapter 2 and Pat Carlen (2011) in Chapter 4. To provide a quick illustration, one may quantify the extent of poverty in a society and 'correlate' this with increases in incarceration rates. In some ways, showing such a correlation disrupts power arrangements insofar as it intimates that prison is being used to control the poor, and that it might be better to tackle inequality if we wish to minimise dependence on the prison. Of course, our 'radical constructivists' from Chapter 1 might not see this as politically progressive knowledge insofar as it reproduces the idea that 'causes' to 'problems' can be 'found'. Accepting that causes can be found legitimises 'representational epistemology' – which is the very same ground upon which those inclined to argue, say for example, that increases in crime explain increases in incarceration rates often stand.

In short, the question is whether any method can be conflated with a particular political standpoint. The cultural criminologist appears to answer in the affirmative: particular methods align with particular political positions. But the problem is much more complicated. Any given method may lead to knowledge that disrupts power asymmetries or it may lead to knowledge that naturalises unjust power relations. Furthermore, whether any given knowledge claim disrupts or normalises power relations is open to interpretation. Linking poverty and incarceration rates may be progressive in some respects, but it may also assume epistemological sensibilities that typically work to normalise power inequalities (as the radical constructivist would argue).

It is worth emphasising that whether cultural criminology actually advances progressive knowledge claims has been subject to debate. Not surprisingly, cultural criminology thinks of itself as providing a counter-punch to authority (see Chapter 3 and the section on 'modes of resistance' found in Chapter 6). However, feminist theorists and critical Marxists have questioned this. For feminist criminology, the resistance thesis advanced by cultural criminology is not necessarily progressive, for it does not recognise how criminalised subcultures may be better explained as enactments of hegemonic masculinity (see above and Chapter 4). Amongst critical Marxists, such as Hall and Winlow (2007), the 'resistance thesis' amounts to an ideological claim: in distorting the meaning of resistance by conflating it with petty crime, the cultural criminologist provides a narrative that protects the interests of capital. 'Real' resistance requires large-scale social movements that directly confront capitalism and its injustices.

Second, in seeing research methods as connected to knowledge claims that advance a political standpoint, cultural criminology often ignores the fact that the research process is a social relationship, one in which a power imbalance between the researcher and the researched is likely to prevail. That is to say, the analyst interacts with people or artefacts (or both), but occupies a privileged position in doing so. This raises issues. Does cultural criminology's preference for ethnography lead it to exploit those it researches? Does the cultural criminologist secure benefits (e.g., an academic career) 'on the backs' of those researched (Stacey 1988)? If textual analysis is utilised, does this lead the researcher to exclude the voices of the marginalised? This latter problem may arise if one analyses the textual outputs of a marginalised social group (Clarke 1990; Williams 2007).

Criminalised behaviour

This brings us to the centre of Figure 0.1, where one will find the categories of 'crime' and 'punishment'. Cultural criminology often focuses on criminalised behaviours that take group form, and this would explain why it often works with a notion of subculture. In this, there is a recognition that crime is much more than a simple infraction of legal codes. Instead, crime is fraught with meaning, it might even be resistant given that it transpires against a backdrop of profound power asymmetries. Imperfect resistance it may be, but resistance nonetheless (Ferrell 1996). Alongside this, and given the preference for textual analysis, cultural criminology often acknowledges the constructed nature of crime, or how it is mediated through language. In Ferrell's *Crimes of Style* (1996), for example, much attention is paid to how public officials and the dominant media construct graffiti as a 'serious crime', something that needs to be eradicated lest the entire urban fabric crumble to pieces.

These are important insights, and they are certainly worth incorporating into how we think about criminalised behaviour. Very few behaviours are likely to be merely instrumental, and which behaviours become appended to the label of 'criminal' is a product of language. The problem is that cultural criminology is not entirely transparent in its fundamental understanding of 'crime'. In some ways, it seems that 'crime' is understood as a real problem that warrants a search for its causes, or the development of theories on crime. The 'resistance' and 'inclusion/exclusion' theses belong to this order of thinking. In the former, some behaviours are regarded as criminal, but they are also moments of political engagement (Ferrell 1996). In the latter, crime is accorded ontological status, but explained by the pathologies of late capitalism (Young 2003. On according crime an ontological status, see Carrier 2006 and Hulsman 1986, cited in Chapter 2).

Against this, there is some sense in which crime is recognised as belonging to the order of discourse, rather than reality. In these respects, the cultural criminologist is much closer to the constructivist, or the view that there is no reality to be found outside language. How we make sense of the world occurs through language, and language always provides a variety of possible frames.

Whether any particular behaviour is linked to the signifier of 'crime' or some other signifier, such as 'pleasure' or 'legal', is arbitrary. This approach to crime is most evident when cultural criminologists analyse society's powerful players and what they do in the realm of representation. Here we find concepts like ideology, discourse, moral panics and, amongst others, loops/spirals (see Chapter 5). The cultural criminologist makes use of these notions, despite their differences and ambiguities.

Relative to Marx's notion of ideology (1994a, 1994b), Foucault's (1972) discourse is found much further down the path of constructivism. That is, whereas ideology asserts that there is a truth that can be found and subsequently represented in language (where inaccurate and distorted representations amount to ideology), discourse rejects the idea that truth can be found in this way. The moral panic concept appears closer to ideology because it often assumes that panics 'over-signify' events and practices, but it also acknowledges that panics may involve pure fabrications. Loops/spirals is difficult to locate: it suggests that the real and its representation collapses in our mediated environment, but tends to generate thick descriptions of how representations and reality form endless feedback loops (Chapter 5).

How, in all of this, is 'crime' to be understood? Is it real, but distorted via its representation, or is it a pure construction, an artefact of discourse? All things considered, I would argue that cultural criminology makes space for both possibilities, but generally veers towards the former view. That is, cultural criminology tends to accept the criminality of some behaviours, but proceeds to explore how the threat posed by them is routinely distorted and blown out of all proportion by powerful social institutions and groups. Although this implies that cultural criminology is relatively consistent in how it understands crime, it is not a view with which the radical constructivist would agree.

Punishment and social control

And, our final entry in Figure 0.1, that of punishment and social control. In these respects, cultural criminology correctly recognises that punishment cannot be adequately comprehended as a simple response to crime. It must be freed from such common-sense views. Once divorced from crime, punishment can be situated within the broader structural contexts in which it invariably transpires. This insight often leads to theories in which cultural logics and power relations are used to explain punitive practices (see Chapters 7 and 8). Across this diversity, it is often assumed that punishment is difficult to justify, if not illegitimate, and this becomes obvious when it is closely examined. Given this generalised scepticism towards state authority and its punitive practices, cultural criminology, feminist criminology, sociological criminology, critical Marxists, radical constructivists – in short, most strands of critical criminology – arguably share common ground here. Any critical scholar worth their salt, it would seem, recognises that punitive practices need to be interrogated and disrupted.

But, perhaps due to its focus on young men, cultural criminology would appear to focus on practices that are obviously punitive, especially those orchestrated by the state. In this, it runs the risk of missing how punishment saturates culture and thus social life. This is a point often made by feminist scholars, who show that women are far more likely to be regulated via cultural norms surrounding femininity and sexuality (Bartky 1988; Carlen 1983; Smart 1976; Young 1990). And, to be sure, men are also regulated by specific norms surrounding masculinity and sexuality, not just their entanglements with formal mechanisms of punishment. If, however, power asymmetries grounded in sex/gender, sexuality, race and so on, are downplayed, it becomes difficult to approach culture as inherently prescriptive and thus punitive.

Escaping contradictions?

Of course, this brief summary of the tensions that transpire within cultural criminology does not necessarily amount to saying that the project should be abandoned. Rather, it is to emphasise that a variety of issues need to be thought through if one accepts that a concept of culture is necessary for making sense of problems that are relevant to criminology. How are we to understand reality? Is there something real that can be represented via language? Or, do we need to interrogate language because it mediates all reality? Is 'crime' real, or is it a discursive category? Is culture to be understood as primary, or as a secondary effect of material relations? Alternatively, is it possible to somehow transcend this dualistic view of culture? How to incorporate power asymmetries? Can one be selective and focus on specific power axes, or is an intersectional approach more desirable? If the former, which power asymmetries should be accorded theoretical primacy? How to manage the political aspects of knowledge production? Can one produce an account that is politically progressive and refrain from exploiting research participants? And, perhaps the most difficult of problems, can one work through these and other dilemmas in a way that leads to a logically coherent position that proceeds to inform the analysis of substantive problems?

To be sure, by no means should it be thought that this line of questioning is unique to cultural criminology. In some way, shape or form, such dilemmas arise the moment one becomes interested in resolving criminological problems. In all likelihood, the idea that there is a perfect perspective out there – one that would enable us to finally understand the world – is illusory. As such, it might be more fruitful to consider what certain perspectives can and cannot give us. Any given approach involves sacrifice: in order for something to be revealed, something will invariably be concealed. What, then, can a cultural criminological perspective reveal? What does it conceal? Is the analyst prepared to make the sacrifices that cultural criminology appears to demand?

REFERENCES

Abercrombie, N., Hill, S., and Turner, B. S. 1988. *Dictionary of sociology (second edition)*. London: Penguin Books.

Adorno, T. 1973. *Negative dialectics*. Translated by E. B. Ashton. New York: Continuum.

Alexander, M. 2012. *The new Jim Crow: Mass incarceration in the age of colorblindness*. New York: The New Press.

Altheide, D. L., and Coyle, M. J. 2006. Smart on crime: The new language for prisoner release. *Crime Media Culture* 2(3): 286–303.

Anderson, C. A., and Bushman, B. J. 2001. Effects of violent video games on aggressive behavior, aggressive cognition, aggressive affect, physiological arousal, and prosocial behavior: A meta-analytic review of the scientific literature. *Psychological Science* 12(5): 353–359.

Anderson, E. 1990. *Streetwise: Race, class, and change in an urban community*. Chicago: University of Chicago Press.

Anderson, E. 1999. *Code of the street: Decency, violence, and the moral life of the inner city*. New York: W.W. Norton and Company.

Australian Productivity Services. 2018. Report on government services 2018: Corrective services. Available: https://www.pc.gov.au/research/ongoing/report-on-government-services/2018/justice/corrective-services. Retrieved: July 16, 2019.

Ayres, T. C., and Jewkes, Y. 2012. The haunting spectacle of crystal meth: A media-created mythology? *Crime Media Culture* 8(3): 315–332.

Babbie, E. 1995. *The practice of social research (seventh edition)*. Belmont: Wadsworth Publishing.

Bagdikian, B. H. 2000. *The media monopoly*. Boston: Beacon Press.

Baker, L. A., Tuvblad, C., and Raine, A. 2010. Genetics and crime. In *The SAGE handbook of criminological theory*, edited by E. McLaughlin and T. Newburn, pages 21–39. London: Sage.

Barak, G. 1988. Newsmaking criminology: Reflections on the media, intellectuals, and crime. *Justice Quarterly* 5(4): 565–587.

Barak, G. 2011. Media, society, and criminology. In *Media, process, and the social construction of crime: Studies in newsmaking criminology*, edited by G. Barak, pages 3–45. New York: Routledge.

Barthes, R. 1973. *Elements of semiology*. Translated by A. Lavers and C. Smith. New York: Hill and Wang.

Barthes, R. 1983. *The fashion system*. Translated by M. Ward and R. Howard. Berkeley: University of California Press.

Bartky, S. L. 1988. Foucault, femininity, and the modernization of patriarchal power. In *Feminism and Foucault: Reflections on resistance*, edited by I. Diamond and L. Quinby, pages 61–86. Boston: Northeastern University Press.

Bataille, G. 1991. *The accursed share, Volume 1*. Translated by R. Hurley. New York: Zone Books.

Bauman, Z. 2001. Consuming life. *Journal of Consumer Culture* 1(1): 9–29.

Beccaria, C. 1963 [1764]. *On crimes and punishment.* Indianapolis: Bobbs-Merrill.

Beck, U. 1992. *The risk society.* London: Sage.

Becker, H. 1963. *Outsiders: Studies in the sociology of deviance.* New York: Free Press.

Becker, H. 1967. Whose side are we on? *Social Problems* 14(3): 239–247.

Belk, R. 1984. Three scales to measure constructs related to materialism: Reliability, validity, and relationships to measures of happiness. In *Advances in consumer research,* edited by T. Kinnear, pages 291–297. Provo: Association for Consumer Research.

Bennett, A. 1999. Subcultures or neo-tribes? Rethinking the relationship between youth, style and musical taste. *Sociology* 33(3): 599–617.

Bennett, W. L. 2009. *News: The politics of illusion.* New York: Pearson.

Bennett, W. L., and Klockner, J. D. 1996. The psychology of mass-mediated publics. In *The psychology of political communication,* edited by A. N. Crigler, pages 89–109. Ann Arbor: University of Michigan Press.

Bennett, W. L., Lawrence, R. G., and Livingston, S. 2007. *When the press fails: Political power and the news media from Iraq to Katrina.* Chicago: Chicago University Press.

Bordo, S. 1988. Anorexia nervosa: Psychopathology as the crystallization of culture. In *Feminism and Foucault: Reflections on resistance,* edited by I. Diamond and L. Quinby, pages 87–117. Boston: Northeastern University Press.

Bottoms, A. E. 1995. The philosophy and politics of punishment and sentencing. In *The politics of sentencing reform,* edited by C. Clarkson and R. Morgan, pages 17–49. Oxford: Clarendon.

Bourdieu, P. 1984. *Distinction: A social critique of the judgment of taste.* Translated by R. Nice. Cambridge, MA: Harvard University Press.

Box, S. 1981. *Deviance, reality and society (second edition).* London: Holt, Rinehart and Winston.

Braverman, H. 1974. *Labor and monopoly capital: The degradation of work in the twentieth century.* New York: Monthly Review Press.

Brisman, A. 2010. 'Creative crime' and the phytological analogy. *Crime Media Culture* 6(2): 205–225.

Brown, M. 2007. Mapping discursive closings in the war on drugs. *Crime Media Culture* 3(1): 11–29.

Brown, M. 2009. *The culture of punishment: Prison, society, and spectacle.* New York: New York University Press.

Brown, M. 2014. Visual criminology and carceral studies: Counter-images in the carceral age. *Theoretical Criminology* 18(2): 176–197.

Buttle, J. 2017. Imagining an Aotearoa/New Zealand without prisons. *Counterfutures* 3(1): 99–127.

Canton, R. 2017. *Why punish? An introduction to the philosophy of punishment.* London: Red Globe Press.

Carlen, P. 1983. *Women's imprisonment: A study in social control.* London: Routledge and Kegan Paul.

Carlen, P. 2011. Against evangelism in academic criminology: For criminology as a scientific art. In *What is criminology?* edited by M. Bosworth and C. Hoyle, pages 95–108. Oxford: Oxford University Press.

Carlson, J. M. 1985. *Prime-time law enforcement: Crime show viewing and attitudes toward the criminal justice system.* New York: Praeger.

Carrier, N. 2006. Academics' criminals. *Champ Pénal/Penal Field* 3: 1–20.

Carrier, N. 2008. Speech for the defense of a radically constructivist sociology of (criminal) law. *International Journal of Law, Crime and Justice* 36(3): 168–183.

Carrier, N. 2011. Critical criminology meets radical constructivism. *Critical Criminology* 19(4): 331–350.

Carrier, N., and Walby, K. 2014. Ptolemizing Lombroso: The pseudo-revolution of biosocial criminology. *Journal of Theoretical and Philosophical Criminology* 1(1): 1–45.

Cavender, G., and Deutsch, S. K. 2007. *CSI* and moral authority: The police and science. *Crime Media Culture* 3(1): 67–81.

Cheliotis, L. K. 2010. The ambivalent consequences of visibility: Crime and prisons in the mass media. *Crime Media Culture* 6(2): 169–184.

Chermak, S. M. 1995. *Victims in the news: Crime and the American news media.* Boulder: Westview Press.

Clarke, G. 1990. Defending ski-jumpers: A critique of theories of youth subcultures. In *On record: Rock, pop, and the written word*, edited by S. Frith and A. Goodwin, pages 81–96. New York: Routledge.

Clarke, J., Hall, S., Jefferson, T., and Roberts, B. 2006 [1975]. Subcultures, cultures and class. In *Resistance through rituals: Youth subcultures in post-war Britain (second edition)*, edited by S. Hall and T. Jefferson, pages 3–59. New York: Routledge.

Clear, T. 1994. *Harm in American penology: Offenders, victims, and their communities.* Albany: State University of New York Press.

Cohen, A. 1955. *Delinquent boys: The culture of the gang.* New York: Free Press.

Cohen, B. 2008. *Mental health user narratives: New perspectives on illness and recovery.* London: Palgrave Macmillan.

Cohen, B. 2016. *Psychiatric hegemony: A Marxist theory of mental illness.* London: Palgrave Macmillan.

Cohen, L., and Felson, M. 1979. Social change and crime rate trends: A routine activity approach. *American Sociological Review* 44(4): 588–608.

Cohen, S. 2011 [1972]. *Folk devils and moral panics: The creation of the Mods and Rockers.* London: Routledge.

Cole, S. A., and Dioso-Villa, R. 2007. *CSI* and its effects: Media, juries, and the burden of proof. *New England Law Review* 41: 435–470.

Cole, S. A., and Dioso-Villa, R. 2011. Should judges worry about the 'CSI effect'? *Court Review* 47: 20–31.

Coleman, J. W. 2005. *The criminal elite: Understanding white-collar crime (sixth edition).* New York: Worth Publishers.

Cook, T. 2005. Freeing the presses: An introductory essay. In *Freeing the presses*, edited by T. Cook, pages 1–28. Baton Rouge: Louisiana State University Press.

Cornish, D., and Clarke, R. 1986. *The reasoning criminal.* New York: Springer-Verlag.

Coulter, A. H. 2002. *Slander: Liberal lies about the American right.* New York: Crown.

Cremin, C. 2016. *Exploring videogames with Deleuze and Guattari: Towards an affective theory of form.* London: Routledge.

Crowther-Dowey, C., and Fussey, P. 2013. *Researching crime: Approaches, methods and application.* London: Red Globe Press.

Davis, A. 2003. *Are prisons obsolete?* New York: Seven Stories Press.

de Saussure, F. 1972. *Course in general linguistics.* Translated by R. Harris. Chicago: Open Court.

Dobash, R. E., Schlesinger, P., Dobash, R., and Weaver, C. K. 1998. 'Crimewatch UK': Women's interpretations of televised violence. In *Entertaining crime: Television reality programs*, edited by M. Fishman and G. Cavender, pages 37–58. New York: Aldine de Gruyter.

Donovan, R. J., and Scherer, R. 1992. *Unsilent revolution: Television news and American public life, 1948–1991.* Cambridge: Cambridge University Press.

Douglas, M. 1984. *Purity and danger: An analysis of the concepts of pollution and taboo.* London: Ark Paperbacks.

Dunn, R. 1998. *Identity crises: A social critique of postmodernity.* Minneapolis: University of Minnesota Press.

Durkheim, E. 1958. *The rules of sociological method.* Translated by S. A. Solovay and J. H. Meuller. Glencoe: The Free Press.

Durkheim, E. 1960. *The division of labor in society.* Translated by G. Simpson. Glencoe: The Free Press.

Durkheim, E. 2001. *The elementary forms of religious life.* Translated by C. Cosman. Oxford: Oxford University Press.

Engels, F. 1999 [1845]. *The condition of the working class in England.* Edited by D. McLellan. Oxford: Oxford University Press.

Erikson, K. 1966. *Wayward puritans: A study in the sociology of deviance.* New York: John Wiley and Sons, Inc.

Fagan, J., and Davies, G. 2000. Street stops and broken windows: Terry, race, and disorder in New York City. *Fordham Law Review* 28(2): 456–504.

Fairclough, N. 1989. *Language and power.* London: Longman.

Feeley, M., and Simon, J. 1992. The new penology: Notes on the emerging strategy of corrections and its implications. *Criminology* 30(4): 449–474.

Ferree, M. M., Gamson, W. A., Gerhards, J., and Rucht, D. 2002. *Shaping abortion discourse: Democracy and the public sphere in Germany and the United States.* New York: Cambridge University Press.

Ferrell, J. 1996. *Crimes of style: Urban graffiti and the politics of criminality.* Boston: Northeastern University Press.

Ferrell, J. 1998. Criminological *verstehen*: Inside the immediacy of crime. In *Ethnography at the edge: Crime, deviance, and field research*, edited by J. Ferrell and M. Hamm, pages 20–42. Boston: Northeastern University Press.

Ferrell, J. 1999. Cultural criminology. *Annual Review of Sociology* 25(1): 395–418.

Ferrell, J. 2013. Cultural criminology and the politics of meaning. *Critical Criminology* 21(2): 257–271.

Ferrell, J., Hayward, K., and Young, J. 2008. *Cultural criminology: An invitation.* London: Sage.

Fishman, M., and Cavender, G. 1998. *Entertaining crime: Television reality programs.* New York: Aldine de Gruyter.

Foucault, M. 1972. *The archaeology of knowledge.* Translated by A. M. Sheridan Smith. New York: Pantheon Books.

Foucault, M. 1973. *Madness and civilization: A history of insanity in the age of reason.* Translated by R. Howard. New York: Vintage Books.

Foucault, M. 1977. *Discipline and punish: The birth of the prison.* Translated by A. Sheridan. London: Penguin.

Foucault, M. 1978. *The history of sexuality. Volume one: An introduction.* Translated by R. Hurley. New York: Vintage Books.

Foucault, M. 1980. *Power/knowledge: Selected interviews and other writings, 1972–1977*. Edited by C. Gordon. New York: Pantheon Books.

Garland, D. 2001. *The culture of control: Crime and social order in contemporary society*. Oxford: Oxford University Press.

Geertz, C. 1973. *The interpretation of cultures: Selected essays*. New York: Basic Books.

Gerbner, G. 1970. Cultural indicators: The case of violence in television drama. *The Annals of the American Academy of Political and Social Science* 388(1): 69–81.

Gerbner, G., and Gross, L. 1976. Living with television: The violence profile. *Journal of Communication* 26(2): 172–199.

Goffman, E. 1961. *Asylums: Essays on the social situation of mental patients and other inmates*. London: Penguin.

Goldberg, B. 2003. *Bias: A CBS insider exposes how the media distort the news*. New York: Harper Collins.

Goode, E., and Ben-Yehuda, N. 1994. *Moral panics: The social construction of deviance*. Oxford: Blackwell.

Goode, J. 2002. How urban ethnography counters myths about the poor. In *Urban life: Readings in the anthropology of the city (fourth edition)*, edited by G. Gmelch and W. P. Zenner, pages 279–295. Prospect Heights: Waveland Press.

Gramsci, A. 1971. *Selections from the prison notebooks*. New York: International Publishers.

Green, D. A. 2009. Feeding wolves: Punitiveness and culture. *European Journal of Criminology* 6(6): 517–536.

Greenham Common Women's Peace Camp. 2018. *Greenham Common Women's Peace Camp: 1981–2000*. Available: http://www.greenhamwpc.org.uk. Retrieved June 19, 2018.

Greer, C., and Reiner, R. 2012. Mediated mayhem: Media, crime, criminal justice. In *The Oxford handbook of criminology (fifth edition)*, edited by M. Maguire, R. Morgan, and R. Reiner, pages 245–278. Oxford: Oxford University Press.

Greitemeyer, T., and Mügge, D. O. 2014. Video games do affect social outcomes: A meta-analytic review of the effects of violent and prosocial video game play. *Personality and Social Psychology Bulletin* 40(5): 578–589.

Hall, S. 1986. The problem of ideology – Marxism without guarantees. *Journal of Communication Inquiry* 10(2): 28–44.

Hall, S. 1997. *Representation: Cultural representations and signifying practices*. London: Sage.

Hall, S., Critcher, C., Jefferson, T., Clarke, J., and Roberts, B. 2006 [1975]. Some notes on the relationship between the societal control culture and the news media, and the construction of a law and order campaign. In *Resistance through rituals: Youth subcultures in post-war Britain (second edition)*, edited by S. Hall and T. Jefferson, pages 60–64. New York: Routledge.

Hall, S., Critcher, C., Jefferson, T., Clarke, J., and Roberts, B. 1978. *Policing the crisis: Mugging, the state, and law and order*. London: Macmillan.

Hall, S., and Winlow, S. 2007. Cultural criminology and primitive accumulation: A formal introduction for two strangers who should really become more intimate. *Crime, Media, Culture* 3(1): 82–90.

Hall, S., Winlow, S., and Ancrum, C. 2008. *Criminal identities and consumer culture: Crime, exclusion and the new culture of narcissism*. Cullompton: Willan.

Hamm, M. 2004. Apocalyptic violence: The seduction of terrorist subcultures. *Theoretical Criminology* 8(3): 323–339.

Hannah-Moffat, K. 2005. Criminogenic needs and the transformative risk subject: Hybridizations of risk/need in penality. *Punishment and Society* 7(1): 29–51.

Haraway, D. 1988. Situated knowledges: The science question in feminism and the privilege of partial perspective. *Feminist Studies* 14(3): 575–599.

Harding, S. 1986. *The science question in feminism.* Milton Keynes: Open University Press.

Harding, S. 1993. Introduction: Eurocentric scientific illiteracy – A challenge for the world community. In *The 'racial' economy of science: Toward a democratic future*, edited by S. Harding, pages 1–22. Bloomington: Indiana University Press.

Harding, S. 2015. *Objectivity and diversity: Another logic of scientific research.* Chicago: University of Chicago Press.

Hayward, K. 2004. *City limits: Crime, consumer culture and the urban experience.* London: Glasshouse.

Hayward, K., and Yar, M. 2006. The 'chav' phenomenon: Consumption, media and the construction of a new underclass. *Crime Media Culture* 2(1): 9–28.

Henry, S., and Milovanovic, D. 1996. *Constitutive criminology: Beyond postmodernism.* London: Sage.

Herman, E. S., and Chomsky, N. 1988. *Manufacturing consent: The political economy of the mass media.* New York: Pantheon Books.

Herman, E. S., and McChesney, R. W. 2001. *The global media: The new missionaries of corporate capitalism.* New York: Continuum.

Hollway, W., and Jefferson, T. 1997. The risk society in an age of anxiety: Situating fear of crime. *British Journal of Sociology* 48(2): 255–266.

Horn, D. 2003. *The criminal body: Lombroso and the anatomy of deviance.* New York: Routledge.

Huey, L. 2010. 'I've seen this on *CSI*': Criminal investigators' perceptions about the management of public expectations in the field. *Crime Media Culture* 6(1): 49–68.

Hulsman, L. H. C. 1986. Critical criminology and the concept of crime. *Crime, Law and Social Change* 10(1): 63–80.

Jewkes, Y. 2007. Prisons and the media: The shaping of public opinion and penal policy in a mediated society. In *Handbook on prisons*, edited by Y. Jewkes, pages 447–466. Cullompton: Willan.

Jones, T., and Newburn, T. 2006. Three strikes and you're out: Exploring symbol and substance in American and British crime control politics. *British Journal of Criminology* 46(5): 781–802.

Katz, J. 1988. *Seductions of crime.* New York: Basic Books.

Kelling, G., and Bratton, W. 1998. Declining crime rates: Insiders' views of the New York City story. *Journal of Criminal Law and Criminology* 88: 1217–1231.

King, A., and Maruna, S. 2009. Is a conservative just a liberal who has been mugged? Exploring the origins of punitive views. *Punishment and Society* 11(2): 147–169.

Kramer, R. 2012. Political elites, 'broken windows', and the commodification of urban space. *Critical Criminology* 20(3): 229–248.

Kramer, R. 2017. *The rise of legal graffiti writing in New York and beyond.* London: Palgrave Macmillan.

Kramer, R., and Oleson, J. 2021, forthcoming. *Overcoming crime science: The indomitable resilience of deviance.* Berkeley: University of California Press.

Kramer, R., Rajah, V., and Sung, H. E. 2013. Neoliberal prisons and cognitive treatment: Calibrating the subjectivity of incarcerated young men to economic inequalities. *Theoretical Criminology* 17(4): 535–556.

Kramer, R., Rajah, V., and Sung, H. E. 2016. Entrapments of consumerism: Adolescent prisoners, cognitive treatment, and consumption. *Journal of Consumer Culture* 16(3): 801–823.

Kuhn, T. 1970. *The structure of scientific revolutions.* Chicago: University of Chicago Press.

Lemert, E. 1967. *Human deviance, social problems and social control.* New York: Prentice-Hall.

Linnemann, T., and Wall, T. 2013. 'This is your face on meth': The punitive spectacle of 'white trash' in the rural war on drugs. *Theoretical Criminology* 17(3): 315–334.

Lippert, R., and Wilkinson, B. 2010. Capturing crime, criminals and the public's imagination: Assembling *Crime Stoppers* and CCTV surveillance. *Crime Media Culture* 6(2): 131–152.

Lombroso, C. 2006 [1876–1897]. *Criminal man.* Translated by M. Gibson and N. Rafter. Durham: Duke University Press.

Lowry, D. T., Nio, T. C. J., and Leitner, D. W. 2003. Setting the public fear agenda: A longitudinal analysis of network TV crime reporting, public perceptions of crime, and FBI crime statistics. *Journal of Communication* 53(1): 61–73.

Lupton, D., and Tulloch, J. 1999. Theorizing fear of crime: Beyond the rational/irrational opposition. *British Journal of Sociology* 50(3): 507–523.

Lyng, S. 1990. Edgework: A social psychological analysis of voluntary risk taking. *American Journal of Sociology* 95(4): 851–886.

Lyng, S. 1998. Dangerous methods: Risk taking and the research process. In *Ethnography at the edge: Crime, deviance and field research,* edited by J. Ferrell and M. Hamm, pages 221–251. Boston: Northeastern University Press.

Macdonald, N. 2001. *The graffiti subculture: Youth, masculinity, and identity in London and New York.* New York: Palgrave Macmillan.

Marx, K. 1906. *Capital: A critique of political economy.* New York: Modern Library.

Marx, K. 1994a. Economic and philosophic manuscripts. In *Karl Marx: Selected writings,* edited by L. H. Simon. Indianapolis: Hackett.

Marx, K. 1994b. The communist manifesto. In *Karl Marx: Selected writings,* edited by L. H. Simon. Indianapolis: Hackett.

Marx, K. 1998. *The 18th Brumaire of Louis Bonaparte.* New York: International Publishers.

Matza, D., and Sykes, G. 1961. Juvenile delinquency and subterranean values. *American Sociological Review* 26(5): 712–719.

McChesney, R. W. 2004. *The problem of the media: U.S. communication politics in the 21st century.* New York: Monthly Review Press.

McGowan, W. 2003. *Coloring the news: How political correctness has corrupted American journalism.* San Francisco: Encounter Books.

McRobbie, A. 1997. Second hand dresses and the role of the ragmarket. In *The subcultures reader,* edited by K. Gelder and S. Thornton, pages 191–199. New York: Routledge.

McRobbie, A. 2002. Clubs to companies: Notes on the decline of political culture in speeded up creative worlds. *Cultural Studies* 16(4): 516–531.

McRobbie, A., and Garber, J. 2006 [1975]. Girls and subcultures: An exploration. In *Resistance through rituals: Youth subcultures in post-war Britain (second edition),* edited by S. Hall and T. Jefferson, pages 177–188. New York: Routledge.

Mead, G. H. 1934. *Mind, self and society from the standpoint of a social behaviorist.* Chicago: The University of Chicago Press.

Merton, R. 1938. Social structure and anomie. *American Sociological Review* 3(5): 672–682.

Miller, W. 1958. Lower-class culture as a generating milieu of gang delinquency. *Journal of Social Issues* 14(3): 5–19.

Mopas, M. 2007. Examining the 'CSI effect' through an ANT lens. *Crime Media Culture* 3(1): 110–117.

Myers, Q. 2018. Five tips for spending New Year's Eve in Times Square without hating your life. *Eventbrite*, October 14. Available: https://www.eventbrite.com/rally/new-york-city/new-years-eve-in-times-square/. Retrieved: August 30, 2019.

NAACP. 2019. Criminal justice fact sheet. Available: https://www.naacp.org/criminal-justice-fact-sheet/. Retrieved: July 16, 2019.

Naegler, L., and Salman, S. 2016. Cultural criminology and gender consciousness: Moving feminist theory from margin to center. *Feminist Criminology* 11(4): 354–374.

National Association of Criminal Defense Lawyers. 2018. *The trial penalty: The Sixth Amendment right to trial on the verge of extinction and how to save it.* Washington, DC: National Association of Criminal Defense Lawyers. Available: https://www.nacdl.org/trialpenaltyreport/. Retrieved: September 12, 2019.

Newburn, T., and Jones, T. 2005. Symbolic politics and penal populism: The long shadow of Willie Horton. *Crime Media Culture* 1(1): 72–87.

Nightingale, C. H. 1993. *On the edge: A history of poor black children and their American dreams.* New York: Basic Books.

O'Brien, M. 2005. What is *cultural* about cultural criminology? *British Journal of Criminology* 45(5): 599–612.

Oleson, J. 2015. Rituals upon celluloid: The need for crime and punishment in contemporary film. *Cleveland State Law Review* 63(3): 599–619.

Pettit, B., and Western, B. 2004. Mass imprisonment and the life course: Race and class inequality in US incarceration. *American Sociological Review* 69: 151–169.

Pratt, J. 2007. *Penal populism.* London: Routledge.

Presdee, M. 2000. *Cultural criminology and the carnival of crime.* London: Routledge.

Reiner, R. 2012. What's left? The prospects for social democratic criminology. *Crime Media Culture* 8(2): 135–150.

Rosino, M. L., and Hughey, M. W. 2017. Speaking through silence: Racial discourse and identity construction in mass-mediated debates on the 'war on drugs'. *Social Currents* 4(3): 246–264.

Rusche, G., and Kirchheimer, O. 2005 [1939]. *Punishment and social structure.* New Brunswick: Transaction Publishers.

Ryan, W. 1976. *Blaming the victim.* New York: Random House.

Schor, J. 1998. *The overspent American: Upscaling, downshifting, and the new consumer.* New York: Basic Books.

Schor, J. 2004. *Born to buy: The commercialized child and the new consumer culture.* New York: Scribner.

Schudson, M. 2005. Why democracies need an unlovable press. In *Freeing the presses*, edited by T. Cook, pages 73–86. Baton Rouge: Louisiana State University Press.

Shaw, J., Crosby, K., and Porter, S. 2014. The impact of a video game on criminal thinking: Implicit and explicit measures. *Simulation and Gaming* 45(6): 786–804.

Sherry, J. 2001. The effects of violent video games on aggression: A meta-analysis. *Human Communication Research* 27(3): 409–431.

Shichor, D. 1997. Three strikes as a public policy: The convergence of the new penology and the McDonaldization of punishment. *Crime and Delinquency* 43(4): 470–492.

Simon, J. 2000. Megan's law: Crime and democracy in late modern America. *Law and Social Inquiry* 25(4): 1111–1150.

Smart, C. 1976. *Women, crime and criminology: A feminist critique*. London: Routledge and Kegan Paul.

Smith, P. 2001. *Cultural theory: An introduction*. Massachusetts: Blackwell.

Smith, P. 2008. *Punishment and culture*. Chicago: University of Chicago Press.

Snyder, G. 2017. *Skateboarding LA: Inside professional street skateboarding*. New York: New York University Press.

Sparks, R. 1992. *Television and the drama of crime: Moral tales and the place of crime in public life*. Buckingham: Open University Press.

Spencer, D. 2009. Sex offender as homo sacer. *Punishment and Society* 11(2): 219–240.

Spencer, D. 2011. Cultural criminology: An invitation… to what? *Critical Criminology* 19(3): 197–212.

Stacey, J. 1988. Can there be a feminist ethnography? *Women's Studies International Forum* 11(1): 21–27.

Steen, S., and Bandy, R. 2007. When the policy becomes the problem: Criminal justice in the new millennium. *Punishment and Society* 9(1): 5–26.

Steinberg, S. 2011. Poor reason: Culture still doesn't explain poverty. *Boston Review*, January 13. Available: http://bostonreview.net/steinberg.php. Retrieved: September 12, 2019.

Summers, A. 1975. *Damned whores and god's police: The colonization of women in Australia*. Melbourne: Allen Lane.

Surette, R. 2015. *Media, crime, and criminal justice: Images, realities, and policies (fifth edition)*. Stamford: Cengage Learning.

Taylor, I. 1996. Fear of crime, urban fortunes and suburban social movements: Some reflections from Manchester. *Sociology* 30(2): 317–337.

Taylor, I., Walton, P., and Young, J. 1973. *The new criminology: For a social theory of deviance*. London: Routledge and Kegan Paul.

Veblen, T. 1899. *The theory of the leisure class: An economic study of institutions*. New York: Modern Library.

Wacquant, L. 2009a. *Punishing the poor: The neoliberal government of social insecurity*. Durham: Duke University Press.

Wacquant, L. 2009b. *Prisons of poverty*. Minneapolis: University of Minnesota Press.

Wacquant, L. 2010. Crafting the neoliberal state: Workfare, prisonfare, and social insecurity. *Sociological Forum* 25(2): 197–220.

Walby, K., and Carrier, N. 2010. The rise of biocriminology: Capturing observable bodily economies of 'criminal man'. *Criminology and Criminal Justice* 10(3): 261–285.

Webber, C. 2007. Background, foreground, foresight: The third dimension of cultural criminology? *Crime Media Culture* 3(2): 139–157.

Weber, M. 1978. *Economy and society: An outline of interpretive sociology*, edited by G. Roth and C. Wittich. Berkeley: University of California Press.

Weber, M. 1979. *The protestant ethic and the spirit of capitalism*. London: Allen and Unwin.

Western, B. 2006. *Punishment and inequality in America*. New York: Russell Sage Foundation.

Wilkins, L. 1964. *Social deviance: Social policy, action and research*. London: Tavistock.

Williams, J. P. 2007. Youth-subcultural studies: Sociological traditions and core concepts. *Sociology Compass* 1(2): 572–593.

Williams, R. 1976. *Keywords*. New York: Oxford University Press.

Wilson, D., and O'Sullivan, S. 2005. Re-theorizing the penal reform functions of the prison film: Revelation, humanization, empathy and benchmarking. *Theoretical Criminology* 9(4): 471–491.

Wilson, J. Q., and Kelling, G. L. 1982. Broken windows: The police and neighborhood safety. *Atlantic Monthly* 249: 1–9. Available at: http://www.theatlantic.com/doc/198203/broken-windows. Retrieved: August 3, 2009.

Wilson, W. J. 1987. *The truly disadvantaged: The inner city, the underclass, and public policy*. Chicago: University of Chicago Press.

World Prison Brief. 2019. United Kingdom: England and Wales. London: Institute for Crime and Justice Policy Research. Available at: https://www.prisonstudies.org/country/united-kingdom-england-wales. Retrieved: November 17, 2019.

Worrall, A. 2002. Rendering women punishable: The making of a penal crisis. In *Women and punishment: The struggle for justice*, edited by P. Carlen, pages 47–66. Cullompton: Willan.

Wright, R. 2000. 'I'd sell you suicide': Popular music and moral panic in the age of Marilyn Manson. *Popular Music* 19(3): 365–385.

Young, A. 1990. *Femininity in dissent*. London: Routledge.

Young, A. 1996. *Imaging crime: Textual outlaws and criminal conversations*. London: Sage.

Young, J. 1971. *The drugtakers: The social meaning of drug use*. London: MacGibbon and Kee.

Young, J. 1999. *The exclusive society*. London: Sage.

Young, J. 2003. Merton with energy, Katz with structure: The sociology of vindictiveness and the criminology of transgression. *Theoretical Criminology* 7(3): 389–414.

Zimring, F. E. 1996. Populism, democratic government, and the decline of expert authority: Some reflections on three strikes in California. *Pacific Law Journal* 28: 243–256.

Zimring, F. E., and Hawkins, G. 1991. *The scale of imprisonment*. Chicago: University of Chicago Press.

INDEX

Printed by Printforce, United Kingdom